Pro OpenSolaris

A New Open Source OS for Linux Developers and Administrators

Harry J. Foxwell, PhD
and Christine Tran

Pro OpenSolaris: A New Open Source OS for Linux Developers and Administrators

Copyright © 2009 by Harry J. Foxwell and Christine Tran

ISBN-13 (pbk): 978-1-4302-1891-3

ISBN-13 (electronic): 978-1-4302-1892-0

Trademarked names may appear in this book. Rather than use a trademark symbol with every occurrence of a trademarked name, we use the names only in an editorial fashion and to the benefit of the trademark owner, with no intention of infringement of the trademark.

Lead Editors: Michelle Lowman, Frank Pohlmann
Technical Reviewer: Sam Nicholson
Editorial Board: Clay Andres, Steve Anglin, Mark Beckner, Ewan Buckingham, Tony Campbell,
    Gary Cornell, Jonathan Gennick, Michelle Lowman, Matthew Moodie, Jeffrey Pepper,
    Frank Pohlmann, Ben Renow-Clarke, Dominic Shakeshaft, Matt Wade, Tom Welsh
Project Manager: Kylie Johnston
Copy Editor: Kim Wimpsett
Associate Production Director: Kari Brooks-Copony
Production Editor: Richard Ables
Compositor: Diana Van Winkle, Van Winkle Design Group
Proofreader: Nancy Sixsmith
Indexer: Becky Hornyak
Interior Designer: Diana Van Winkle, Van Winkle Design Group
Cover Designer: Kurt Krames
Manufacturing Director: Tom Debolski

Distributed to the book trade worldwide by Springer-Verlag New York, Inc., 233 Spring Street, 6th Floor, New York, NY 10013. Phone 1-800-SPRINGER, fax 201-348-4505, e-mail orders-ny@springer-sbm.com, or visit http://www.springeronline.com.

For information on translations, please contact Apress directly at 2855 Telegraph Avenue, Suite 600, Berkeley, CA 94705. Phone 510-549-5930, fax 510-549-5939, e-mail info@apress.com, or visit http://www.apress.com.

Apress and friends of ED books may be purchased in bulk for academic, corporate, or promotional use. eBook versions and licenses are also available for most titles. For more information, reference our Special Bulk Sales–eBook Licensing web page at http://www.apress.com/info/bulksales.

The source code for this book is available to readers at http://www.apress.com.

To my sons, Andrew, Michael, and Edward, as inspiration and example,
and to my wife, Eileen, for making it all possible.
—Harry J. Foxwell

This book is dedicated to my parents. You are the mountain and the spring;
you made everything possible.
And to Steve, who kept the lights on every night I came home late.
—Christine Tran

Contents at a Glance

About the Authors. xiii

About the Technical Reviewer xv

Acknowledgments xvii

Introduction xix

PART 1 ■ ■ ■ Getting Started

CHAPTER 1   Introducing OpenSolaris 3

CHAPTER 2   The Advantages of Developing with OpenSolaris 17

CHAPTER 3   Getting and Installing OpenSolaris 27

CHAPTER 4   A Familiar User and Developer Environment and More 51

PART 2 ■ ■ ■ Working with OpenSolaris

CHAPTER 5   SMF: The Service Management Facility. 69

CHAPTER 6   The ZFS File System. 89

CHAPTER 7   OpenSolaris and Virtualization 111

PART 3 ■ ■ ■ Exploiting OpenSolaris's Unique Features

CHAPTER 8   A Development Environment on OpenSolaris. 153

CHAPTER 9   Innovative OpenSolaris Features 205

PART 4 ■ ■ ■ Appendixes

APPENDIX A   Recommended Reading and Viewing. 233

APPENDIX B   OpenSolaris 2009.06 239

INDEX 243

Contents

About the Authors. xiii

About the Technical Reviewer xv

Acknowledgments xvii

Introduction xix

PART 1 ■ ■ ■ Getting Started

■CHAPTER 1   **Introducing OpenSolaris** 3

The True Name of Open Source Software 5

What You'll Find and Learn in This Book 7

The Origin of OpenSolaris. 9

Goals and Future Directions. 10

That Troublesome CDDL License 11

The OpenSolaris Community: OpenSolaris.org. 12

Essential URLs 15

Summary. 15

■CHAPTER 2   **The Advantages of Developing with OpenSolaris** 17

OpenSolaris Qualities 17

OpenSolaris Is Free 18

OpenSolaris Is Open Source. 19

OpenSolaris Runs on "Commodity" Hardware Platforms 20

OpenSolaris Runs High-Quality Application Software 22

You Can Get a Software Support Subscription for OpenSolaris 22

OK, It's Like Linux. So What?...23

    Scalability 23

    Service Management..23

    ZFS 24

    DTrace 24

    Virtualization 25

    Security 25

Summary...26

CHAPTER 3   **Getting and Installing OpenSolaris** 27

Installation Choices...29

Checking Your System 30

Live CD Booting 34

Direct "Bare-Metal" Installation 36

Multiboot Installation...36

Installing OpenSolaris as a Guest VM (Recommended) 37

Are We There Yet?...47

Summary...50

CHAPTER 4   **A Familiar User and Developer Environment and More**...51

At Home with GNOME..51

The CLI, for the GUI-averse 55

To su, or Not to sudo?..56

Boot and Reboot..57

    Updating Your Kernel Build....................................59

Other Administrative Tasks 62

    Adding New Users 62

    Printing..64

Summary...65

PART 2 ▪ ▪ ▪ **Working with OpenSolaris**

▪**CHAPTER 5**   **SMF: The Service Management Facility** 69

What's a Service? 70
A Bit About Milestones 74
More About Services 74
Creating Your Own Services 81
Summary 88

▪**CHAPTER 6**   **The ZFS File System** 89

Exploring the Basic ZFS Features 91
Creating and Managing ZFS Storage Pools 94
Creating a ZFS Pool 95
Managing Boot Environments with ZFS 108
Summary 110

▪**CHAPTER 7**   **OpenSolaris and Virtualization** 111

Zones and Containers 118
Creating a Zone 120
Global and Local Zone Environments 124
Cloning a Zone 127
Managing Zones 128
Using the Zone 129
Managing Zone Resources 130
More OpenSolaris Virtualization 133
VirtualBox 134
The xVM Hypervisor 136
Installing the OpenSolaris 2008.11 xVM Hypervisor 138
BrandZ 145
LDoms 148
Summary 150

PART 3 ▪▪▪ Exploiting OpenSolaris's Unique Features

▪CHAPTER 8 A Development Environment on OpenSolaris 153

Introducing the Web Stack and AMP 154
Getting the AMP Stack 154
    Taking a Tour of the Command-Line Package Manager 156
Making a Case for Containers 162
Building Applications for a Container Environment 163
    Introducing Zones and Discrete Privileges 163
    Qualifying Your Application for Zones 164
Installing Tomcat in a Container 165
Installing MySQL 172
Taking a Quick Tour of NetBeans IDE 175
Using Subversion 179
    Creating the Repository and Managing Files 179
    Using the Manage Access Control Method 183
Integrating NetBeans with Other Products 191
    Integrating with Tomcat 191
    Integrating with Subversion 193
Putting It All Together with IPS 200
Summary 204

▪CHAPTER 9 Innovative OpenSolaris Features 205

DTrace 205
    Probes 207
    Providers 208
    DTrace Scripts 208
    A Simple Example 209
    DTrace Aggregations 210
    DTrace Community Contributions 212
    DTrace and Java 218

The Tracker Utility: Where's That File? 219

The OpenSolaris Distro Constructor 220

The Device Driver Utility 222

And Now for a Little Entertainment 223

OpenSolaris Educational Resources 226

    The OpenSolaris Curriculum Development Resources 226

    OpenSolaris Learning Cloud Service 227

Summary 229

PART 4 ■■■ **Appendixes**

■APPENDIX A   **Recommended Reading and Viewing** 233

Books 233

Blogs and Wikis 234

Developer Resources 234

Learning and Training 235

Linux to OpenSolaris Translation 235

Newsletter 235

User Groups 236

Videos 236

Web Sites 236

White Papers 237

■APPENDIX B   **OpenSolaris 2009.06** 239

SPARC Support 239

Project Crossbow 240

Encrypted ZFS File System 240

CUPS Printing 241

Other Anticipated Features 241

■INDEX 243

About the Authors

**HARRY J. FOXWELL** is a senior system engineer and OS ambassador for Sun Microsystems Federal, Inc., in the Washington, D.C., area, where he is responsible for solutions consulting and customer education on Solaris, OpenSolaris, Linux, open source software, and virtualization technologies.

Harry has worked for Sun Microsystems since 1995; he also authors Sun's internal web site of Linux technical information and has been a Linux user since 1995. He has been influential in developing and promoting Sun's Linux and open source strategies and messages. He is coauthor of two Sun BluePrints: "Slicing and Dicing Servers: A Guide to Virtualization and Containment Technologies" (Sun BluePrints Online, 2005) and "The Sun BluePrints Guide to Solaris Containers: Virtualization in the Solaris Operating System" (Sun BluePrints Online, 2006).

Harry received his doctorate in Information Technology in 2003 from George Mason University (in Fairfax, Virginia) and has since taught graduate-level computer science courses at GMU about operating systems and electronic commerce. His students use OpenSolaris, VirtualBox, MySQL, and other open source software from Sun in their course assignments and projects.

CHRISTINE TRAN is a software developer for Assured Decisions, LLC. Before that, she spent ten years at Sun Microsystems as a solutions architect and OS Ambassador, guiding customers through all aspects of working on the Solaris platform. She is the author of the online OpenSolaris Service Management Facility FAQ.

Christine is working on shipping her first product, built on Solaris 10 and Trusted Extensions. She has recently gone through First Customer Shipment (FCS) and finds the experience exhilarating and crushingly stressful at the same time, much like writing this book. She hopes to survive the support phase.

Christine holds a BSE in Electrical and Computer Engineering from Johns Hopkins University in Baltimore, Maryland.

About the Technical Reviewer

SAM NICHOLSON began his Solaris trip as a SunOS system administrator in the late 1980s, just in time to work on the conversion to 3.5.1. He has been an adherent ever since. He has earned his keep by writing file system bits, SCSI device drivers, and network management apps for Solaris and other Unixen. He has consulted in the fields of network services and information security. Having ridden two waves (the telecom and mortgage booms) to shore, he is now combining his experiences to design and deploy a nationwide satellite content delivery system. He's still enjoying the ride.

Acknowledgments

Writing a technical book in a short few months about a new and rapidly changing operating system like OpenSolaris is a challenge, but with the help of a great Apress team we were able to meet it.

Thanks to Frank Pohlmann, editorial director for Linux, for agreeing to the need for this book; to open source editor Michelle Lowman for her guidance and for giving us the freedom to write our own occasionally not-so-humble opinions; and to technical reviewer Sam Nicholson for keeping us from getting too carried away with our enthusiasm for this still evolving OS and yet-to-be perfected development environment. Special thanks to Apress project manager Kylie Johnston for her good-natured but insistent nagging that kept us (approximately) on schedule, and to copy editor Kim Wimpsett for her diligent efforts to make our perfect sentences even perfecter. ☺

The value of this book owes much to Christine Tran, for enthusiastically sharing her time to write on a difficult schedule and for sharing her extensive development experience. I don't think she knew what she was signing up for when we asked her to contribute, but I couldn't have found a better coauthor, and I sincerely thank her for her valuable work on this book.

We both wrote Pro OpenSolaris in our "spare time," and this book is not sponsored or supported in any way by Sun Microsystems other than agreeing to let me write it. Sun does, however, provide very useful and interesting technologies to write about!

And thanks most of all to my family for patiently (most of the time) tolerating my many "spare time" hours writing at the computer.

Harry J. Foxwell

I got an email in late December 2008 from Harry, asking me whether I would like to contribute a chapter to a book about OpenSolaris. I nonchalantly wrote Harry back saying, "Sure, whatever I can do to help," at the time thinking it would occupy, at most, one weekend banging out stuff I'd already known and written about. Besides, the project was probably not going to happen anyway. Little did I know it would explode to at least eight weekends and two all-nighters of writing, revisions, rewrites, one dead laptop, and more espresso and anxiety than is medically advisable. Now that our project is a reality, I couldn't be happier that Harry asked me and that I decided to do it, against all inclinations to make excuses and run away. Thanks, Harry! I'm honored to make a small contribution to this book.

There are no good writers, only good editors, project managers, and proofers. I could not have done this without Michelle Lowman, Kylie Johnston, and Kim Wimpsett, the Apress team who kept us on schedule and smoothed our way with their mastery of the production process. Thank you, publishing goddesses!

Finally, I thank my employer, Assured Decisions, and the MDeX team for their support of this project. I couldn't wish for a better crew.

Christine Tran

Introduction

If you're familiar with the UNIX operating system, perhaps you wonder what it will look like in the future given its long and varied history. We think it will look a lot like OpenSolaris, which is heavily influenced by the open source developer communities, especially by Linux developers.

In 2005, Sun Microsystems released the source code for one of its "crown jewels," Solaris 10, under an OSI-approved open source license and created the OpenSolaris.org community. Since that time, the numbers of OpenSolaris end users, user groups, application developers, and contributing kernel engineers have grown worldwide to several hundred thousand participants, and the number continues to increase.

We recognized that although there are myriad documents, tutorials, and software examples about OpenSolaris and its special features on the Web, a book on this "new" operating system was needed that would give readers an important perspective and organization of what's familiar and what's innovative about this software. So, we begin this book with a gentle reminder of what open source software is really about—community development—and then introduce you to the most recent version of OpenSolaris, the 2008.11 release. The next release is expected to be 2009.06.

OpenSolaris's roots are in Sun's Solaris 10 operating system. It therefore inherits decades of OS advances by Sun engineers, now enhanced and extended by the broader development community. It includes advanced features like the ZFS file system, OS virtualization, and DTrace, while providing an open source–based development environment that should be familiar to Linux users.

We hope you will do more than just satisfy your curiosity about OpenSolaris and that you will begin to use it as a foundation for your open source–based solutions.

Who This Book Is For

We assume that you are a professional system administrator or developer of an open source software environment based on Linux or on Solaris and that your learning style needs only an orientation and an indication of what should be learned first in order to take advantage of OpenSolaris. This is *not* an introductory book on how to replace Windows with OpenSolaris. We don't cover all the basics of GNOME, networking, and shell use, only indicating important concepts and details you will need to get started. We do give you detailed examples of key OpenSolaris technologies in order to illustrate their power and utility, and we give you helpful web references for further study. Both of us have extensive experience teaching and presenting Solaris and OpenSolaris, and our approach is to introduce you to OpenSolaris based on what you already know about similar operating systems.

How This Book Is Structured

Pro OpenSolaris is divided into three major sections. In the first part, "Getting Started" (Chapters 1 through 4), we describe the philosophy and origins of OpenSolaris and discuss the advantages of its unique features. We show you where to get the software, we review several methods of installing it on your systems, and we give you a tour of the OpenSolaris environment, highlighting its similarities to many Linux distributions.

In Part 2, "Working with OpenSolaris" (Chapters 5 through 7), we present details on how to use OpenSolaris's unique features, including the Service Management Facility (Chapter 5), the ZFS file system (Chapter 6), and virtualization (Chapter 7).

In Part 3, "Exploiting OpenSolaris's Unique Features" (Chapters 8 and 9), we present practical examples and innovative OpenSolaris technologies that enhance and extend your development environment. The extensive Chapter 8 brings all of these technologies together and shows you how to use OpenSolaris's development tools and familiar open source applications to build your AMP stack solutions. The final chapter highlights a number of innovative OpenSolaris features and includes a brief introduction to the DTrace observability tool, gives an overview of the Distribution Constructor, and directs you to some online resources to help you learn more about OpenSolaris.

Prerequisites

You should be familiar with downloading and installing software on your laptop, workstation, or server, and you should be generally familiar with the GNOME-based user environment found on most Linux distributions, as well as with basic network tools for such systems.

This book is based on the OpenSolaris 2008.11 release of the operating system; you should obtain and install the latest release as described in Chapter 3 from http://www.opensolaris.com/get/index.jsp and then use it to work through the book's examples. No programming experience is required, but the ultimate goal of the book is to get you to use OpenSolaris for your open source programming and administration projects.

Downloading the Code

The source code for this book is available to readers in the Source Code section at `http://www.apress.com`. Please feel free to visit the Apress web site and download all the code there. You can also check for errata and find related books from Apress.

Contacting the Authors

If you have comments, corrections, or questions about *Pro OpenSolaris*, please visit the book's web site at `http://apress.com/book/view/1430218916`. You can email Harry J. Foxwell at `hfoxwell@cs.gmu.edu`, and you can email Christine Tran at `christine.tran@gmail.com`.

PART 1

■ ■ ■

Getting Started

OpenSolaris is a community-developed and community-supported operating system platform you can use to host your open source applications and web solutions. Although its look and feel is purposely designed to appeal to Linux developers, OpenSolaris has unique features that make it an attractive alternative. In this part of the book, you'll learn about these features and the growing community that supports this new operating system.

CHAPTER 1

■■■

Introducing OpenSolaris

To change this rock into a jewel, you must change its true name.

—Kurremkarmerruk, the Master Namer, in *A Wizard of Earthsea*, by Ursula Le Guin

Welcome, open source solution developers! If you've purchased and are reading this book (thanks!) or if you're scanning it in the bookstore (please keep reading!), you probably think of yourself as a "Solaris developer" or a "Linux developer." You Solaris users, administrators, and developers may already know that as Sun Microsystems' commercial version of Solaris continues to evolve, it will look more and more like today's OpenSolaris, so it's great that you've chosen this book to learn more about it.

But if you call yourself a "Linux developer," is that your *true name*? Are you really among the less than 1 percent of all Linux users who download the kernel source code, change it or add to it, recompile it, and use the result for highly specialized purposes? Or are you truly an *open source solutions developer* who just happens to use one of the popular Linux operating system kernel distributions as the foundation for your work? If you're among the latter, *why* have you chosen Linux (if, in fact, you were the one who made the choice)?

The typical answers that we hear when we ask this question is that Linux distributions:

- "are free,"
- "are open source,"
- "support commodity platforms,"
- "run high quality application software," and
- "have vendor support available."

Well, so do other open source operating systems and their associated user and development environments. This book is about another such operating system with these characteristics, OpenSolaris.

If you're an open source solutions developer, you should realize that the true name of your development environment is not limited to Linux and that there is generally no such thing as a "Linux application." Rather, you're likely using a packaged distribution of open source user interface tools and developer tools that have been compiled for the Linux kernel. Red Hat's Enterprise Linux, Novell's SUSE Linux Enterprise, and Ubuntu Linux are among the most popular of such distributions. So-called Linux applications are really "open source applications" that happen to have been compiled and distributed with the Linux kernel; they could just as easily have been compiled for other kernels, as indeed many of them have. Some of these applications and tools have even been compiled for so-called proprietary environments such as Microsoft Windows. Indeed, calling an open source application like the Apache web server a "Linux application" actually limits its consideration for use on other platforms. There's even a term for this view of the typical collection of web software technologies that Linux developers use—the *LAMP stack*, comprising Linux, Apache, MySQL, and PHP—and there are many books on this specific combination of software. In this book, we'll be showing you that there are some advantages to substituting something else for that *L*.

To make it clear what we're emphasizing, look at the typical open source stack of software you're probably using in Table 1-1. The Linux kernel *can* provide the operating system foundation for the stack, but it's *not required*; other commercial or community operating systems such as AIX, HP-UX, Solaris 10, OS X, FreeBSD, or OpenSolaris are widely used as well, since virtually all the "standard" open source tools in the stack are available for these systems. So, it's useful to examine the relative advantages of the available operating system kernels.

Table 1-1. *A Typical Open Source User and Developer Stack*

Stack Component	Tools and Utilities
User and developer tools	Firefox browser, Thunderbird email, OpenOffice, gcc and Java compilers; Perl, Ruby, other languages; IDEs, vi/vim and emacs, bash and csh shells
Desktop environment	GNOME and/or KDE Desktop tools
Window system	X Window System and tools
Services and utilities	UNIX and GNU programs, services, and utilities, web servers, application servers, databases, Apache, JBoss, GlassFish, MySQL
APIs and system libraries	POSIX libraries and extensions, language libraries
Operating system kernel and services	Process scheduling, security, network, resource management, virtualization support; Linux, FreeBSD, OS X, or OpenSolaris
System hardware	Multicore, multithreaded processors; Intel, AMD, SPARC, PowerPC

Clearly, what you are most concerned with when designing and creating your open source solutions is the availability of a familiar, productive, efficient, and comprehensive user and development environment. This is provided by the open source components that have been compiled for and integrated with the underlying operating system kernel. And of course you'll want the operating system to provide high-quality services for performance, scalability, and security; special features such as virtualization support, debugging aids, and resource management would be a bonus. The various open source operating system kernels, along with their "distribution" tools and accessories, each have specific advantages for open source development and deployment. This book focuses on the advantages of using the OpenSolaris distribution for such work.

The *True Name* of Open Source Software

While we're discussing open source software, let's call it by its true name. The term *open source software* is often misunderstood to mean Linux software, free software, shareware, or other terms that emphasize the method of acquiring the programs or the fact that you can obtain and inspect the programs' source code.

The names we give to concepts can either enhance understanding or confuse practitioners and users. The term *virtualization*, for example, includes some technologies that have no true virtualization components; we prefer *workload containment*, which includes true virtualization but also includes other concepts.

Open source is another somewhat misused and misunderstood term that focuses on the wrong component of modern software development. A better phrase to use is *community-developed software*, which focuses on the true methodology (yes, you obviously can't have community development without access to the source code, but the source code itself should not be the main focus...Microsoft could publish the entire Vista source and still severely restrict its sharing and use!). We'll have more on the community aspect of OpenSolaris later.

We also avoid the term *free* and prefer using *freely sharable* or some other words that focus on the community rather than on the object of the community's activity. Then we can emphasize the distinction between community-supported software and commercially supported software, *regardless of the software's origin* (community developers and/or commercial developers).

When you think about it, much of what so-called open source businesses such as Red Hat, Novell, Sun, HP, IBM, and others are selling is commercially supported community software. It's not as pretty sounding as *open source software*, but it's more accurate nevertheless. However, we do not expect businesses or developers to change their vocabulary simply for the sake of accuracy.

Speaking of the commercial software developers, it's very interesting to observe the recent trend of such companies acquiring the trademarks, distribution rights, and support rights to popular and mature community-developed tools. For example:

- Novell acquires SuSE Linux (2004).

- Red Hat acquires JBoss (2006).

- Oracle acquires the Sleepycat database (2006).

- Citrix acquires XenSource and Xen (2007).

- Sun Microsystems acquires MySQL (2008), Lustre (2007), and Innotek/VirtualBox (2008).

These vendors and others are also taking advantage of the community development model for their own internally originated software in order to expand their user bases and to obtain the hoped-for benefits of community support. Sun, notably, has released much of its own as well as its acquired software under various OSI-approved open source licenses, including the following, to name just a few:

- Java

- GlassFish Application Server

- NetBeans IDE

- StarOffice (now OpenOffice)

- Grid Engine

- Solaris 10 (now OpenSolaris)

You should therefore anticipate a future open source development environment with a variety of support and distribution models, from the traditional "totally free" approach to the multitier approach that provides both "community" and "enterprise" editions and support levels for open source software on a wide selection of hardware and operating system platforms. Sun Microsystems does provide subscription support services for OpenSolaris (see `http://www.sun.com/service/opensolaris/faq.xml`), and these services are still evolving as Sun enhances its operating system offerings from Solaris 10 to OpenSolaris. In the meantime, we'll concentrate on describing the features and benefits of this new, community-developed operating system.

What You'll Find and Learn in This Book

Pro OpenSolaris assumes you're already generally familiar with either Linux or Solaris 10 as an end user, software developer, or system administrator. It explains the origin and intent of Sun Microsystems' effort to move from the internally developed Solaris 10 operating system to the community-developed OpenSolaris. Later in this chapter, we'll detail the projects and activities of the OpenSolaris community and will encourage you to become part of it. Chapter 2 will highlight the advantages of using OpenSolaris as your solutions development platform, including advanced technologies such as the DTrace observability tool, the ZFS file system, virtualization with zones, and Service Management, all typically not found in any of today's Linux distributions. In Chapters 3 and 4, we'll discuss the various options for installing OpenSolaris, and we'll review the common features that both Linux and Solaris users will find familiar, such as the GNOME user environment shown in Figure 1-1. Then we'll get to work, showing you how to exploit OpenSolaris's unique technologies such as containers, including how to set up and use the AMP software stack for OpenSolaris-hosted web solutions.

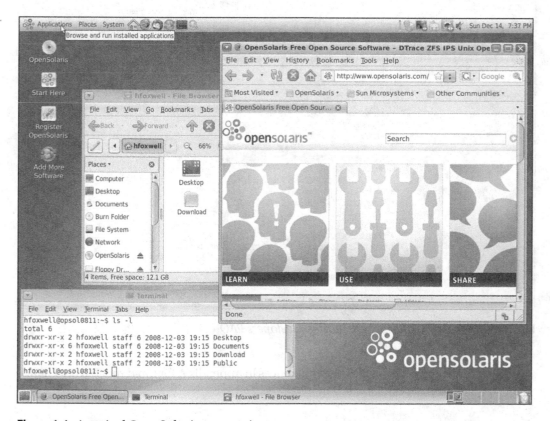

Figure 1-1. *A typical OpenSolaris user session*

We won't be digging into the internals of the OpenSolaris source code or covering how to write OpenSolaris device drivers, because this book focuses on *using* OpenSolaris rather than its design or development. Readers interested in those topics can go directly to the source at http://www.opensolaris.org/os/get/ and http://www.solarisinternals.com or to the OpenSolaris device drivers community at http://www.opensolaris.org/os/community/device_drivers/. If you're willing and able to contribute new features or bug fixes to the OpenSolaris community, there is an active contributor community FAQ on how to get involved (see Figure 1-2).

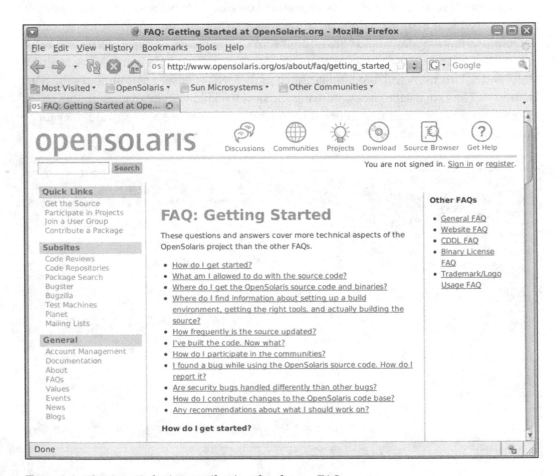

Figure 1-2. *The OpenSolaris contributing developers FAQ*

Don't forget to check out the other references in Appendix A for topics not covered here.

The Origin of OpenSolaris

OpenSolaris has a long and rather unique history as an open source operating system, and its origins go all the way back to the early days of UNIX, which, ironically, was one of the first major open source projects. We don't need to review all of its detailed history except to highlight some key events relevant to today's OpenSolaris:

- *1965–1972*: Ken Thompson and Dennis Ritchie develop UNIX at AT&T's Bell Laboratories; AT&T distributes UNIX source code to universities and industry users.

- *1976–1979*: Bill Joy at UC Berkeley enhances UNIX memory management; AT&T continues UNIX technical development.

- *1982–1983*: AT&T releases commercial UNIX System V; Sun Microsystems founded and releases UNIX-based SunOS.

- *1984–1987*: AT&T releases additional versions of UNIX System V.

- *1988–1992*: AT&T works with Sun on UNIX development; Open Software Foundation and UNIX International formed; Novell purchases AT&T's UNIX Software Lab; *Sun acquires rights to UNIX SVR4 code for distribution of source, binaries, and derivatives.*

- *1991*: Linus Torvalds releases the first implementation of Linux.

- *1994–1995*: First Red Hat Linux distribution released; Red Hat Software founded, first SuSE Linux distribution released.

- *1999*: Sun Microsystems announces intent to release Solaris under open source license.

- *2001*: National Security Agency (NSA) releases Linux-based SELinux.

- *2002*: Sun Microsystems reenters x86 server market, considers own Linux distribution, and later decides to OEM and support Red Hat and SuSE Linux.

- *2004*: Novell acquires SuSE Linux.

- *2005*: Solaris 10 is released, which is the first release of Solaris source code under the OSI-approved CDDL license; OpenSolaris.org founded.

- *2007*: Sun Microsystems hires Debian developer Ian Murdock to guide the OpenSolaris project.

- *2008*: First OpenSolaris binary is release, with source code; IDC reports Sun rises to no. 4 provider of x86 servers; NSA announces collaboration with OpenSolaris community to integrate mandatory access control (MAC), based on the Flux Advanced Security Kernel (Flask) architecture into OpenSolaris.

Being derived from the first UNIX, OpenSolaris has evolved from one of the original collaborations between the industry and the general software development community, passing through a period of commercial ownership with restricted access to the source code and arriving today as an enterprise-quality open source operating system that is developed, distributed, and supported by Sun, by other technology vendors, and by a growing community of users and developers.

Why did Sun start down this open source path with its highly regarded core operating system technology? In part, the answer has to do with you, the developer. In recent years, the two largest groups of developers have been for Windows and for Linux. And although today's Solaris 10 arguably has compelling advantages as an open source deployment platform, one of its target developer groups—Linux users and programmers—found its user interface and tools to be unfamiliar and sometimes lacking when compared to what they were accustomed to in modern Linux distributions.

Sun has now started what might be called the "Linuxification" of Solaris. Future versions of Solaris will look more like today's OpenSolaris, and that's good news for Linux users and developers because they now have a powerful yet familiar alternative environment on which to host their open source solutions. Obviously, Sun's strategy is to attract more developers to OpenSolaris, and that appears to be working considering the rapid growth of the OpenSolaris.org community.

Goals and Future Directions

Having finally released a stable, well-designed binary distribution of OpenSolaris, what's next? Sun would certainly like to preserve the high quality and popularity of Solaris 10 while transforming it into the preferred community-developed operating system. It wants to keep Solaris's scalability, stability, and binary compatibility features; develop a profitable product support model; and continue to expand OpenSolaris's user base. It also wants to continually add to the operating system's list of useful features, both those unique to OpenSolaris and those popular in Linux distributions.

According to the public road maps for Solaris 10 and OpenSolaris on http://www. sun.com and on http://www.opensolaris.org, you'll eventually see the expansion of Sun's OpenSolaris support subscription offerings, support for SPARC platforms (especially for the new multicore chips), a growing base of ISVs supporting their applications on Open-Solaris, and encouragement of contributing community software developers. Sun is also increasing its focus on the academic research and student communities. There is already a comprehensive OpenSolaris-based curriculum for university computer science courses that some schools have started to use, and hundreds of thousands of students and computer science faculty from around the world have downloaded OpenSolaris for their research and coursework.

New builds of OpenSolaris will be posted on the web site every two weeks. As with Solaris, these builds include bug fixes, new features, and support for newly released hardware. Officially supported, stable binary releases, such as the 2008.11 release, are targeted for a 6-month update cycle, along with an 18-month support subscription cycle for each release. Also on the road map are enhancements of the OpenSolaris application software repositories' content and features, including specialized repositories for supported, experimental, and ISV packages.

Note There have been several Solaris-related binary release downloads available: Solaris 10 for x86 and SPARC, the Solaris Express Community and Developer Edition releases, and the OpenSolaris releases. The Solaris Express releases, which gave periodic snapshots of future Solaris 10 technologies, will be replaced by the OpenSolaris distributions for x86 and SPARC.

That Troublesome CDDL License

Nothing seems to arouse the passions of open source developers more than discussions of how source code is licensed. Whole books, thousands of web pages, and innumerable blogs argue the merits and deficiencies of the various "open source" or "free software" licenses. The Open Source Initiative (OSI) organization, which works with community software developers, is the caretaker of the official definition of *open source* and has approved more than 70 different licenses for such software. Two of these approved licenses, the GNU General Public License (GPL) and the Common Development and Distribution License (CDDL), are the focus of much of the controversy over how Sun has released the code for OpenSolaris.

It is important to understand how community-developed source code is licensed if you use such code to build new programs. To put it as briefly as possible, the GPL's goal is to encourage the broadest sharing of community-developed software; all projects using GPL-licensed code, including derived works, require the public sharing of any changes or enhancements to the code.

After more than 5 years of legal review and documentation effort, Sun released the nearly 10 million lines of source code for OpenSolaris under the file-based CDDL, which essentially requires that source files derived from common files must be shared but that executables of derived works may use other licenses, including those that permit protection of software patents, which many GPL proponents consider "evil."

Under the CDDL, you can combine your program files with those covered by other licenses, you can release your code under more than one license, you're *not* required to release the source of your "proprietary" value-added code, and you can distribute and sell binaries derived from OpenSolaris source files.

The controversy will no doubt continue, and the CDDL might be reexamined for new OpenSolaris components in light of new business requirements and community needs and the development of new licenses such as the GPLv3, which attempts to address some of the concerns about the commercialization of open source software.

The OpenSolaris Community: OpenSolaris.org

No open source project survives for long without a large, actively contributing community of developers and users. Founded by Sun in 2005, OpenSolaris.org now includes more than 150,000 registered community members, more than 300 discussion groups with more than 250,000 postings, and nearly 100 registered OpenSolaris User Groups worldwide. More than half of the visitors to the OpenSolaris web site, shown in Figure 1-3, are from outside the United States, including many from Germany, the United Kingdom, Japan, India, China, and South America.

OpenSolaris community members support the development and deployment of the operating system and tools by participating in online help forums and mailing lists, promoting and explaining the project and its activities to the press and to developer communities, creating and contributing marketing materials, and of course writing and debugging kernel components and user applications and tools. In addition to the Sun kernel development engineers who now work on Solaris and OpenSolaris almost exclusively through the public web sites, hundreds of contributors who do not work for Sun are refining and adding to this project.

You might wonder, who decides what goes into OpenSolaris? Like with Linux, Java, JBoss, Xen, MySQL, and other open source software, it's the owner of the trademark who has the final say of what that trademark means. Linus Torvalds is the owner of the Linux trademark and is therefore the "benevolent dictator" for what goes into the Linux kernel. Sun Microsystems, advised by members of the Java Community Process (JCP, at http://www.jcp.org), does the same for open source Java. Similarly, Sun currently is the final arbiter of OpenSolaris content and features, with significant input from the OpenSolaris Community Advisory Board (CAB) and community members, whose charter is "...the collaborative production of open source software related to the OpenSolaris family of operating systems and committed to fostering the evolution and adoption of the Open-Solaris code base." The CAB has a community-developed governance charter and open elections, along with well-defined roles and responsibilities of board members, regular members, and technical contributors to projects.

OpenSolaris users, developers, and contributors have gathered for tutorials, technical presentations, and BoF sessions at many of the traditional Linux and annual open source conferences and workshops such as JavaOne, OSCON, ApacheCon, Community-One, and Usenix, as well as at Tech Days sponsored around the world by Sun in Europe, India, China, the United States, and Japan. As the OpenSolaris community grows, active users are posting wikis and blogs to share what they've learned. One of the most popular blogs is the OpenSolaris Observatory at http://blogs.sun.com/observatory, which includes video demonstrations and tutorials (see Figure 1-4).

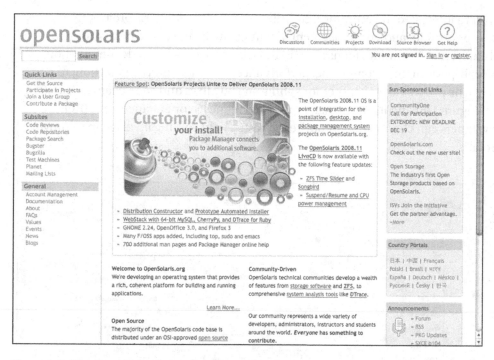

Figure 1-3. *The OpenSolaris community web page*

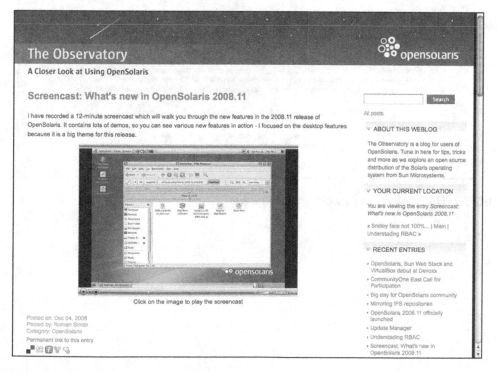

Figure 1-4. *The OpenSolaris Observatory blog*

If you're interested in becoming a contributor to the OpenSolaris project, there is ample opportunity and encouragement to participate in any of the nearly 50 special-interest communities focused on issues such as accessibility, documentation, games, high-performance computing, performance, security, and virtualization, to name but a few. The process and web sites for submitting bug fixes and code changes is well defined (Figure 1-5) and includes many suggested requests for enhancement (RFEs) that developers can choose from if they're interested in becoming involved in improving OpenSolaris.

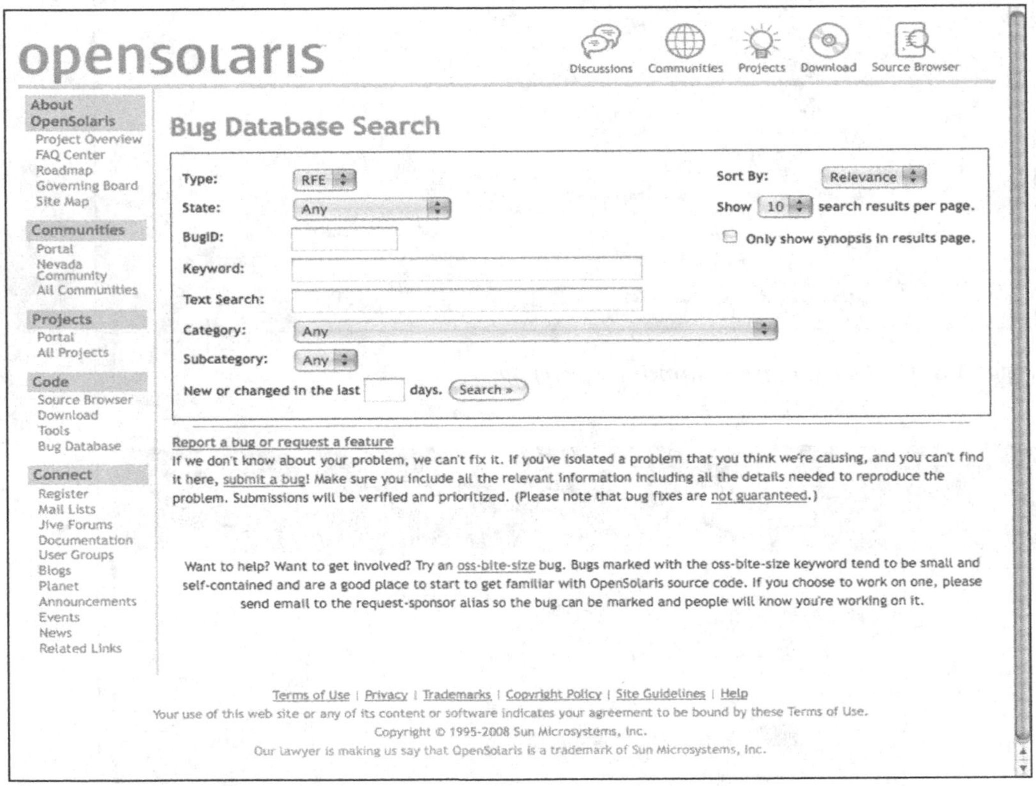

Figure 1-5. *The OpenSolaris bug-tracking and RFE site*

Essential URLs

Be sure to visit these web sites frequently to learn what's going on in the OpenSolaris communities and to learn about new software features, bug fixes, and opportunities to participate:

- The OpenSolaris community: http://www.opensolaris.org

- The OpenSolaris FAQs: http://www.opensolaris.org/os/about/faq/

- Getting started as an OpenSolaris contributor: http://www.opensolaris.org/os/about/faq/getting_started_developers/

- OpenSolaris downloads and learning resources: http://www.opensolaris.com/learn/

Summary

OpenSolaris is already a successful open source project because of its historical roots in Sun's Solaris operating system and its large and active development community. You can participate as an end user and application developer or as a contributor to OpenSolaris to improve its features, documentation, or usage. Next, you'll learn about some of the technologies that make OpenSolaris a good choice for open source development.

CHAPTER 2

The Advantages of Developing with OpenSolaris

When people say they want Linux, they want the user environment that the various distributors have built around the Linux kernel. It's the GNU utilities, the GNU Desktop environment, the compiler tool chain, Apache, MySQL, Ruby on Rails, and so on.

—Ian Murdock, now at Sun Microsystems, founder of the Debian Linux distribution

Netscape founder Marc Andreessen somewhat famously remarked in 2006 that "Solaris is a better Linux than Linux." That comment raised a bit of ire from many Linux proponents, but what he was referring to at the time was Solaris 10's excellent reputation for code quality, reliability, performance, and scalability. OpenSolaris inherits those characteristics.

Note Some of the OpenSolaris documents and web sites you'll find on the Internet refer to Solaris 10 information on Sun web sites. Sun is continually updating these sites, and, in most cases, technical details listed for Solaris 10 are applicable to OpenSolaris.

OpenSolaris Qualities

We mentioned in Chapter 1 that Linux distributions are widely used today because they:

- "are free,"
- "are open source,"
- "support commodity platforms,"
- "run high-quality application software," and
- "have vendor support available."

OpenSolaris has all these qualities and more. Let's look at each of these key points.

OpenSolaris Is Free

As with nearly all other community-developed software, OpenSolaris can be legally downloaded, shared and redistributed, and deployed in your projects and IT infrastructure without charge. You can use it to study how it works, and you can fix things you think are broken or enhance it for your own specific purposes and projects. Software vendors and developers may incorporate OpenSolaris code into their products and may charge for them, just as companies like Red Hat, Novell, Sun, and others package and support Linux kernels and other community-developed software. You can get the OpenSolaris sources and binaries at http://opensolaris.com (see Figure 2-1).

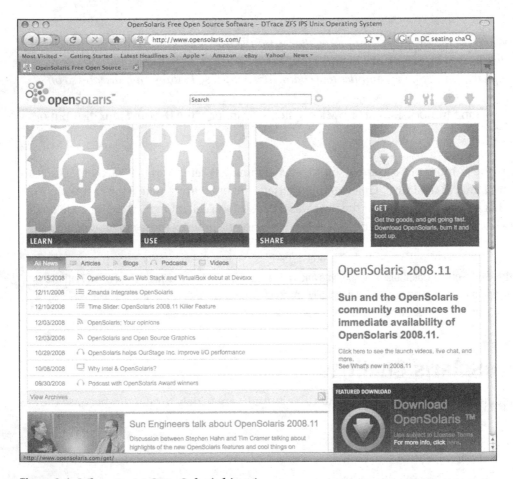

Figure 2-1. *Where to get OpenSolaris binaries*

OpenSolaris Is Open Source

It's really "community developed," remember? We already mentioned that OpenSolaris is distributed under the CDDL license that lets you share, use, integrate, change, and add to the source code, as well as protect your intellectual property investments and patents. This means that you have the same OSI-approved license responsibilities and opportunities with OpenSolaris as you do with Linux distributions. OpenSolaris's Source Code web site at http://opensolaris.org/os/get, shown in Figure 2-2, is the place to go for all code related information; it includes a source code search and browser tool (Figure 2-3) that you can use to find the sections of the code that you need

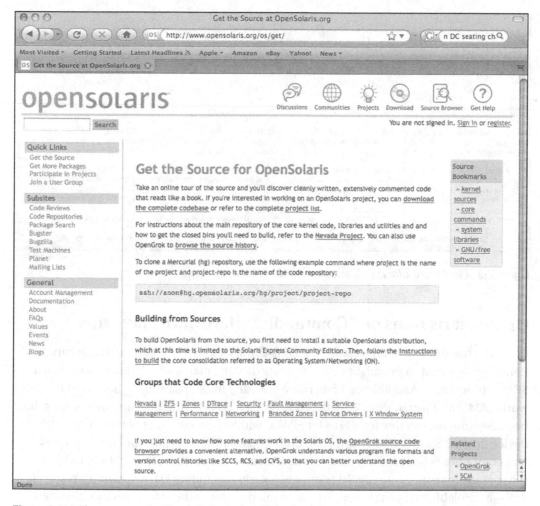

Figure 2-2. *Where to get the OpenSolaris source code*

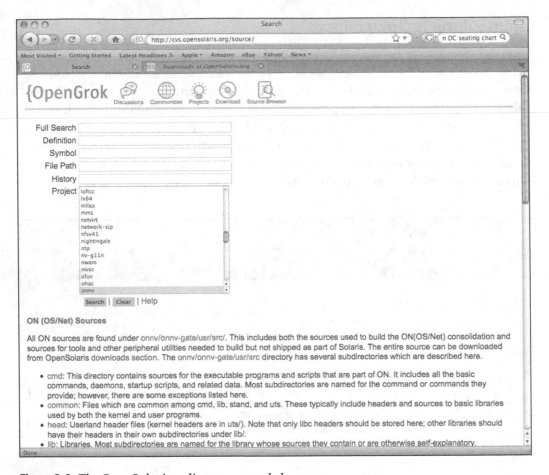

Figure 2-3. *The OpenSolaris online source code browser*

OpenSolaris Runs on "Commodity" Hardware Platforms

For some reason, one of the best-kept secrets about OpenSolaris is where it can run. Longtime Sun customers might recall the early days of Solaris, which ran only on Sun's SPARC processors. And although Sun had a few early missteps bringing Solaris to the x86 world (AMD and Intel), since 2004 the code base for Solaris, and now for OpenSolaris, has been essentially the same for x86 as for SPARC with the exception of platform-specific device drivers. So, OpenSolaris runs on thousands of different AMD and Intel systems and components from hundreds of manufacturers such as IBM, HP, and Dell, not just those made by Sun. Every special feature of Solaris—including DTrace, containers, and ZFS—is available on both processors; OpenSolaris inherits these features too. New versions of OpenSolaris will be available for SPARC systems, although SPARC support has lagged a bit because the boot process for such systems needed to be changed to use ZFS like the x86 systems do.

If you're not sure whether OpenSolaris will run on your laptop, workstation, or server, you can check out Sun's Hardware Compatibility List at `http://www.sun.com/bigadmin/hcl/` (see Figure 2-4).

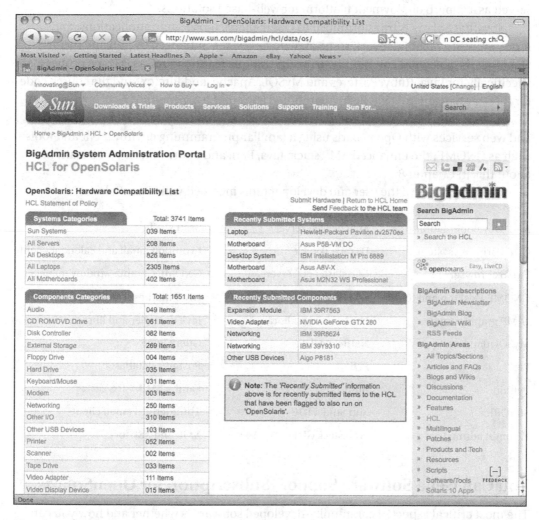

Figure 2-4. *The OpenSolaris Hardware Compatibility List*

Sun and Toshiba recently announced that laptops with OpenSolaris preinstalled will be available on certain models; similar plans for other laptops are underway.

There is also a Sun Device Detection Tool that you can run at `http://www.sun.com/bigadmin/hcl/hcts/device_detect.jsp` to determine whether OpenSolaris can run on your specific system. You can use this tool on AMD and Intel systems running Solaris, Windows, Linux, and even OS X prior to OpenSolaris installation to examine devices on your system and to report whether built-in or downloadable drivers are available for those devices. We'll show you how to use this tool in the next chapter.

OpenSolaris Runs High-Quality Application Software

For many years Solaris has been distributed with both supported and unsupported open source tools such as Apache, Perl, Postgres, Webmin, MySQL, and many others, and it has served as a superb deployment platform for web-based solutions.

Now that Solaris is transforming into OpenSolaris, those same applications, and more, are still available. In fact, some of them have been enhanced by Sun and by the OpenSolaris developer community to include unique features such as DTrace probes specifically for Java, Ruby, Postgres and MySQL, Apache, and Firefox, and the source code for these enhancements has been contributed back to the community.

So, *and this is the main point of this book*, you can build highly capable applications and web services with OpenSolaris using a familiar programming environment and tools such as GNOME, the enhanced AMP stack, Java, Perl, and many others. You'll learn more about this in Chapter 8.

These are some of the user and developer tools included with OpenSolaris:

AMP Developer Library	Apache web server	Bash shell
CUPS printing system	DTrace Toolkit	Evolution email and calendar client
Firefox browser	GlassFish app server	GNOME Compiz window manager
GNOME Desktop and tools	GNU gcc compiler and tools	GNU utilities
GIMP graphics tool	HPC developer library	Java compiler and libraries
MySQL database	NetBeans IDE	OpenOffice
Perl	PHP	Postgres database
Python	Ruby	Samba SMB/CIFS server
StarOffice	Sun Studio IDE	Thunderbird email client
Webmin admin tool	Web stack GUI	XML and XSL tools

You Can Get a Software Support Subscription for OpenSolaris

The most critical aspect of community-developed software is whether and how you can get immediate support when you deploy it on mission-critical systems. In today's business environment, people wonder how anyone can make money when the software is "free." That doesn't seem to bother successful companies such as Red Hat and Novell; like other open source businesses, they make money through support subscriptions.

Can you get support for OpenSolaris? Certainly! Look here: http://www.sun.com/service/opensolaris/index.jsp. You can get 24/7 production use and escalation support from Sun at prices comparable to those for Linux distributions, as well as lower-tier email support. Currently, each new supported OpenSolaris binary release comes out every 6 months and is supported for 18 months. Longer-term support cycles will emerge as Sun enhances its OpenSolaris support to match what has been available for Solaris.

OK, It's Like Linux. So What?

You might think that the characteristics we just reviewed make OpenSolaris "just like Linux." If they're really the same now, why consider any alternative to Linux? Well, they're not the same. Here are some of the key advantages of OpenSolaris. You'll learn how to exploit these benefits in later chapters.

Scalability

Because OpenSolaris is derived from Solaris 10, it has essentially the same scalability characteristics. Solaris has proven itself to scale nearly linearly to hundreds of processors on traditional SMP systems, on the new generation of CMP/CMT SPARC processors, and on the new multicore processors from Intel (Dual Quad Core Xeon) and AMD (Dual Quad Core Opteron). New virtualization features on Intel's Xeon and AMD's Opteron processors are also supported.

In general, the OpenSolaris kernel, like Solaris, scales and performs more stably under heavy CPU, memory, and I/O loads than on other UNIX kernels or on Linux. Recent SPECjAppServer2004 benchmarks using all open source web stack software on OpenSolaris, and including the GlassFish application server, have produced world-record results.

OpenSolaris is a 64-bit-addressing operating system and takes full advantage of 64-bit processors from Intel, AMD, and SPARC; 32-bit mode and applications are supported as well. This means that you can have up to 2TB of memory on current hardware, and even more as future server hardware and memory modules evolve to support larger memory systems.

Service Management

It's no longer acceptable for production servers to crash because of a hardware or software failure. Because of the 24/7 global use of your systems, there are no more "windows" of time during which you can plan to fix or upgrade servers. So, there must be both hardware and software frameworks that allow you to monitor system services, keep them running in spite of errors or failures, provide intelligible error codes and diagnostics, and allow for configuration of service dependencies. Fortunately, server hardware from nearly all the major equipment vendors has advanced to include component redundancy and "hot swap" capabilities. When fans, power supplies, and even memory boards and CPUs fail, they can usually be replaced without service interruption. But the operating systems on such hardware must be smart enough to provide software fault management as well. That's what the OpenSolaris Service Management Facility (SMF) provides—monitoring, management, and failure recovery for critical software that starts when your system boots such as database startup, secure login and network services, and web service daemons.

The old way of managing these services through *ad hoc*/etc/rc scripts is insufficient for today's server uptime requirements. SMF helps keep your servers running and helps you quickly determine what's wrong when and if a service fails.

ZFS

The ZFS file system provides a unique advantage for OpenSolaris. It includes data integrity checks, RAID-like features, and storage management services. OpenSolaris boots and updates using ZFS, allowing you to try patches and upgrades and to back them out if necessary. ZFS's 128-bit addressing eliminates traditional UFS size restrictions, supporting "ginormous" file systems and file sizes of thousands of terabytes. ZFS also includes both file system compression and encryption options. It allows both end users and system administrators to take instant and periodic point-in-time snapshots, to roll back to earlier snapshots, and to easily recover lost files. It also makes sharing file systems across different storage architectures very easy since it automatically converts between big-endian and little-endian bit order.

ZFS is one of the "foundation" technologies of OpenSolaris; it supports booting the root file system, safe and easy upgrading and patching using file system snapshots, and an automatic backup/recovery desktop tool called Time Slider, which is similar to Apple OS X's Time Machine.

ZFS recently won *InfoWorld*'s 2008 Storage Technology of the Year Award, and because, again, it's an open source community project, it's now included in FreeBSD and Apple's OS X operating systems. But because of licensing issues, ZFS is not yet generally available for any of the major Linux distributions.

DTrace

If you can't see it, you can't fix it. The OpenSolaris kernel is fully instrumented for full observability, allowing performance tuning and bug tracing from application function calls all the way down the software and hardware stack to hardware interrupts, using one powerful tool. It's nonintrusive, meaning you can't hurt your system while using DTrace, which in turn means it's ideal if you want to use it to diagnose application and operating system issues on your production systems. It's like an MRI for OpenSolaris instead of brain surgery—it won't hurt.

A wide range of developer and performance-monitoring tools are now available to help you use DTrace, including an open source DTrace GUI, the DLight tool integrated with the Sun Studio developer IDE, and hundreds of clever and useful DTrace scripts contributed by OpenSolaris.org members.

DTrace has gotten extraordinary attention from the developer community, has been recognized with the *Wall Street Journal*'s 2006 Innovation Award, and (because it's open source, remember?) it's now integrated with FreeBSD and with Apple's OS X operating system's "Instruments" programming and monitoring tools, so there is now an even larger community of DTrace experts with which to share ideas.

Virtualization

OpenSolaris actually supports several types of virtualization:

- *Single-kernel mode*: On both SPARC and x86 systems in the form of containers (zones)

- *Multikernel modes*: Xen-based guest virtual machine (VMs) on the x86 processors and soon Logical Domains (LDoms) on Sun's Sun4v UltraSPARC processors

This provides a choice for how you want to deploy and manage virtualization/consolidation efforts. There's even a special form of virtualization in OpenSolaris that lets you run Linux applications in a container without requiring a full Linux kernel. You'll learn more about this in Chapter 7.

Several virtualization software providers—notably VMware, XenSource, Microsoft, and Sun—provide commercial and open source hypervisor software that allow you to run OpenSolaris as a guest operating system on Windows, Linux, OS X, and even on OpenSolaris itself. Installing OpenSolaris as a virtual machine (VM) is an ideal way for you to learn about its features and advantages. We'll review how to install OpenSolaris as a virtual machine in the next chapter.

Security

OpenSolaris includes modern security capabilities such as role-based access control (RBAC) and full configuration of all user and process permissions. Recognizing that very few applications really need to run as root, OpenSolaris enables administrators to configure only the execution and access privileges needed by each program. The OpenSolaris root account is now just another user role all of whose privileges can be explicitly controlled; the operating system checks for these privileges rather than simply inspecting for UID 0 and granting all privileges when running programs as root.

A cryptographic framework and APIs are provided for you to develop applications that communicate with smart cards, biometric devices, crypto accelerator boards, and on-chip crypto stream processors. OpenSolaris also supports digitally signed executables, disabling stack execution, and secure by default installation. Of course, your familiar security tools such as SSH, OpenSSL, IPFilter, VPN support, and sudo are also included.

A sudo-like utility, pfexec, is available to allow for delegating administrative tasks and for granting root privileges to other users.

The U.S. government's National Security Agency (NSA) has worked with open source communities to enhance operating system and application security. For example, its SELinux kernel modifications have been integrated with Linux distributions such as Fedora and Red Hat Enterprise Linux. The NSA also started working in March 2008 with both Sun and with OpenSolaris developers to support Flexible Mandatory Access Control (FMAC) and the Flux Advanced Security Kernel (FLASK).

OpenSolaris adds a unique feature called Trusted Extensions, which supports the Trusted Computing feature known as labeled objects; labels define the security sensitivity of files, processes, and devices and specify access rights based on a user's security policy profile. OpenSolaris implements this through the use of labeled containers. Solaris 10 with Solaris Trusted Extensions has achieved the U.S. government's Common Criteria Certification for the Labeled Security Protection Profile (LSPP) at Evaluation Assurance Level (EAL) 4+, the highest commonly recognized global security certification. Open-Solaris inherits Solaris 10's security technologies, which you can use to enhance data privacy and to create safer web services and application environments; Sun plans to submit future versions of OpenSolaris for formal security evaluations.

You'll read more about containers' security features in Chapter 7 and more about how to use the advanced security features of OpenSolaris in Chapter 8.

Summary

OpenSolaris is not "just another open source operating system." Although it is indeed designed to give you all of the tools, behavior, and appearance that you're already familiar with as a "Linux developer," it has distinct advantages that make it a preferred foundation for your web infrastructure projects. Because it descends directly from Sun's very successful and capable Solaris 10 operating system, OpenSolaris gives you a flexible, highly scalable, and secure development environment along with advanced technologies not found in other operating systems. Try it. We think you'll like it!

CHAPTER 3

Getting and Installing OpenSolaris

I was dumbfounded to discover that installing Linux was easy. Why? Well, the world has changed.

—John Schwartz, *Washington Post*, December 2000

Linux has a justifiably good reputation for being easy to install, and that process has become even easier and with more useful options since Schwartz's report so long ago. On the other hand, Sun's Solaris for x86 systems has had a reputation, also somewhat deserved, of being difficult to install and configure, along with doubts as to whether it would run at all on any randomly chosen "commodity" laptop, workstation, or server. But the world has indeed changed. As we pointed out in Chapter 2, Solaris and OpenSolaris run on thousands of differently configured Intel and AMD systems; installation of Solaris and now OpenSolaris has been steadily improving using the same boot technologies and methods found in Linux distributions. Yes, now OpenSolaris is also easy to install.

The primary web site for getting OpenSolaris is `http://www.opensolaris.com/get/` (Figure 3-1), although additional download mirrors such as `http://genunix.org` are becoming available worldwide; several open source magazines and books are even now including the OpenSolaris CD. On the web site, you will find two choices: downloading the current version's `.iso` file to your system so that you can make your own CD or registering with the Sun Developer Network so they can send you a current OpenSolaris CD.

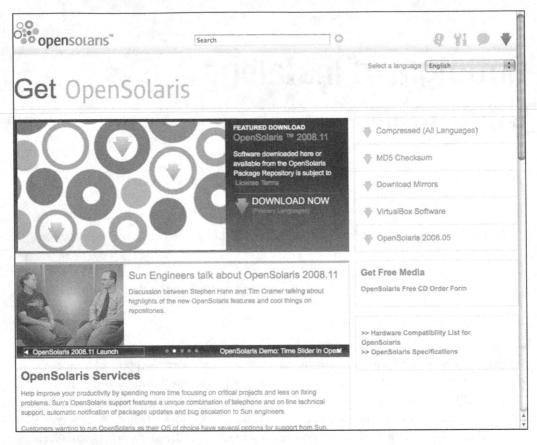

Figure 3-1. *Where to download the OpenSolaris CD* `.iso` *file*

Note Unlike Solaris 10, which requires a full installation DVD to hold all its files and programs in addition to a companion DVD of precompiled open source tools, OpenSolaris is distributed on a CD containing only the basic operating system, the GNOME environment, and some general user and administration programs. As with Ubuntu Linux, you get the rest of what you need for OpenSolaris development by updating your newly installed OS environment over the Internet from remote repositories.

In addition to the resources available through the OpenSolaris developer community web sites, a wealth of Solaris 10 information is available on the Sun Developer Network (SDN) that is directly relevant to OpenSolaris (Figure 3-2). Joining the SDN is free and gives you access to online forums, developer tools, and notification of technical events.

Figure 3-2. *The Sun Developer Network*

Installation Choices

Not so long ago, the only choice you had for installing an operating system was to put it on the "bare metal"—installing it directly, and exclusively, on the system hardware. Microsoft's aggressive tactics led to its virtual ownership of the laptop and PC markets so that you could not even purchase such systems without Microsoft Windows preinstalled. You could overwrite Windows with Linux or another operating system, but you would lose the ability to run Windows software if you really needed it. Open source community developers wanting to run Linux eventually created several tools such as LILO (Linux Loader) and GRUB (Grand Unified Bootloader) that supported "multiboot" systems, allowing users to select which OS their system would boot. This method, however handy, permitted the user to run only one operating system kernel at a time on their system— switching operating systems required a reboot. But two additional technologies have evolved that don't require rebooting or overwriting the system's original OS: Live CDs and virtualization.

Many Linux distributions such as Ubuntu and the innumerable customized Linux kernel projects come packaged as Live CDs. These CDs allow you to boot an operating system on your computer from that media without overwriting or changing your installed OS. Essentially, the Live CD process creates a memory-resident operating system and file system that you can use to explore the distribution, trying it out before deciding to install it. This boot technique has been expanded recently to include "live" boot from USB flash memory drives (also called *memory sticks* or *thumb drives*). The advantage of this boot technique is that, unlike the read-only CD, USB drives are writable so that you can actually carry around a complete working OS and file system on a tiny portable device and boot it on almost any system without disturbing that system's files. There is a derivative distribution of OpenSolaris called MilaX (http://www.milax.org/) that supports a multi-boot environment from USBs, memory cards, and other devices.

Virtualization software, such as VMware's Workstation and Fusion products, Parallels, Sun's VirtualBox, and the open source Xen and KVM projects, now easily allows testing and exploring new operating systems as "guests" that you can install as virtual machines on a wide range of host operating systems and processors.

Tip Installing an OS as a *virtual machine* is the easiest and least risky method of trying new operating systems such as OpenSolaris. We'll describe the other methods, but we strongly recommend the VM approach.

The good news about OpenSolaris is that you can use *any* of these techniques to load, test, learn about, and install it: Live CD, bare-metal install, multiboot install, and virtual machine guest install. But first you need to answer a key question: how do you know that OpenSolaris will run on your system?

Checking Your System

The "typical" laptop, workstation, or server you'll probably select for installing Open-Solaris will have a 64-bit Intel family processor such as the Intel Xeon, the Core 2, or a similar 64-bit AMD family processor such as the Athlon or Opteron, although many other 32-bit and 64-bit x86/x64 processors are also supported. For best performance, these processors should have a least a 1GHz clock rate. OpenSolaris will run in 512MB of memory, but 1GB or more of RAM is recommended, especially if you plan to use the system for any form of virtualization. You should have at least 10GB of disk space available, either in a disk partition or reserved in a virtual disk file. Of course, you will also need either Ethernet or wireless network devices for network access.

Note The active OpenSolaris community at http://www.opensolaris.org/os/community/laptop/ focuses on laptop issues. They work on and contribute solutions to wireless communications, power management, and other issues specific to running OpenSolaris on the myriad laptops that are available.

Although many first-time OpenSolaris users successfully install it without problems, you might want to see what others have experienced with your specific system. The OpenSolaris Hardware Compatibility List (HCL) displays a growing collection of systems and components where OpenSolaris has been successfully installed and run: hundreds of AMD and Intel servers, laptops, workstations, and motherboards; and thousands of component devices (see Figure 3-3). For the commercial Solaris 10, there are three general categories on its HCL:

- *Sun Microsystems certified*: Sun has tested and certified that the system or component will run Solaris 10, for example, Sun's own x86 servers and workstations.

- *Hardware vendor certified*: Using the available Hardware Certification Test Suite, the vendor has tested and certified that its system or component will run on Solaris 10.

- *Reported to work*: Users who have successfully installed Solaris 10 on their system can register and report their success.

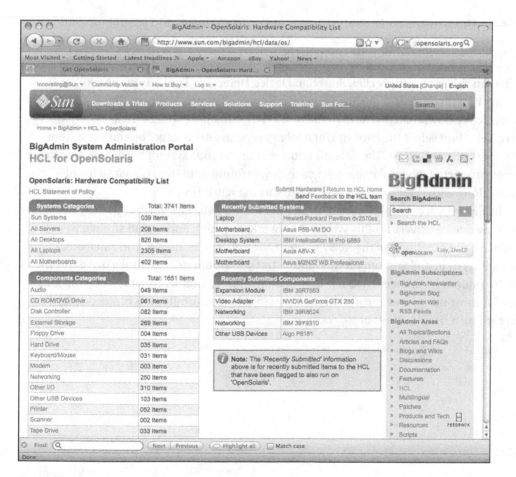

Figure 3-3. *The OpenSolaris Hardware Compatibility List*

Currently, the only official category for OpenSolaris is the "Reported to Work" category, although it includes many of the systems and components listed for Solaris 10 in the other two categories. The OpenSolaris HCL web site reports that Sun plans to provide an OpenSolaris hardware certification program.

For a more specific test of what components are supported on your particular system, you can download and run the Sun Device Detection Tool if your component is not listed in the HCL. This tool is a Java program that runs on Windows, Linux, and other operating systems; it will probe your hardware and let you know whether there are already device drivers for your system components included with OpenSolaris. The program generates a report that indicates the driver support status of each of your system's devices:

- A driver for your component is *bundled with* OpenSolaris.

- A third-party driver is *available* for your component *but not included* with your OpenSolaris installation.

- An OpenSolaris community driver is *under development* and *possibly available*.

- *No known driver* for your component.

To run this tool, simply click Start Sun Device Detection Tool 2.1 on the tool's web site. When you accept the license, a Java Network Launch Protocol (JNLP) file will automatically download and launch the tool's GUI using Java Web Start, as shown in Figure 3-4. Then select the current OpenSolaris version as the target operating system, and click the Start button. The detection tool will probe your system hardware, search its current supported device database for each device found, and then display a list of all the devices along with their driver support status, as in Figure 3-5.

The Figure 3-5 example was run on an Acer Ferrari 3400 laptop, and you can see that all the key device drivers for this system's network, graphics, audio, and storage were found with the exception of the AC97 modem controller. This means you can expect OpenSolaris to install and run on this laptop, but you would need to find a driver for the built-in modem if you needed to use dial-up networking. That's probably not a big issue today for most users, and a search of the OpenSolaris community web projects might even turn up a usable driver or workaround.

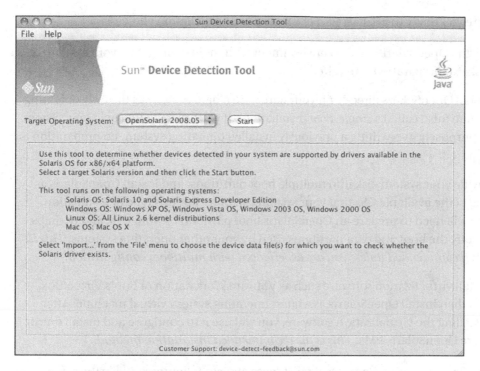

Figure 3-4. *The Sun Device Detection Tool*

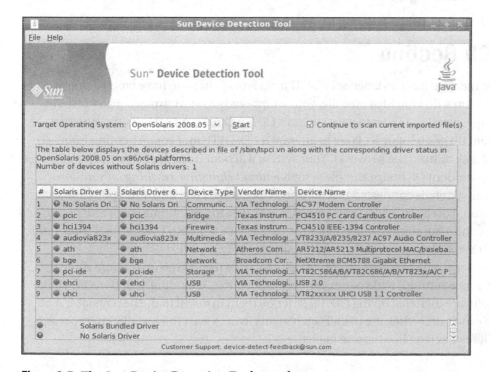

Figure 3-5. *The Sun Device Detection Tool sample output*

OK, are you ready to get started? Let's review your installation choices:

- Try the OpenSolaris Live CD environment without installing it on your system disk. No preparation is required.

- Install OpenSolaris directly on your hardware ("bare metal") as the only operating system (also called a *single-boot* installation). If you are installing on a new system or purposely overwriting a previously installed operating system, no preparation is required.

- Divide your system disk into multiple boot partitions, and install OpenSolaris as one of the available OSs that your system can boot. For this type of installation, you will need to prepare an OpenSolaris boot partition on your disk and perhaps modify the boot and data partitions used by your other operating systems. *This is not recommended unless you are experienced with multiboot configuration!*

- Install virtualization software such as VMware Workstation or Sun's VirtualBox, and then install OpenSolaris as a guest operating system virtual machine. After installing the virtualization software, you will use it to configure and install one or more OpenSolaris VMs. *This is the recommended installation method.*

After a few initial differences, several of these choices follow essentially the same installation and configuration steps. Let's look at each of these choices in more detail.

Live CD Booting

Assuming that you have an OpenSolaris CD from Sun or that you have created one of your own from a downloaded .iso file, you're now ready to start exploring and installing it. Simply insert the CD into your system's CD/DVD drive and reboot (be sure that your system BIOS's boot order is set to attempt a CD/DVD boot *before* booting from your hard disk or from the network). Your system will boot from the CD, creating a memory-resident OS image and file system *without changing anything on your local disk*. If your system is connected to a network, OpenSolaris will also attempt to initialize a connection. You'll see a fully functional GNOME desktop, including icons and menus for Firefox and Thunderbird, an icon for the Getting Started With OpenSolaris guide, and an Install OpenSolaris icon, like the screen shown in Figure 3-6.

At this point, you can start exploring OpenSolaris's navigation menus and directories, preference settings, and system administration tools, including selections for all the default software included on the CD. I'll describe them in detail in the next chapter. For now, you can double-click the Install OpenSolaris icon to start the installation process, and you'll see a screen like the one in Figure 3-7.

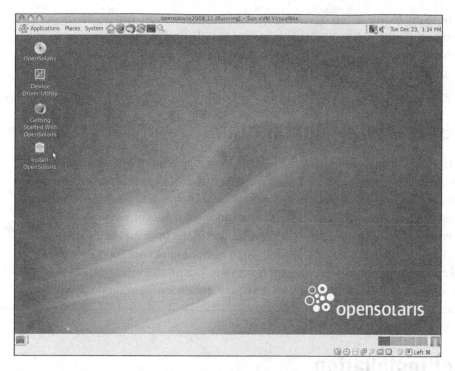

Figure 3-6. *The OpenSolaris Live CD screen (booted in VirtualBox)*

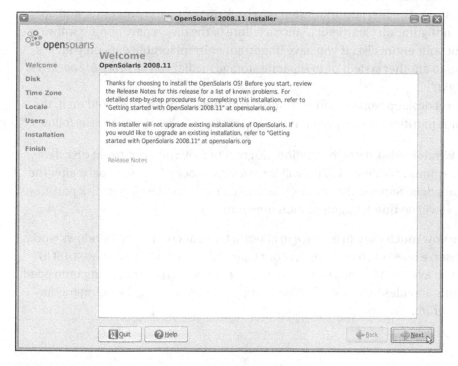

Figure 3-7. *The OpenSolaris Installer Welcome screen*

Now you're ready to install the operating system on your system. But let's stop here and examine the other paths to this point in the installation process, because once you reach this installation screen from any method, nearly all the subsequent steps are the same.

Direct "Bare-Metal" Installation

Boot the Live CD, and immediately click the Install OpenSolaris icon. *Be sure that this is what you intend to do, since you will now have the opportunity to wipe out any other OS and data partitions on your disk!* Additionally, you should know what hardware your system has and have at least a rough idea of how you want to allocate your disk resources. For example, you may want to plan for multiple data partitions or to configure a large root partition. Later in the installation process, you'll have a chance to organize your disk the way you want. In any case, when you boot from the CD with the intention of installing only OpenSolaris, you'll still arrive at the same Installer Welcome screen shown in Figure 3-7.

Multiboot Installation

This installation scenario requires the most planning and understanding of your disk drive configuration. The first important step is to back up your data, programs, and operating system configuration parameters, since a failure of the disk repartitioning software could wipe out your entire disk. If you have important or irreplaceable data on your system, back it up to another system or to separate storage media. *You've probably backed it up already, right?*

If you have a desktop workstation or a laptop with only Windows installed on it, the basic steps for repartitioning it in preparation for your OpenSolaris install are as follows:

1. Run a Windows disk defragmentation program to move all the current disk data to the beginning of the disk. This will leave a large block of unused space after the Windows data. Some of the commercial and community-developed disk partitioning tools will do this defragmentation preparation for you.

2. Decide how much extra disk space to allocate for your continuing Windows work, and observe how much remains for your OpenSolaris installation; at least 10GB should be available for this. If you don't have enough, consider deleting unneeded programs and files from the Windows partition and rerunning the defragmentation program.

3. Use the Windows `fdisk` program, a third-party commercial disk utility such as Symantec's PartitionMagic, or the community-developed `gparted` program to truncate the Windows partition at a convenient location that will still leave some additional working space and create a new "Solaris partition" for OpenSolaris.

4. Reboot your system from the OpenSolaris Live CD, click the Install OpenSolaris icon, and arrive at the installation screen. If you've previously set up your system for multiboot with Windows, Linux, or other operating systems, ensure that you have an appropriately sized free disk partition for your installation.

Having outlined this multiboot installation procedure, we should mention that this method of installing multiple operating systems on a single machine is rapidly becoming obsolete because of the introduction of virtualization software. With multiboot configurations, you can run only one operating system at a time, and you must reboot each time you want to change OSs. With virtualization software, described next, you can install additional guest operating systems such as OpenSolaris without worrying about disk repartitioning, you can run multiple operating systems simultaneously without rebooting, and you can easily and instantly switch among them with a simple key sequence or mouse click. Additionally, as emphasized earlier, there is less risk of endangering your currently installed OS and data when installing OpenSolaris as a virtual machine.

Installing OpenSolaris as a Guest VM (Recommended)

Because there are now so many choices for virtualization software, we'll briefly review just a few of the currently available ones here and then show you how to use one of them to install OpenSolaris as a guest operating system.

We'll explain more about the various types of virtualization in Chapter 7, but for now you need to understand that there are two types of virtualization software, called *hypervisors*, which can serve as hosts for other operating systems. A *Type 1* hypervisor is installed directly on your system's hardware and supports the installation of multiple guest operating systems. This type of hypervisor must be the first software installed on your system; it's essentially a special operating system kernel designed to abstract, that is, *virtualize*, access to your system's devices by other operating system guests. A *Type 2* hypervisor runs as an application within a host operating system that has already been installed as the primary OS on your system. Type 2 hypervisors also support the installation of multiple guest operating systems. You can find and install Type 2 hypervisors for any of today's popular x86 operating systems.

OpenSolaris can be installed as a guest VM on any one of the virtualization platforms listed in Table 3-1.

Table 3-1. *Some Virtualization Software for Running OpenSolaris as a Guest VM*

Virtualization Software	Hypervisor Type	Source and Support	Description
VMware ESX, ESXi	1	Commercial	Server-based virtualization on Intel and AMD systems
VMware Workstation	2	Commercial	For Intel and AMD laptops and desktops; runs on Windows and Linux
VMware Fusion	2	Commercial	Runs on Apple systems with Intel processors
Microsoft Virtual Server 2005	2	Commercial	Runs on Windows Server 2003 and XP Professional
Microsoft Hyper-V	1	Commercial	Enhanced version of Windows Server 2008
Parallels Workstation	2	Commercial	Available for Windows and Linux
Parallels Desktop for Mac	2	Commercial	Runs on Apple systems with Intel processors
Xen	1	Commercial and community	Commercial availability from Citrix, community from Xen.org
Linux KVM	1	Commercial and community	Supports wide variety of guests, Windows, Linux, BSD, Solaris, OpenSolaris, and others
Sun Microsystems xVM Server	1	Commercial and community	Supports Windows, Linux, and Solaris/OpenSolaris guests
Sun Microsystems VirtualBox	2	Commercial and community	Free, open source tool for desktop and laptop virtualization; supports Solaris, OpenSolaris, Windows, Macintosh OS X, and Linux hosts; Solaris, OpenSolaris, Windows, and Linux guests

Let's take a look at one of these, VirtualBox. We recommend this because it is free, open source, and easy to install and configure. Installing OpenSolaris as a guest VM on any of the other virtualization platforms requires generally similar configuration decisions, so you can use VirtualBox as a model. Early in 2008, Sun Microsystems acquired the German company Innotek GmbH, developer of this popular desktop virtualization software; shortly thereafter, Sun released the VirtualBox source code under the GPL. Available versions of this Type 2 hypervisor run on Linux, OS X, Windows XP and Vista, Solaris, and OpenSolaris. Supported guest operating systems include nearly the entire Windows family (Vista, 2000, XP, Server 2003, and NT), many of the popular Linux distributions (Ubuntu, Debian, SUSE,

Fedora, and Red Hat), FreeBSD, Solaris 10, OpenSolaris, and even DOS and OS/2. You can download and install the current version of VirtualBox for your Intel or AMD system and your choice of operating system from http://www.virtualbox.org. When you start the VirtualBox program, you'll see a Registration dialog box, followed by a welcome screen like the one in Figure 3-8.

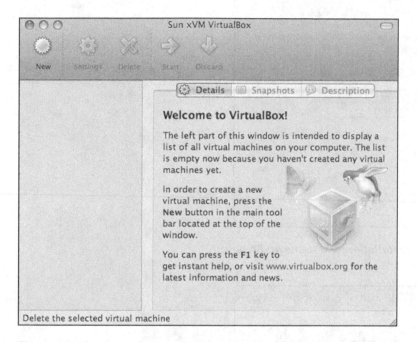

Figure 3-8. *The VirtualBox welcome screen*

Click the New button to start the installation process. Most of the installation screens are self-explanatory, so we'll review only the key configuration options. First, of course, you need to assign a name to the VM and to select OpenSolaris as its type, as in Figure 3-9.

The next screen asks you to allocate memory for the VM. The minimum is 512MB, and more is better while leaving enough for the host operating system; 1GB is a good starting point for general VM use, assuming you have sufficient total memory on your system. Then you need to allocate a new virtual disk and specify its size. In most cases, selecting a dynamically expanding virtual disk is preferable, as shown in Figure 3-10.

VirtualBox will then display a summary screen, like the one in Figure 3-11. At this point, you have two important specifications to make: where OpenSolaris will boot from (CD or .iso file) and the type of networking your VM will use (NAT or host).

If you have an OpenSolaris CD, ensure that it's mounted and ready; if you're using a downloaded .iso file, specify its location. To connect your VM to the external network, select Network Address Translation (NAT) or host-based addressing.

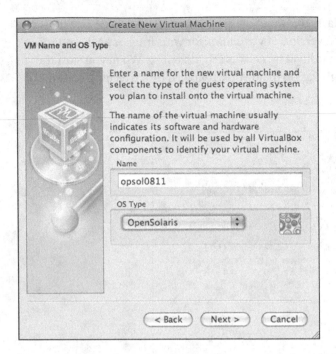

Figure 3-9. *VirtualBox installation: VM name and type*

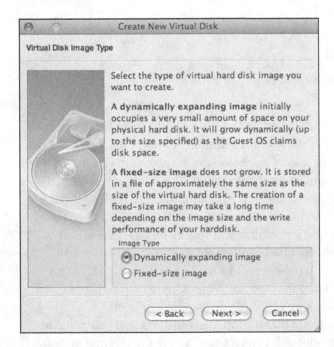

Figure 3-10. *VirtualBox installation: virtual disk type selection*

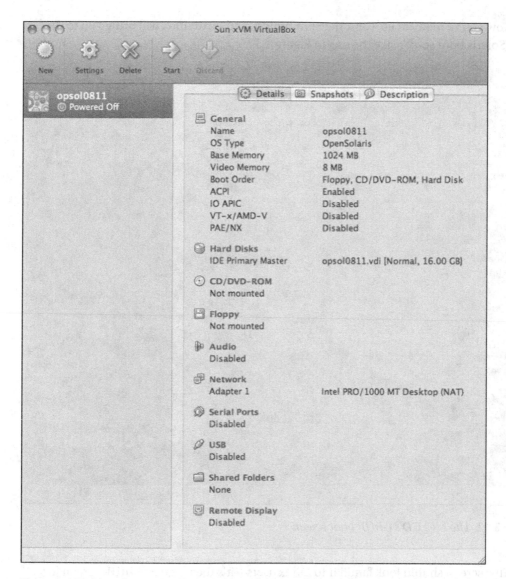

Figure 3-11. *VirtualBox installation: boot device and network configuration*

Now you're ready to go. Click the Start button, and VirtualBox will bring you to the OpenSolaris boot screen like the one in Figure 3-12.

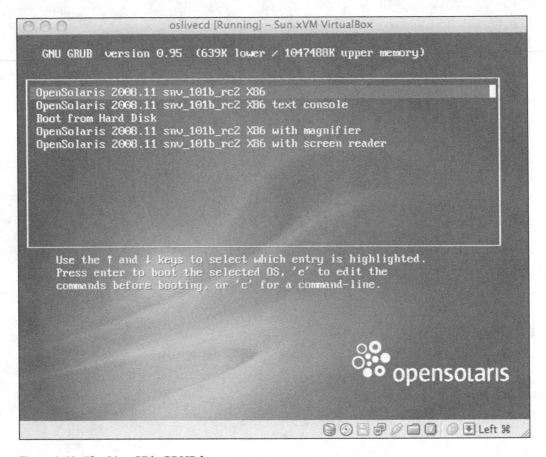

Figure 3-12. *The Live CD's GRUB boot screen*

This screen should look familiar to Linux users—it's the standard GRUB screen for selecting a boot option. Now the *real* installation begins!

Note The decisions you made in this example using VirtualBox—VM memory size, virtual disk size and type, boot device or file, and network addressing mode—are basically the same ones you must make for other virtualization software; only the screen layouts, configuration order, and some additional options are different.

Select the first OpenSolaris 2008.11 menu item and hit Return; the installation boot process will begin. You'll be asked to choose the keyboard layout and desktop language, and if all goes well, you'll see the same OpenSolaris screen you saw with the Live CD boot. Basically all you've really done up to this point is boot the Live CD in a VM. And if you now double-click the Install OpenSolaris icon, you'll start the actual OS install using the memory and disk parameters you specified in your VirtualBox VM configuration session; you should see the OpenSolaris Installer Welcome screen (Figure 3-13).

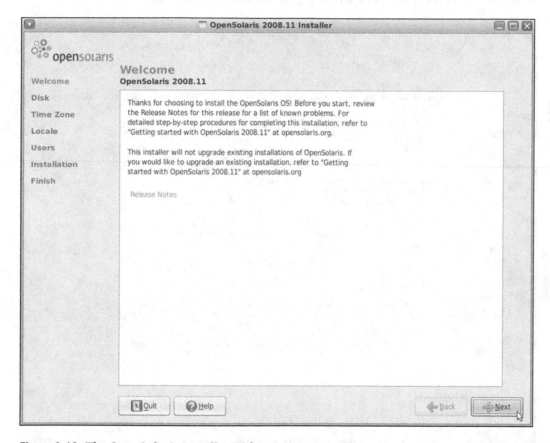

Figure 3-13. *The OpenSolaris Installer Welcome screen*

Click the Next button, and you will see the installer's Disk configuration screen (Figure 3-14). If you're installing OpenSolaris using VirtualBox or other virtualization software, you can select the "whole disk," which is really the virtual disk you defined earlier. Otherwise, you should select one of the true disk partitions, again remembering that OpenSolaris needs at least 10GB for a usable installation. You can modify the disk layout and partition sizes to suit your needs at this point if you anticipate needing a larger root partition or a separate data partition. Click the Next button; select your location, time zone, date and time, locale, and language; and then click Next again.

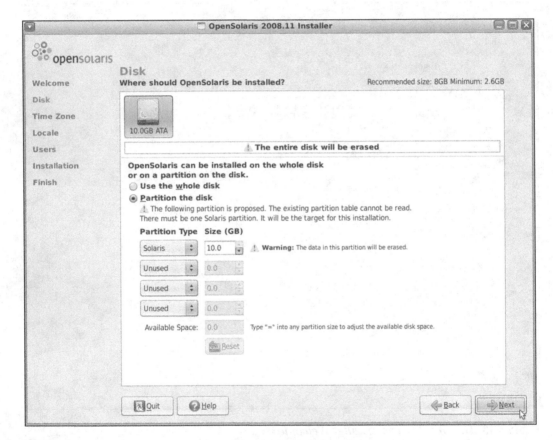

Figure 3-14. *The OpenSolaris Disk configuration screen*

The last screen of the operating system installation process is for entering the root password and for defining a Primary Administrator user who becomes the default root administrator (Figure 3-15). *Be sure to record the passwords for these accounts.*

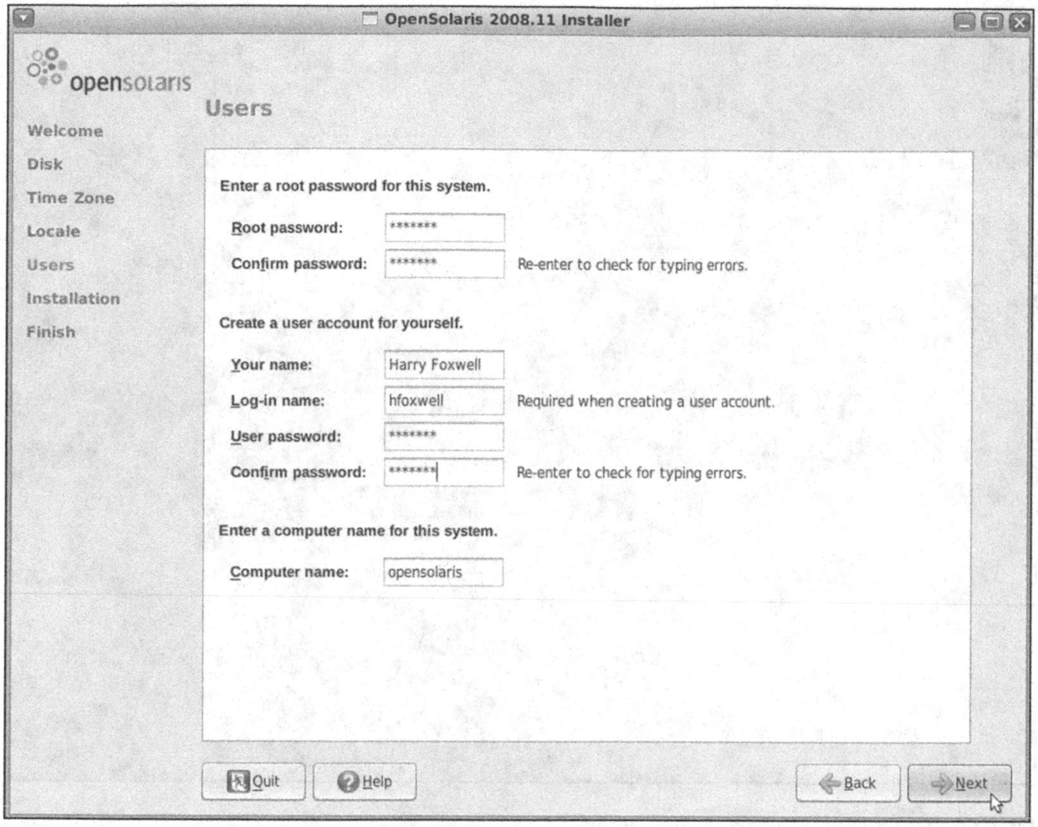

Figure 3-15. *The OpenSolaris root and user account setup screen*

Click the Next button, and go get a cup of coffee and something to read; OpenSolaris will start copying its files from the CD or `.iso` file onto the virtual or real disk. When it's finished, it will ask you to reboot, and you'll be the proud owner of your very own OpenSolaris installation (Figure 3-16).

■**Tip** VirtualBox (and most other virtualization software) includes a feature that lets you copy, or *clone*, a virtual machine to create a new image with the same characteristics without having to go through all the usual OS installation steps; you can then quickly customize this copy. As you explore OpenSolaris, use your virtualization software's snapshot or cloning features to create different configurations; you can also use the OpenSolaris boot environment tools described in Chapter 5 to accomplish the same thing.

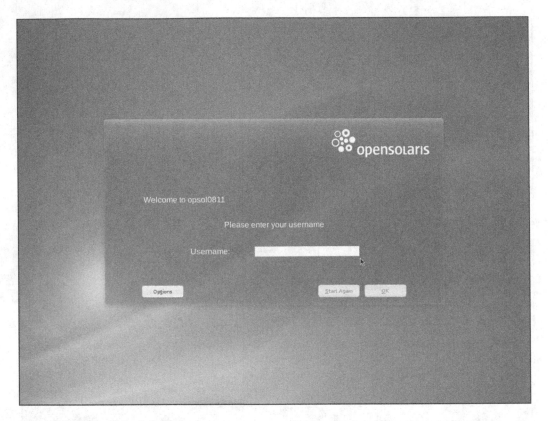

Figure 3-16. *The OpenSolaris login screen*

Now try to log in as root. Even when you enter the correct password, you can't log in, and OpenSolaris will politely inform you that "Roles can only be assumed by authorized users." This is a security feature; the root role can be used only after you log in as the Primary Administrator user and then su to root. This enables the system to track who becomes root and to track and record their actions. You'll have to log in as the Primary Administrator user you defined earlier. Log in and double-click the Start Here icon, and you'll see a window containing links to OpenSolaris news, customization instructions, community participation information, and marketing/support information from Sun (Figure 3-17).

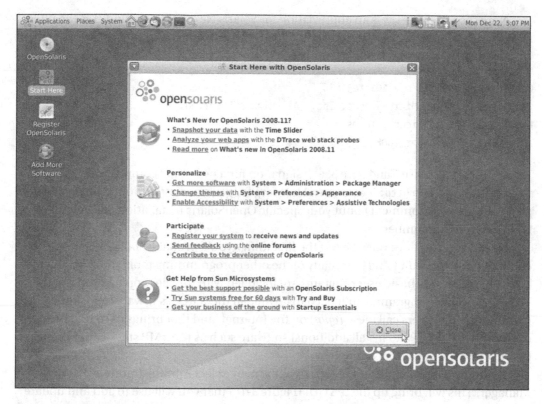

Figure 3-17. *The OpenSolaris Start Here with OpenSolaris page*

Are We There Yet?

You now have access to all the software and tools that were copied from the CD or .iso image. In the next chapter, we'll explore these tools in more detail, but now you need to know how to update your newly installed operating system and how to add software using OpenSolaris's Image Packaging System (IPS). But first, a few words about build numbers.

Earlier we mentioned that new binary versions of OpenSolaris become available every two weeks. Each of these new compilations, called *builds*, has a sequence number. You'll read discussions in the OpenSolaris online community forums referring to a particular *build number*—comments like "This bug is fixed in build 101" or "That feature will be included in build 104." So, your first question should be "How do I find out my build number?" As with almost every UNIX and Linux system, use the uname command in a terminal window:

```
$ uname -a
SunOS opsol01 5.11 snv_101 i86pc i386 i86pc Solaris
```

Note the snv_101—snv is an abbreviation for Solaris Next Version, and 101 is the build number. More specific information about your build is contained in the /etc/release file:

```
$ cat /etc/release
OpenSolaris 2008.11 snv_101_rc3 x86
Copyright 2008 Sun Microsystems, Inc.  All Rights Reserved.
Use is subject to license terms.
Assembled 05 November 2008
```

rc3 means Release Candidate 3, a designation for a near-final compilation expected to be posted soon on http://www.opensolaris.org for general distribution. Whenever you post a question or comment about your specific OpenSolaris installation, it's helpful to mention its build number.

Now if you're a developer, one of the first things you'll probably look for is the gcc compiler, but you won't find it or many of the other programming tools you'll need. That's because only basic user programs are included with the files copied from the CD. To get additional programs, you'll need to download them from software repositories (community members call these *repos*) on the Internet, and that brings us to IPS. In later chapters, we'll use IPS to install additional software such as the AMP stack components, but first let's look at a brief example.

From the System menu at the top of your screen, select Administration ➤ Package Manager. This will bring up the IPS GUI (Figure 3-18) that you will use to add and update software to your installation.

Note that this tool lists several categories of available software packages, their current versions and whether they are already installed, and the repository to be used; in this example, it's OpenSolaris.org. In the Search text box, enter **gcc**; IPS will query its database and list the available version of the gcc development package (Figure 3-19).

Check the selections you need, and click the Install/Update icon to start the installation. IPS will identify any additional packages needed for your choice and then download and install the program and its dependencies. It will also add selections for the new software to your desktop's menus if that's appropriate. IPS can also download and install groups of related software, such as the AMP stack group that you'll read about in Chapter 8.

Now would be a good time to explore the package repository and decide what additional software you'll need for your work. For example, you will probably want to install OpenOffice (in the Office package group) on your system. You'll find a growing number of online software repositories for OpenSolaris users and developers; Table 3-2 lists some of them, and more are being added by Sun, ISVs, and the user community.

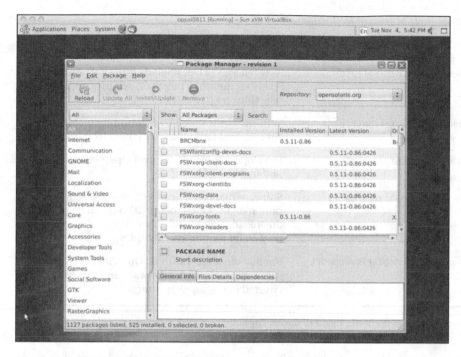

Figure 3-18. *The Image Packaging System GUI*

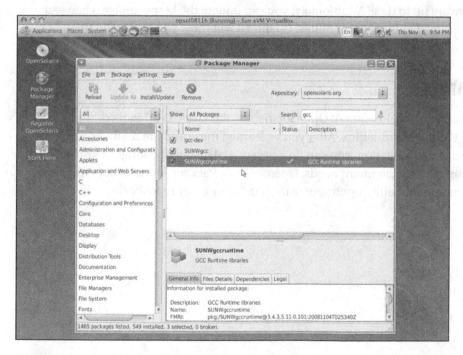

Figure 3-19. *Installing gcc using the Package Manager GUI*

Table 3-2. *OpenSolaris Software Repositories**

Repository	Description
http://pkg.opensolaris.org/release	New releases of OpenSolaris milestone builds (every six months), bug fixes, security updates, and new software packages.
http://pkg.opensolaris.org/contrib	Software contributed by community members; not yet reviewed for inclusion in the release repository.
http://pkg.opensolaris.org/dev	Developer repository for next OpenSolaris release; updated biweekly.
http://pkg.sun.com/opensolaris/extra	Software that is not licensed for initial redistribution on the OpenSolaris CD but can be freely downloaded and used. VirtualBox and the Flash plug-in for Firefox are examples.
https://pkg.sun.com/opensolaris/support	For Sun customers with an OpenSolaris support subscription; includes software and bug fixes covered in the support contract.

* Select the Settings ➤ Edit Repositories menu in the Package Manager GUI to change repositories.

You can now use the Image Packaging System's GUI or its command-line tool to review OpenSolaris's preinstalled software, to add new software, and to keep your installed software up to date. Additionally, you can update the kernel image whenever you learn of the availability of new builds; Chapter 4 will show you how to do this.

Summary

It's easy to start your exploration of OpenSolaris; use the Live CD or, as recommended, install it in a VM using VirtualBox. After you've learned more and are ready to create a more permanent installation, you can do a bare-metal install or configure VMs that reflect your specific development needs. OpenSolaris's Package Manager lets you conveniently add and update other open source tools using Internet repositories.

CHAPTER 4

■ ■ ■

A Familiar User and Developer Environment and More

It's like déjà vu all over again.

—Yogi Berra, U.S. baseball player, coach, and manager

At Home with GNOME

Long before Sun Microsystems even thought about OpenSolaris, it recognized the benefits of community-developed desktop environments such as KDE and GNOME, especially since many Sun engineers contributed extensively to these systems. GNOME was selected as the default Solaris desktop, replacing the Common Desktop Environment (CDE) originally developed by the corporate consortium comprising IBM, Digital Equipment Corporation (DEC), Novell, and Sun. GNOME is now standard on most UNIX and Linux systems, and GNOME 2.24 is the current default desktop for OpenSolaris (Figure 4-1).

Since we're assuming you're already generally familiar with how GNOME menus, icons, and windows work, we'll focus on the application components included with OpenSolaris's desktop environment.

The first thing you'll notice when you log in if your system's network interface is active is an alert that your network interface has been configured by nwamd, the Network Auto-Magic Daemon. Such network autoconfiguration is standard behavior on most laptops and workstations, and it connects you using your predefined or DHCP-assigned IP address. Although this is very convenient, you can manually set up your network interfaces by selecting System ➤ Administration ➤ Network and then selecting the Manual item from the page that appears.

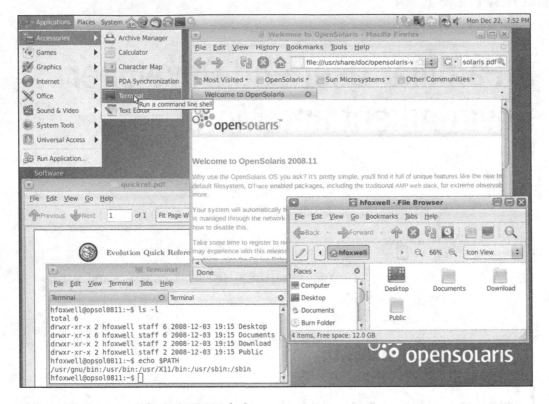

Figure 4-1. *The OpenSolaris GNOME desktop*

Under the Applications menu, you will see a list of programs typically distributed with systems such as Ubuntu Linux:

- Calculator

- Terminal

- Games

- Image Manipulation Software

- Evolution Mail/Calendar

- Firefox Web Browser

- Pidgin Instant Messenger

- Thunderbird Email Client

- Evince PDA Viewer

- Rhythmbox Music Player

- System Monitoring Tools

- Accessibility Aids

You'll note that some programs, such as OpenOffice, are missing. Recall that you installed OpenSolaris from a CD that has limited capacity and that you'll want to download additional programs from the network repositories discussed in Chapter 3. You'll learn more about that in a moment. This approach—distributing the operating system on a CD-sized file rather than on a multigigabyte DVD—reduces the size of the downloaded .iso file needed to get started with OpenSolaris and also allows you to download and customize your installation with only the software you need.

The System ➤ Preferences menu lists the functionality you will use to customize your system and desktop behaviors such as screen resolution, GNOME themes, laptop power management, and many other settings (Figure 4-2). Again, there's nothing unusual here since these are the same kinds of working environment personalizations you find in Linux distributions; in fact, many of them are simply ports of open source configuration tools to OpenSolaris.

Figure 4-2. *The OpenSolaris System ➤ Preferences menu*

The System ➤ Administration menu is where you'll see some familiar system configuration tasks along with some that are unique to OpenSolaris, as shown in Table 4-1.

Table 4-1. *OpenSolaris System Administration Menu*

Menu Item	Description
Keyring Manager	The GNOME keyring manager used to store security credentials such as names and passwords
Network	Configures and activates network interfaces, host names, and DNS information, manually or using nwamd
Package Manager	GUI for the Image Packaging System (IPS); installs and updates application and system software; also includes Boot Environment Management
Print Manager	Manages local and network printers and queues, OpenSolaris version
Register OpenSolaris	Registers your installation with OpenSolaris.org for news and updates
Services	GUI for the Service Management Facility (SMF); starts and stops system and network services
Shared Folders	Specifies NFS shared directories
Solaris LP Print Manager	Selects naming service for local and network printers; adds, modifies, removes printers; Solaris version
Time and Date	Sets your system time zone, time, and date manually or using a specified NTP server
Time Slider Setup	ZFS-based automatic data backup service similar to Apple OS X Time Machine
Update Manager	IPS notification service for application updates
Users and Groups	Adds, deletes, and manages user and group accounts, profiles, and RBAC roles

The CLI, for the GUI-averse

Linux users who've tried Solaris have criticized it for a number of annoyances, in particular for the lack of a modern and familiar default shell for users and for root, as well as for the differences in functionality between the older System V utilities and the newer GNU utilities. Solaris has actually included a directory of GNU programs for several releases, but you had to know its location and alter your PATH environment variable to use it. OpenSolaris addresses these complaints.

The default shell for root and users is now /usr/bin/bash; the old System V Bourne Shell, /usr/bin, is now implemented with KSH93. Developers often have very strong preferences for UNIX or Linux shells, and we won't argue the advantages and differences among all the choices here. OpenSolaris uses bash because of its ubiquity among Linux developers and its advantages over older shell implementations such as command-line editing, shell history, and file name completion. If you prefer other shells, such as the C Shell (/usr/bin/csh) or the Korn Shell (/usr/bin/ksh), they are also included. You can change your default shell using the System ➤ Administration ➤ Users and Groups menu.

Your default path starts with the /usr/gnu/bin directory, which contains links to the GNU versions of the typical UNIX tools (Figure 4-3). Many of the programs in the /bin directory have also been replaced with their GNU or community-developed equivalents, including the venerable /bin/vi, which is now a link to the vim editor. GNU emacs can be easily added using the Package Manager GUI from the Text Tools group. The OpenSolaris terminal shell also enables cursor-driven command-line history and editing, and file name completion by default, a capability that Linux has had forever and that Solaris probably should have included by default long ago.

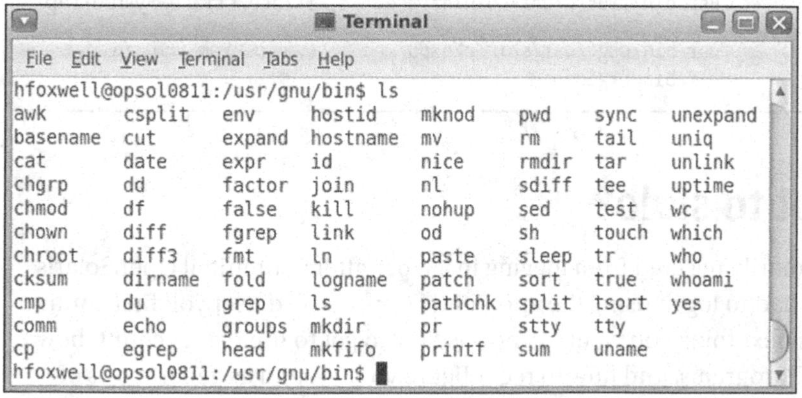

Figure 4-3. *The /usr/gnu/bin directory*

As you explore OpenSolaris, you'll find many of the common UNIX/Linux utilities and find that they work in the expected manner. However, some programs are unique to OpenSolaris because of their Solaris heritage, and some familiar programs behave differently because of their interaction with special features such as ZFS or zones. We'll explain the differences for ZFS in Chapter 6 and for virtualization in Chapter 7. Table 4-2 shows some of the OpenSolaris-specific programs and their approximate Linux equivalents.

Table 4-2. *OpenSolaris Administrator Tools*

Tool	Program/Command Line	Linux Distribution Equivalents
Examine Network Packets	/usr/sbin/snoop	etherfind or tcpdump
Manage Boot Images	/usr/sbin/beadm	(Varies) Startup Manager, GNOME Grub Conf
Manage RBAC Roles	/usr/bin/roles, /usr/sbin/roleadd, /usr/sbin/rolemod	sudo
Manage Service Daemons	/usr/bin/svcs, /usr/sbin/svcadm, /usr/sbin/svccfg	/etc/rc*, /etc/init.d
Manage ZFS Pools	/usr/sbin/zpool, /usr/sbin/zfs	(None)
Modify Process Privs	/usr/bin/ppriv	sudo
Reset System Identity	/usr/sbin/sys-unconfig	(Varies) sysconfig
Show Processor Info	/usr/bin/isainfo -v, /usr/sbin/psrinfo -v	(Varies) dmesg
Show System Hardware	/usr/sbin/prtconf -v	(Varies) dmesg
Trace System Calls	/usr/bin/truss, /usr/sbin/dtrace	ltrace, strace, SystemTap
Manage IPS and SysV Software Packages	/usr/bin/pkg, /usr/sbin/pkgadd, /usr/bin/pkginfo	(Varies) rpm, yum, apt-get

To su, or Not to sudo?

Since you were summarily rejected from logging in as root after your initial OpenSolaris installation and you had to log in using the apparently unprivileged user you first configured, we assume the next thing you want to know is how to get to the root account, how to execute privileged programs, and how to reconfigure your system as generations of UNIX administrators before you have done for decades. As with all UNIX/Linux systems, simply execute the su command, and enter the root password you specified at installation; then you can happily roam around your system at will. But there is another way.

Because the root ID has traditionally been so powerful, it's been the target of hackers and system abusers and the enabler of catastrophic user errors. Modern systems now restrict the privileges of root and administrator accounts, assigning limited privilege sets to specific users (including root), granting only what's needed to perform each task. This restricted permission approach is called *role-based access control* (RBAC). Special programs also permit execution of privileged tasks by nonadministrator users. The most common such program is the venerable sudo, ported years ago to Linux; it's also delivered with the OpenSolaris CD, and it works as expected, allowing you or designated users to run root-privileged programs and to log their actions.

Although OpenSolaris includes sudo, it also includes RBAC software for defining users' roles. The first non-root user you defined when installing OpenSolaris has the Primary Administrator role, similar to the administrator accounts on Apple's OS X and on Microsoft Windows. The rough equivalent to sudo on OpenSolaris is the pfexec program; commands run by the Primary Administrator using pfexec run with root privileges without requiring you to enter the root password. These privileges are defined (and therefore controlled) by this user's entry in the /etc/user_attr file and its associated role and privileges in the /etc/security/exec_attr file; you alter the administrator and other users' privileges using the /usr/sbin/usermod command or the user administration GUI.

Boot and Reboot

OK, you've installed and explored your first OpenSolaris, downloaded and modified software, reconfigured system parameters, and deleted unwanted files; now that you've familiarized yourself with your new environment, you're ready to go back and start all over and set up the system the way you *really* want it. Here's where ZFS comes to your rescue. Because OpenSolaris installs and boots from a ZFS file system, you get all the advantages that file system provides, including file system snapshots. We'll have much more to say about ZFS in Chapter 6, but for now look at what the capability of taking unlimited root file system snapshots buys you. At any point after your initial installation, you can take a ZFS snapshot of the root file system, make any additions and changes you want, and easily revert to your earlier snapshot if you're unhappy with your changes. OpenSolaris makes this process extraordinarily easy by providing a tool to manage these snapshots: beadm.

The beadm program lets you quickly create a named snapshot of your existing boot environment and files. For example, the following command:

```
# beadm create MyNewBoot
```

creates a ZFS snapshot of the currently active root file system and adds an appropriate entry in the GRUB boot file located at /rpool/boot/grub/menu.lst (Figure 4-4). Note that your current boot image remains the default; beadm has simply added a new image named MyNewBoot to your GRUB boot menu.

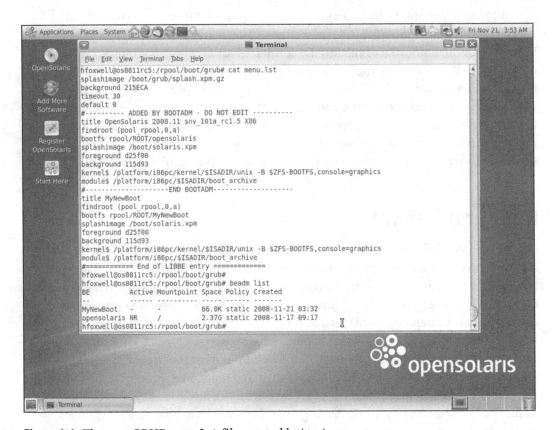

Figure 4-4. *The new GRUB menu.lst file created by beadm*

You can activate any of the images in the menu.lst file using beadm or the File ➤ Boot Environment Manager selection from the Package Manager GUI discussed earlier (Figure 4-5).

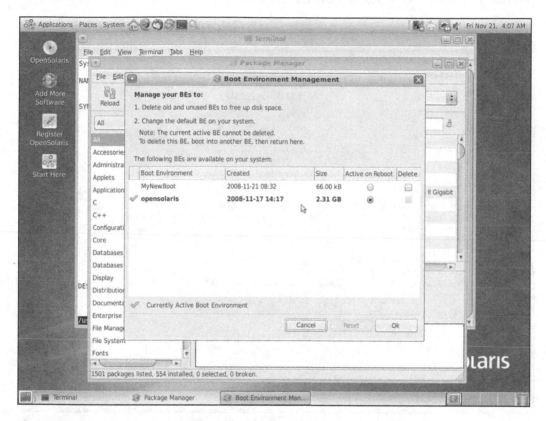

Figure 4-5. *The Boot Environment Management GUI*

Updating Your Kernel Build

As you work with OpenSolaris, you may want to update your OS kernel image to the most recent development builds that are posted to the online repository every two weeks. You don't have to worry about a painful upgrade process, however. From the Primary Administrator account, enter the following:

```
pfexec pkg image-update
```

The IPS will update your package database and then begin the process of updating your OpenSolaris build image. This process will take several minutes as IPS downloads and replaces packages and builds a new boot environment. When it's finished, it alerts you that your new build image is ready (Figure 4-6).

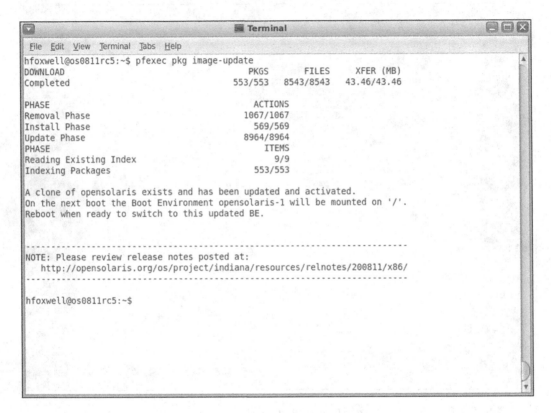

Figure 4-6. *The OpenSolaris image-update process*

IPS has not simply updated your system kernel. First it took a ZFS snapshot of your current system, and then it performed the update of all the kernel and related application files. Next it created a new boot image, appended the new image's configuration details to your GRUB menu.lst file, and set that image as your default boot environment (Figure 4-7). It also gave you a URL for the most recent OpenSolaris Release Notes document.

Now all you need to do is reboot, and you will see the new boot option in your GRUB menu (Figure 4-8). Of course, you can alter this by editing the menu.lst file directly or by using the Boot Environment Management GUI discussed earlier.

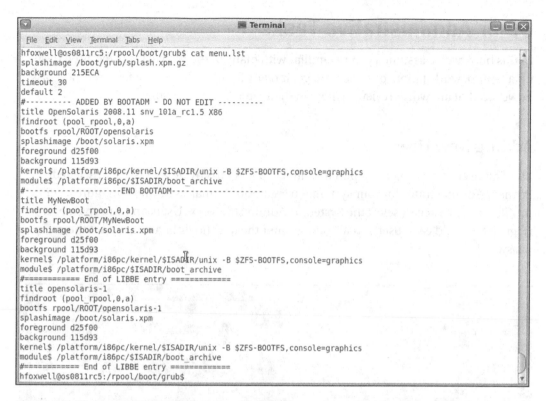

```
hfoxwell@os0811rc5:/rpool/boot/grub$ cat menu.lst
splashimage /boot/grub/splash.xpm.gz
background 215ECA
timeout 30
default 2
#--------- ADDED BY BOOTADM - DO NOT EDIT ----------
title OpenSolaris 2008.11 snv_101a_rc1.5 X86
findroot (pool_rpool,0,a)
bootfs rpool/ROOT/opensolaris
splashimage /boot/solaris.xpm
foreground d25f00
background 115d93
kernel$ /platform/i86pc/kernel/$ISADIR/unix -B $ZFS-BOOTFS,console=graphics
module$ /platform/i86pc/$ISADIR/boot_archive
#-------------------END BOOTADM-------------------
title MyNewBoot
findroot (pool_rpool,0,a)
bootfs rpool/ROOT/MyNewBoot
splashimage /boot/solaris.xpm
foreground d25f00
background 115d93
kernel$ /platform/i86pc/kernel/$ISADIR/unix -B $ZFS-BOOTFS,console=graphics
module$ /platform/i86pc/$ISADIR/boot_archive
#============ End of LIBBE entry =============
title opensolaris-1
findroot (pool_rpool,0,a)
bootfs rpool/ROOT/opensolaris-1
splashimage /boot/solaris.xpm
foreground d25f00
background 115d93
kernel$ /platform/i86pc/kernel/$ISADIR/unix -B $ZFS-BOOTFS,console=graphics
module$ /platform/i86pc/$ISADIR/boot_archive
#============ End of LIBBE entry =============
hfoxwell@os0811rc5:/rpool/boot/grub$
```

Figure 4-7. *The updated GRUB* menu.1st *file for the new kernel image*

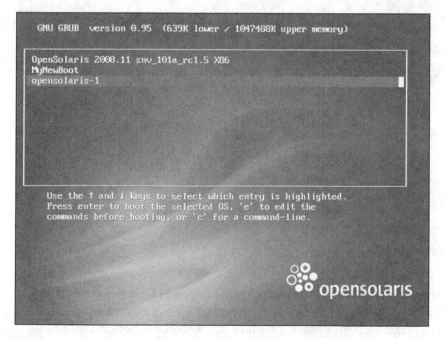

Figure 4-8. *The updated GRUB boot menu listing your new kernel image*

Other Administrative Tasks

In this book we've assumed you're familiar with many of the typical tasks required to set up a laptop, workstation, or server and get it ready for use. There are a few common tasks, however, that are worth reviewing here in their OpenSolaris versions.

Adding New Users

The first user you configured upon installing OpenSolaris by default is the privileged Primary Administrator for your system. To create additional users and configure their profiles and privileges, select the System ➤ Administration ➤ Users and Groups menu (Figure 4-9). Add each user's "real" name, enter the user (login) name, and set their password.

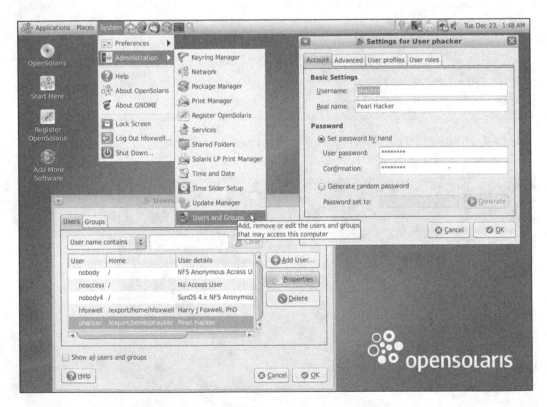

Figure 4-9. *Adding a new user*

You can then select and modify the user's properties, such as their group memberships, shell, and home directory (Figure 4-10); their permissions to execute administrative tasks (Figure 4-11); and the administrative roles they may become to perform special tasks such as taking ZFS snapshots (Figure 4-12).

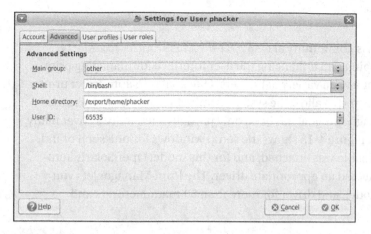

Figure 4-10. *Advanced user settings*

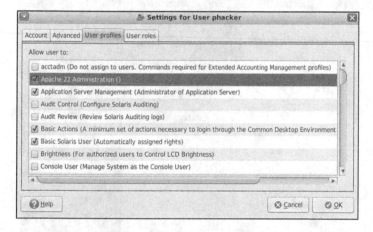

Figure 4-11. *Setting a user's permission profile*

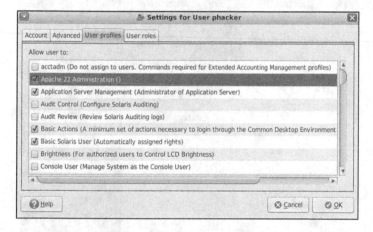

Figure 4-12. *Assigning a user's roles*

Printing

There is an active OpenSolaris community at `http://opensolaris.org/os/community/printing/` devoted to developing and enhancing the user interface for managing printers and to adding support for a wide variety of printers. One goal is to autodetect printer hardware when it is attached and to allow the system administrator to customize the printer configuration. Although this goal has been only partially met, it does cover many common brands of printers. Figure 4-13 shows the setup windows for one such brand, Lexmark. The printer's USB cable was attached, and for this model OpenSolaris automatically detected it and selected an appropriate driver. The Print Manager lets you select and test the brand, model, and driver for more than 50 manufacturers and hundreds of models.

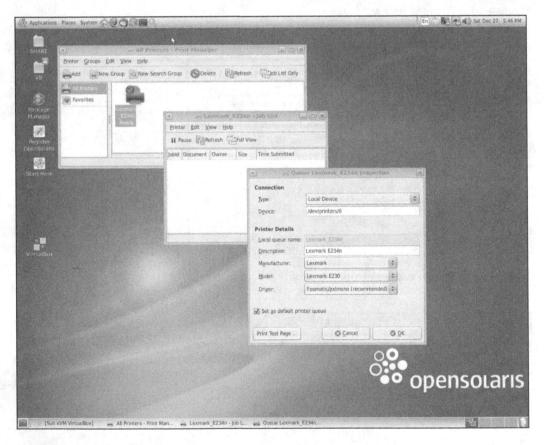

Figure 4-13. *Configuring a printer*

Summary

You've installed OpenSolaris, explored some of its similarities to familiar Linux environments as well as its differences, learned how to add software packages to it, and learned how to keep your OS and applications up to date using the Image Packaging System. Now you're ready to start using OpenSolaris and its special features to host your web applications and other software.

## PART 2

Working with OpenSolaris

Three foundation technologies give the OpenSolaris operating system its great flexibility and power for your applications, especially those for the Web: the Service Management Facility (SMF), the ZFS file system, and several types of virtualization. These are covered in detail in this part of the book.

CHAPTER 5

■■■

SMF: The Service Management Facility

I get knocked down, but I get up again, 'cause you're never gonna keep me down.

—From the song *Tubthumping* by Chumbawamba

Much of modern computer hardware is self-monitoring and self-correcting. It tests itself and reports real and impending errors so that preemptive maintenance can be performed, often in the form of "hot swap" components that can be replaced without interrupting system activity. What would a similar approach to system software look like? It would need a framework for identifying and classifying services and their dependencies, for monitoring and reporting their status, and for some form of autorecovery. UNIX has historically lacked such a framework, relying instead on ad hoc solutions to determine which services are running, which services are not running that should be and why, and which potential services are available.

Think about how you have typically configured service programs in early versions of UNIX and Linux. You created a shell script in one of the /etc/rc.d directories, prefixed the script name with an *S* or a *K* to identify it as a start or kill script, and gave the script a number that determines when it is run. Thus, the /etc/rc.d/rc5.d/S80sendmail script starts the sendmail service when the system enters run level 5. It starts up *after* the sshd service specified in /etc/rc.d/rc5.d/S55sshd. So, does sendmail *depend* on the sshd service being ready before it starts? You can't tell from the scripts! An error in the name or location of your service script can prevent it from running; locating such errors has also been difficult. Administrators usually resort to searching the system log files and process tables using grep; such a simplistic approach often results in incomplete information about the nature of the problem:

- Service processes cannot be easily identified and listed separately from user processes.

- It's difficult to determine or define *when* services should run.

- There is no standard framework for defining service *dependencies*; if two services have no interdependencies, they can't start in parallel, saving boot time.

- There are no standard rules for *restarting* services.

- There are too many differing configuration files in too many different locations, each with its own format and syntax rules.

To address these issues, OpenSolaris includes the Service Management Facility (SMF), which defines a framework and administrative tools for configuring and monitoring system services.

What's a Service?

You already know what a service is; it's a persistently running application, usually started at system boot time and generally not associated with an interactive user's login session. Programs such as the Apache web server, the MySQL database, NFS file servers, the sendmail email daemon, firewalls, DNS servers, and the sshd login daemon are all typical examples of services started when you boot your system. Services listen for and respond to requests for some action such as opening and sending a file with NFS, queuing and printing files, delivering and forwarding email, or responding to database queries.

SMF provides a framework to assign OpenSolaris services a standard state model, naming standards, dependency assignments, and restarter methods, all under control of a service daemon (svc.startd), which is notified of service outages and recovers them according to your specifications. You can install OpenSolaris and use it to develop and run applications without using its special features such as containers and DTrace, but because SMF replaces the familiar /etc/rc* files and methods for managing services, this is one new feature of OpenSolaris that you shouldn't ignore.

Note Your custom rc service scripts and those installed by certain ISV application software will still work; they are executed within their assigned run level *after* SMF-managed services are started. You just won't be able to manage these services with SMF until you prepare and register a service manifest that calls your script.

To understand OpenSolaris services, you need to learn how to refer to them by their true names. Services are referenced using a Fault Managed Resource Identifier (FMRI), which is a character string that looks a lot like a URL. For example, the sshd service daemon's full FMRI on your local system is svc://localhost/network/ssh:default.

FMRIs have the following components:

- A *scheme*, which indicates the type of service, either svc for an SMF-managed service or lrc for a legacy rc script–managed service.

- A *location*, which indicates the host name where the service is running. Usually this will be localhost, but later versions of SMF will allow other locations for dependency purposes.

- A *functional category*, which indicates the type of service. Some types of service are as follows:

  - Application: User service program or daemon

  - System: Platform-independent system service

  - Device: I/O and other hardware devices (generally used for dependencies)

  - Network: Network services, including those converted from inetd

  - Milestone: Run levels, such as those in SVR4

  - Platform: Services specific to the local hardware

  - Site: Services specific to the organization's site

- A *description*, which names the service.

- An *instance*, which is used to indicate services that may have multiple copies running, such as NFS service daemons.

So, the FMRI for the sshd service daemon, svc://localhost/network/ssh:default, indicates that ssh is an SMF-managed network service running with one default instance on the local system.

When you need to refer to a service using any of the SMF programs, you often don't need to give its full FMRI. Like with OpenSolaris's path conventions for file names, you can use the FMRI's *absolute* or *relative* name depending on where you are or what program you are using. So, when referring to the FRMI of the sshd service, you could use any one of the following:

```
svc://localhost/network/ssh:default
svc:/network/ssh:default
network/ssh:default
ssh
```

Now that you've seen how to refer to services by their names, you can start using the SMF tools shown in Table 5-1 to monitor and manage services.

Table 5-1. *Service Management Tools**

Program Name	Description
svcs	Reports service status information, dependencies, instances, and error diagnostics
svcadm	Administers individual service instances, enables, disables, and restarts
svccfg	Configures service parameters and data files
svcprop	Reports service properties and privileges

* svcs *and* svcprop *are in* /usr/bin, *and* svcadm *and* svccfg *are in* /usr/sbin; *set your path appropriately.*

Every service has a *state* that indicates its current functional activity. Services move from one state to another because of system events (such as run-level changes), error conditions, or administrator actions. A service might not be able to move to a desired state because of unfulfilled dependencies or other conditions. Table 5-2 shows the possible states for OpenSolaris services.

Table 5-2. *Possible Service States*

State	Description
uninitialized	This is the starting state for all services before svc.startd moves the service to a new state.
disabled	The service has been disabled by the administrator.
offline	The service is enabled but not yet online, usually because it's waiting for a dependency to be satisfied.
online	The service has been enabled and has successfully started; all its dependencies have been satisfied.
degraded	The service is enabled and running but with a level of degraded performance that is specified in the service's configuration.
maintenance	The service cannot be started by svc.startd because of an error or unsatisfied dependency and must be manually administered to clear the fault conditions.

You can now explore the services on your OpenSolaris system using the SMF tools and observe their states. We'll show some examples next to get you started. First, list the services on your system using the svcs command; use the -a flag to list all the registered services. Figure 5-1 shows typical output from this command (some output lines have been deleted to shorten the list for printing).

```
hfoxwell@opsol0811:~$ svcs -a
STATE          STIME    FMRI
legacy_run     18:11:38 lrc:/etc/rc2_d/S47pppd
disabled       18:09:24 svc:/network/physical:default
disabled       18:09:27 svc:/system/console-login:vt6
disabled       18:09:37 svc:/application/time-slider:default
disabled       18:09:39 svc:/application/print/server:default
disabled       18:09:44 svc:/network/ntp:default
disabled       18:09:45 svc:/network/nis/client:default
disabled       18:09:48 svc:/network/nfs/server:default
disabled       18:09:50 svc:/network/nfs/client:default
disabled       18:09:51 svc:/network/dns/server:default
disabled       18:09:58 svc:/network/smb/client:default
disabled       18:10:06 svc:/network/device-discovery/printers:snmp
disabled       18:10:06 svc:/network/ipfilter:default
disabled       18:11:40 svc:/network/telnet:default
online         18:09:43 svc:/milestone/name-services:default
online         18:10:02 svc:/network/physical:nwam
online         18:10:07 svc:/milestone/network:default
online         18:10:29 svc:/system/filesystem/usr:default
online         18:10:32 svc:/system/device/local:default
online         18:10:33 svc:/system/filesystem/root:default
online         18:10:34 svc:/system/cryptosvc:default
online         18:10:39 svc:/milestone/single-user:default
online         18:10:39 svc:/system/filesystem/local:default
online         18:10:45 svc:/system/cron:default
online         18:11:27 svc:/network/ssh:default
online         18:11:29 svc:/network/smtp:sendmail
online         18:11:37 svc:/network/inetd:default
online         18:11:38 svc:/milestone/multi-user:default
online         18:11:40 svc:/application/graphical-login/gdm:default
online         18:11:45 svc:/milestone/multi-user-server:default
online         18:11:46 svc:/system/zones:default
hfoxwell@opsol0811:~$
```

Figure 5-1. *Sample output (abbreviated) from the* svcs *-a command*

Notice the variety of service types and their states. The pppd point-to-point network protocol daemon, for example, which is started by the /etc/init.d/pppd script, is listed as an lrc, or legacy rc, service. Remember that this is all you can learn from SMF about such services—the fact that they are running and the time that they were started—because only svc services are managed by SMF. Also note that some services are in the disabled state, while some are running, that is, in the online state.

A Bit About Milestones

You'll notice in the output listed in Figure 5-1 that there are several *milestone* services listed. Milestones group services for administrative and end user availability. These groups correspond with the traditional UNIX/Linux run levels shown in Table 5-3.

Table 5-3. *OpenSolaris Boot Milestones (Run Levels)*

SVR4 Run Level	SMF Milestone
-	none; no services are enabled, and only the kernel is running
s, S	single-user; traditional single-user mode for administrative purposes
2	multi-user
3	multi-user-server
5	all

If you need to put your system into single-user mode, for example, you can still use the /usr/sbin/init s command for this. SMF recognizes that run levels are *groupings* of services, so it provides specific FMRIs for each run level. Thus, the "SMF way" of going to single-user mode is as follows:

```
# svcadm milestone single-user
```

and the command to return to run level 3 would be as follows:

```
# svcadm milestone multi-user-server
```

The following command will enable all services dependent on the multi-user-server milestone:

```
# svcadm milestone all
```

More About Services

Let's examine the ssh service in more detail. The old ways of stopping this service would be to kill its process or to run its rc script with the stop parameter, something like this:

```
# /etc/rc.d/init.d/sshd stop
```

If you kill the OpenSolaris sshd process, as shown in Figure 5-2, and then check to see whether it's been stopped, you see that it's still there but running with a new process ID! How did *that* happen? It was restarted by the SMF service daemon, svc.startd.

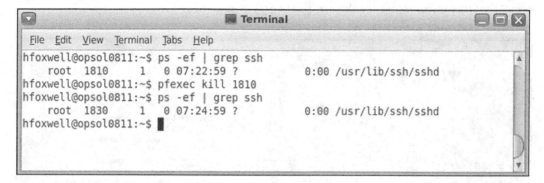

Figure 5-2. *Automatic restart of sshd by SMF*

So, how *do* you stop the sshd service? You use the svcadm command-line program, as shown in Figure 5-3, or use the System ➤ Administration ➤ Services menu and uncheck the SSH Server box, as shown in Figure 5-4.

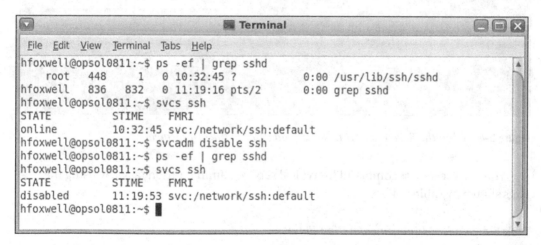

Figure 5-3. *Disabling the ssh service using the svcadm command*

Note that in Figure 5-3 we first used both the `ps` command and the `svcs ssh` command to show that the `ssh` service was running. We then disabled the service with `svcadm` and verified that it was indeed disabled and that its process was gone. Also note that we did not need to give the full FMRI for the service since there was only one local instance; recall that this is like using absolute or relative path names for files.

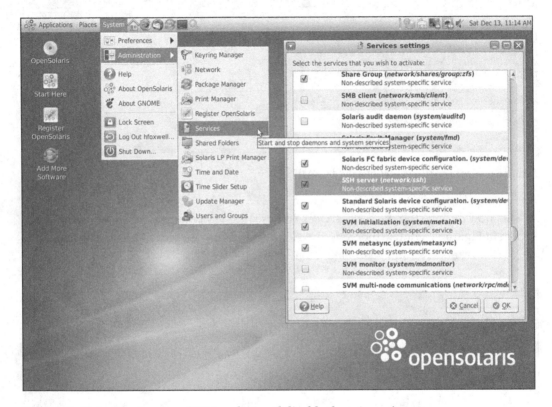

Figure 5-4. *Using the Services GUI to select and disable the* `ssh` *service*

You use the `svcadm` command for typical service administration tasks by using the flags shown in Table 5-4.

Table 5-4. *Service Management Action Flags*

Action Flag	Description
enable	Sets the service as enabled and starts it if all of its dependencies are satisfied
disable	Sets the service as disabled; stops it and doesn't restart it
restart	Stops and restarts the service, assuming its dependencies are satisfied
refresh	Reloads the service's configuration files and restarts the service
clear	Removes the "maintenance" state after a repair; if the service was previously set as enabled, restarts it

When you disable a service, it stays disabled even after a system reboot unless you indicate that the service is being disabled only for the current boot session. For example, the following command will disable the ssh service, and it will *not* restart at the next reboot:

```
# svcadm disable ssh
```

If you intended to disable ssh for only the *current* boot session, you would use the –t (temporary) flag so that normally enabled services will start again at the next system reboot:

```
# svcadm disable -t ssh
```

The power of SMF is really revealed in your ability to define and manage interservice dependencies in the service's manifest file; if a service is not working, you need to know whether something is amiss with the service program itself or with some file or process that the service needs in order to function. SMF's svcs program lets you display a service's dependency relationships along with critical state information. Figure 5-5 shows a series of example svcs commands.

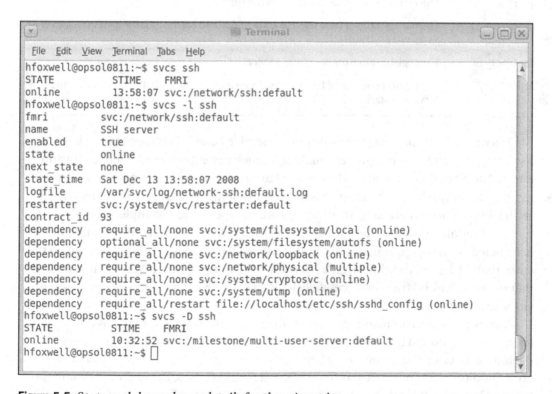

Figure 5-5. *State and dependency details for the ssh service*

The first command, svcs ssh, simply displays the current state and start time of the default instance of the ssh service. More detail is shown in the "long" listing using svcs -l ssh; this listing provides a wealth of information about the service. Table 5-5 briefly explains this output. Later in this chapter you'll see where all this configuration detail is defined.

Table 5-5. *Example State and Dependency Detail for the ssh Service*

Field	Description
fmri	The registered FMRI of the service
name	The name given to the service by the writer of the service definition
enabled	Indicator of whether the service has its enabled state set (true/false)
state	The current state of the service
next_state	Indicator of whether the service is transitioning from one state to another, the next state
state_time	The time the service entered its current state
logfile	The location of the log file used by the service
restarter	The name of the service used to restart; this can be the default system restarter or a custom procedure
contract_id	The registration number of the service
dependency	Listing of services and files needed to be online and available in order for the service to start

It's worth reemphasizing the value of such service details. Each service can have its own log file and restarter process, making it much easier to diagnose service startup errors. Additionally, all of the services needed to support a service are easy to determine. It's almost always the case that services fail because some dependency is not met. Let's see how that works by creating an artificial missing dependency example.

You may already know that sshd needs the /etc/sshd/sshd_config file to configure itself before starting up. Suppose this file is missing. What can SMF tell you when you discover that sshd is not running? Figure 5-6 shows this scenario. The administrator notices that ssh is offline and tries unsuccessfully to enable it. The -x flag of the svcs program provides an explanation.

The svcs -x ssh command reveals that the reason the service is offline is the missing configuration file. Additionally, it refers you to the man page for the service daemon and its log file, along with a URL that provides an online interpretation of the error condition (Figure 5-7). On other UNIX and Linux systems, depending on your system and logging configuration, information about the missing file might not even be logged by sshd in /var/adm/messages. SMF identifies the exact problem for you.

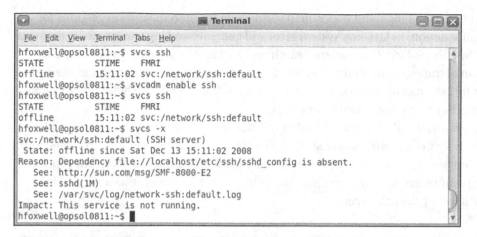

Figure 5-6. *Detail on why the* ssh *service is not running*

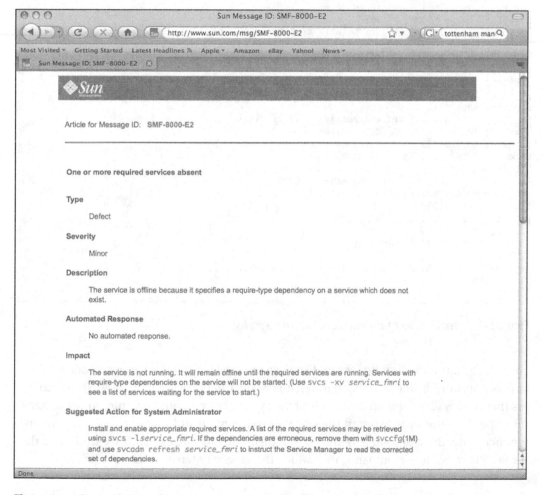

Figure 5-7. *The SMF URL that suggests a reason for the* ssh *service's failure to start*

The URL lists details about the error, its impact on the system, and suggestions for administrator action. In fact, any system error will generate and log a message ID that you can enter into the Solaris/OpenSolaris search tool at http://www.sun.com/msg/ to get an explanation of the error condition. Admittedly, some of the explanations and suggested actions at this site can be somewhat generic, but even that is far more helpful than silent service failures or indecipherable error codes.

Occasionally, simply fixing a dependency is not enough to restart a service; it will remain in an *offline* or *maintenance* state until all the error conditions are eliminated and all dependencies are met. After you have diagnosed the problems and taken appropriate administrative actions, you can clear the maintenance state and restart the service. Figure 5-8 shows you such a scenario.

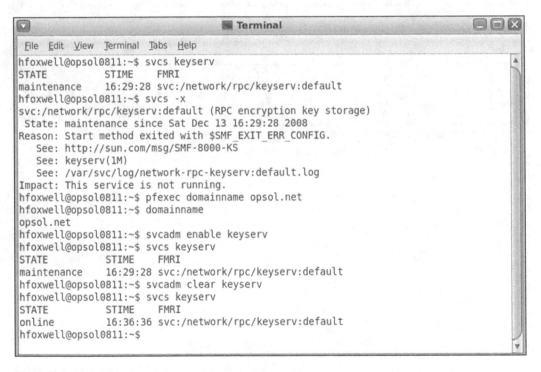

Figure 5-8. *Clearing the maintenance state of a service*

Say the administrator notices that the keyserv service for storing private encryption keys is not running and is in the maintenance state. Checking the man page, she discovers that the keyserv daemon won't start if the system has no domain name, so she assigns one. She then attempts to restart the keyserv service, but it stubbornly remains in a maintenance state. But she soon remembers that this state must be explicitly cleared using the svcadm clear keyserv command, after which the service enters the online state.

> **Tip** If a service has multiple dependencies that are not yet enabled, you can enable them all recursively at one time using the -r flag of the svcadm command: svcadm enable -r ssh.

If you take another look at Figure 5-5, you'll note that the ssh service has a contract_id. A contract defines a relationship (dependency) between a service process and another resource managed by the kernel, such as processors, memory, devices, or other service processes. SMF uses contracts to organize notification events; if a device or service fails, the kernel will notify the owner of the contract for that resource. SMF services are contracted to the svc.startd daemon so that if they fail or exit, then the appropriate restarter action can be taken. The default restarter will try to restart a service if any of the service's contract members fail.

You can examine and monitor service contract relationship activities using the ctstat and ctwatch commands; they provide a means to get detailed information on failing services.

Creating Your Own Services

You've seen that existing OpenSolaris services have their own FMRIs, service names, log files, restarters, and dependencies. Where are these characteristics defined? And, more importantly, how can you define your own services?

Each OpenSolaris service is configured using a *manifest* file that defines the service's name, start and stop methods, restart conditions, and dependencies. Manifests are XML files that reside in the /var/svc/manifest directory tree; each service functional category has its own subdirectory for its manifest files. For example, the manifest file for the ssh service that we have been examining is /var/svc/manifest/network/ssh.xml.

> **Tip** Before you decide to create your own service manifest, remember that you are part of the OpenSolaris developer community and that there are other users who may have already created one that you can use. You can find sample manifest files for many types of services at http://blastwave.org/smf/manifests.php and at http://opensolaris.org/os/community/smf/manifests.

Service manifests can be easily created by copying and modifying existing manifests or by using generic manifest templates such as the one at `http://www.sun.com/bigadmin/content/selfheal/smf-hds/template.xml`, shown in Figure 5-9 (note the `"REPLACE_ME"` locations in this template; that's where you define the service name, timeout values, and other characteristics of your service).

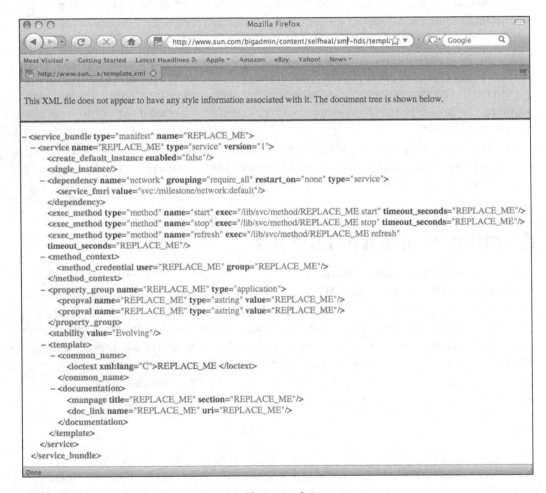

Figure 5-9. *A sample generic service manifest template*

These are the key manifest components you need to define:

- *Service name*: The service name includes the functional category and a character string that names the service, such as `application/oracle` or `network/nfsV4`.

- *Start/stop methods*: These are shell scripts, typically residing in the `/lib/svc/method` directory, which call the service programs. These scripts are very much like the familiar `rc` scripts.

- *Dependencies*: Identifying dependencies is often the most difficult part of creating service manifests, and it's a good idea to examine existing OpenSolaris manifests to see how other services define them. You need to know what your service needs in order to function, such as network services, file systems, crypto services, or local device availability.

- *Dependents*: Are you creating a service that is needed by some other service? For example, if your service starts a firewall program, additional network services can be listed that depend on your service (without modifying those services' manifests).

- *Milestone (run level)*: Your service may need to start within a particular milestone because other services depend on it; that milestone will not complete until your service and all the other services for that milestone have started.

Other manifest components include the number of service instances, service model, fault response, and reference documentation. Let's continue examining the ssh manifest, /var/svc/manifest/network/ssh.xml, to see how each of these components have been defined; because the file is rather long, we'll show only the relevant sections of the manifest and highlight the key components in bold.

The ssh service name tag also includes a version number for change documentation purposes:

```
<service
        name='network/ssh'
        type='service'
        version='1'>
```

The ssh service is dependent on other services such as the local file system, network, and crypto services. It's also dependent on the presence of the sshd_config file and is started within the multi-user-server milestone; in turn, that milestone is defined to be dependent on the ssh service and will not complete until the ssh service is online.

```
<dependency name='fs-local'
                grouping='require_all'
                restart_on='none'
                type='service'>
                <service_fmri
                        value='svc:/system/filesystem/local' />
...
<dependency name='net-physical'
                grouping='require_all'
                restart_on='none'
                type='service'>
                <service_fmri value='svc:/network/physical' />
        </dependency>
```

```
        <dependency name='cryptosvc'
                grouping='require_all'
                restart_on='none'
                type='service'>
                <service_fmri value='svc:/system/cryptosvc' />
        </dependency>
...
<dependency name='config_data'
                grouping='require_all'
                restart_on='restart'
                type='path'>
                <service_fmri
                    value='file://localhost/etc/ssh/sshd_config' />
        </dependency>
...
<dependent
                name='ssh_multi-user-server'
                grouping='optional_all'
                restart_on='none'>
                        <service_fmri
                            value='svc:/milestone/multi-user-server' />
        </dependent>
```

The service's start and refresh methods reference shell scripts in the /lib/svc/method
directory that accept the parameters start or refresh as input and execute the sshd daemon. The stop method executes a kill on the service's process, as you would expect. All
of these actions, however, are performed under the control of the SMF daemon to provide and manage the service's states and transitions.

You can also specify online documentation references for the service; this assists
administrators when error reports are logged:

```
<template>
        <common_name>
                <loctext xml:lang='C'>
                SSH server
                </loctext>
        </common_name>
        <documentation>
                <manpage title='sshd' section='1M' manpath='/usr/share/man' />
        </documentation>
    </template>
```

After you have copied or created your service's manifest file, move it to the appropriate functional category directory. You can verify that your file is valid using the svccfg command since it has a built-in XML validator. The following command will validate your file and register it with the SMF service daemon:

```
# svccfg import yourmanifest.xml
```

You will then be able to see that your service is available (using the svcs command), and if you've specified your dependencies correctly, you can use the svcadm command to enable your service and the svcs command to examine its state.

Service manifests can be complicated, but you can create some that are quite basic, such as this simple example for starting the MySQL database (*after* downloading and installing mysql using Package Manager). Create a file, mysql.xml, containing the following:

```
<?xml version="1.0"?>
<!DOCTYPE service_bundle SYSTEM "/usr/share/lib/xml/dtd/service_bundle.dtd.1">
<service_bundle type="manifest" name="MySQL">
<service name="application/database/mysql" type="service" version="1">
<single_instance/>
<dependency name="filesystem" grouping="require_all"
restart_on="none" type="service">
    <service_fmri value="svc:/system/filesystem/local"/>
</dependency>
<exec_method type="method" name="start" exec="/etc/sfw/mysql/mysql.server start"
timeout_seconds="120"/>
<exec_method type="method" name="stop" exec="/etc/sfw/mysql/mysql.server stop"
timeout_seconds="120"/>
<instance name="default" enabled="false"/>
<stability value="Unstable"/>
<template>
<common_name>
    <loctext xml:lang="C">MySQL RDBMS</loctext>
</common_name>
<documentation>
    <manpage title="mysql" section="1" manpath="/usr/sfw/share/man"/>
</documentation>
</template>
</service>
</service_bundle>
```

Note the service name, MySQL; its dependency on the local file system service svc:/system/filesystem/local; the start and stop methods that call the /etc/sfw/mysql/mysql.server executable; and the documentation pointer to the mysql man page.

Copy the file into the /var/svc/manifest/application/database directory, activate it by running svccfg import mysql.xml, and then enable the service using svcadm enable mysql.

Editing manifest files can be tedious, and it's easy to introduce XML syntax errors as well as SMF errors. Fortunately, there are tools to assist you in creating and managing these files. One such tool is the Java-based SMF Manifest Creator that was a prize winner in the OpenSolaris Community Innovation Awards contest; download it at http://opensolaris. org/os/project/awards/awards_land/Entries/. Another tool that we've mentioned in earlier chapters is Webmin, a community-developed system management tool for Linux and UNIX systems, including OpenSolaris (see http://webmin.com/). Webmin is also in the OpenSolaris software repository's Administration and Configuration collection, so you can download and install it using Package Manager. After it's installed, you access it with your browser at http://localhost:10000, as shown in Figure 5-10.

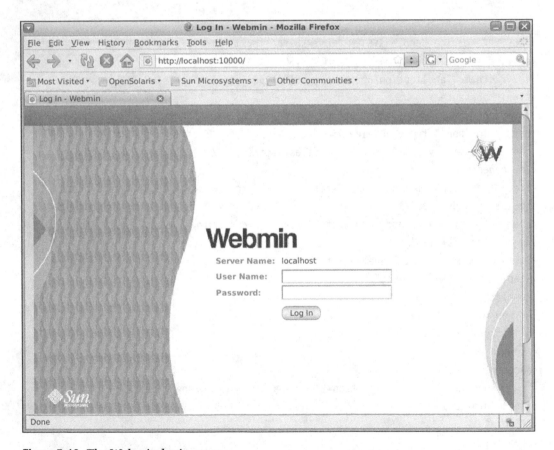

Figure 5-10. *The Webmin login page*

Webmin includes interfaces to most OpenSolaris system management and configuration tasks (Figure 5-11) including the creation and activation of SMF services, which creates the service manifest files for you (Figure 5-12).

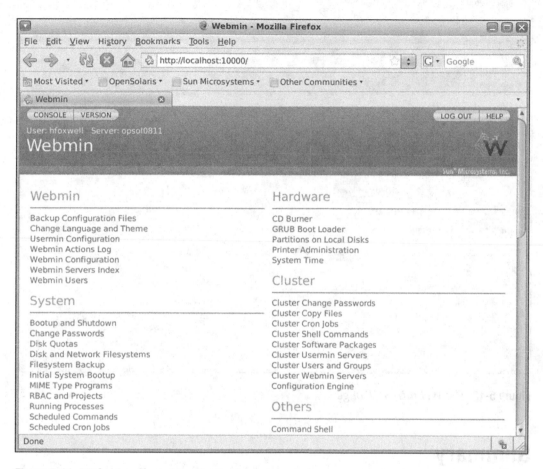

Figure 5-11. *Webmin administrative task menu*

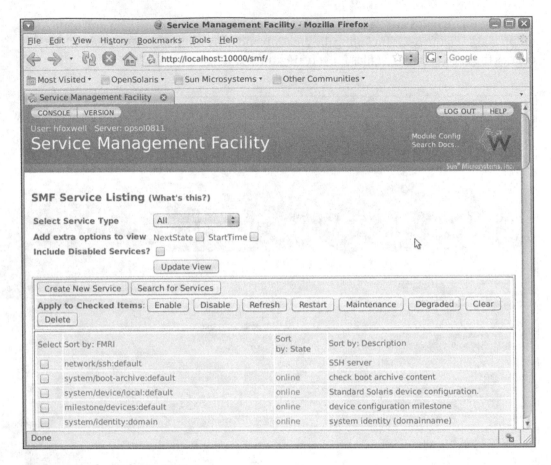

Figure 5-12. *The Webmin SMF page*

Summary

OpenSolaris's Service Management Facility is designed to provide better control over system services and daemons than traditional UNIX/Linux initialization/termination scripts. It's the one "different" OpenSolaris feature you shouldn't ignore. Even though your legacy rc script methods still work, you will benefit from converting these scripts to SMF-managed services.

CHAPTER 6

■ ■ ■

The ZFS File System

There are places I'll remember all my life, though some have changed.

—From the song *In My Life* by the Beatles

Stored data must be remembered perfectly. Many computer technologies have been invented in an attempt to achieve perfect data recall in the presence of electronic, mechanical, and human errors. RAID disk technologies, tape backup systems, error correcting memory, remote data replication, and other techniques are used today to ensure that when data is written it can be quickly and reliably retrieved even after much time has elapsed, perhaps years.

There are numerous commercially developed and community-developed disk file systems; Wikipedia lists almost 100 at http://en.wikipedia.org/wiki/Comparison_of_file_systems. Nearly all file systems have a common functional goal: to provide reliable and secure storage and recall of data organized into files and directories using standardized data object naming conventions. Some file systems are specifically designed for high-performance access to large numbers of disks (open source Lustre), for distributed write access by multiple hosts (Sun Microsystems' QFS), or for hierarchical storage management of online disk and offline tape data (IBM's HFS). The standard file system for UNIX systems, UNIX File System (UFS), originated in the early 1980s and has continued to evolve with new features such as journaling, performance, and scalability enhancements. Linux file systems have also progressed since that OS's introduction in 1991. The Linux Extended File System (ext) was introduced in 1992 and was limited to 2GB; later enhancements included increasing the supported file system size to 4TB but kept the 2GB maximum file size (ext2), journaling (ReiserFS and ext3), size increases (ext3, supporting up to 2TB files and 16TB file systems), and journal checksumming (ext4).

INTERNATIONAL SYSTEM OF UNITS PREFIXES

For reference, here are the standard prefixes for commonly used decimal multiples of bytes for describing data storage quantities:

- 10^3, *kilo*-: Thousands
- 10^6, *mega*-: Millions
- 10^9, *giga*-: Billions
- 10^{12}, *tera*-: Trillions

- 10^{15}, *peta*-: Quadrillions
- 10^{18}, *exa*-: Quintillions
- 10^{21}, *zetta*-: Sextillions
- 10^{24}, *yotta*-: Septillions

Significant problems can occur with disk-based file systems when there is an operating system crash, a hardware failure, or a sudden power outage. The OS may not have completed all the operations needed to write the data to the disk, leaving the data in an inconsistent or corrupted state. The failure of a disk drive or controller can have a similar effect. Restoring data to its correct state and retrieving it successfully can be done somewhat transparently by using RAID techniques such as mirroring or manually using file system repair tools such as fsck, but even these methods sometimes can't retrieve all lost data.

The ZFS file system was initially developed at Sun Microsystems in 2004 and was released as an OpenSolaris project in 2005. ZFS is now the default file system for OpenSolaris. Its primary design goals include the following:

- Support for extremely large storage capacities

- Elimination of many storage management tasks

- Active data integrity checks with automatic error detection and correction

ZFS has earned an incredible amount of attention, including *InfoWorld*'s 2008 Storage Technology of the Year Award. Numerous web sites and blogs are devoted to its features, even more so because of its open source base; ZFS is now available in early access in read-only mode for Apple's current OS X operating system release and is planned for full read/write access in its next release. ZFS is also available in other OSs as well, including FreeBSD (http://wiki.freebsd.org/ZFS).

Full details on ZFS could fill an entire book or more, but in this chapter we'll review the basics you need in order to understand ZFS and to use it for general storage management. We won't include details on ZFS's internal design or specialized performance tuning; for that you may want to browse the ZFS wiki at http://www.solarisinternals.com//wiki/index.php?title=Category:ZFS. But ZFS is a critical component of OpenSolaris's operation for users and system administrators, and there's still a lot to learn, so we'll include information on the following:

- Basic ZFS design features

- Storage management features and commands

- The Time Slider file manager

- OpenSolaris boot environment management

As with all OpenSolaris technologies, you'll find a large community of ZFS users and contributing developers at http://opensolaris.org, as well as a wealth of information on the Sun Microsystems' web sites. To keep up with the latest news on ZFS, visit the following:

- http://www.sun.com/software/solaris/zfs_learning_center.jsp, Sun Microsystems' ZFS Learning Center

- http://opensolaris.org/os/community/zfs/, the OpenSolaris ZFS community

- http://opensolaris.org/os/community/zfs/faq/, the OpenSolaris ZFS FAQ

Exploring the Basic ZFS Features

When you add RAM memory to a system, you almost never care about which DIMM device on which your applications are running. And you generally don't worry about memory boundaries; all you really care about is the *total pool of memory* available to your operating system and to your applications. When you need more memory, you physically install another module, and the OS takes care of adding it to the memory pool and presents you with a single memory resource. You can think of ZFS in similar terms. With earlier file systems, you needed to recognize, configure, and manage individual disk devices and their partitions, and your resulting storage was fragmented and often limited in capacity because of the individual size limits of each device. You had to know and to care exactly where your data was located. With ZFS, you simply add a disk device to a pool of disks, and as with RAM, you see a *total pool of storage* not limited by individual device characteristics (Figure 6-1).

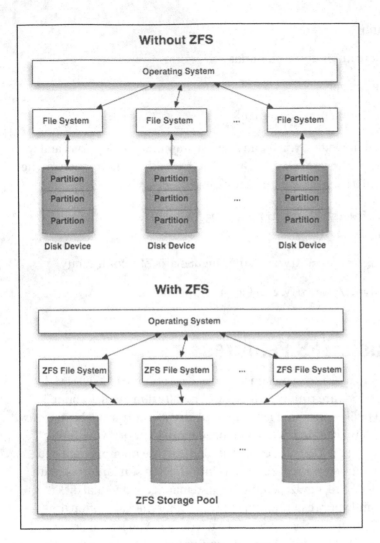

Figure 6-1. *File systems with and without ZFS*

Instead of creating file systems on each disk or partition whose sizes are constrained by the hardware, you create virtual file systems inside the ZFS storage pool. If the size of your file system exceeds that of a partition or disk, ZFS takes care of that for you. As with RAM, if you need more space in the pool, just add another storage device to expand the available size of the pool (and you can do that without shutting down your system). And because of ZFS's 128-bit addressing capability, storage pools can be enormous, encompassing billions of terabytes (Table 6-1); multiple file systems of any size up to 16 exabytes can be created on a ZFS pool.

Table 6-1. *File System Capacities*

File System	Max File Size*	Max Volume Size*
UFS	Up to 32 petabytes	Up to 1 yottabyte
ext3	Up to 2 terabytes	Up to 32 terabytes
ext4	Up to 16 terabytes	Up to 1 exabyte
FAT32	4 gigabytes	Up to 8 terabytes
NTFS	16 exabytes	16 exabytes
ZFS	16 exabytes	2^{18} exabytes

* The max file and volume sizes listed are implementation dependent and vary according to vendor, operating system, and supported disk hardware.

In addition to using a storage pool approach to hosting file systems, ZFS includes active data integrity checking of all I/O operations. Data is *never* overwritten on the disk; ZFS uses a Copy On Write (COW) model for storing new data. This method allocates new disk blocks for the data, writes the new data to them, and then updates the file system *metadata* blocks using the same method. Multiple writes are grouped and cached into an *intent log* to improve performance and to provide a record of transactions in the event that some form of recovery is needed. All write requests use new disk blocks, and both data and metadata blocks are verified using a 256-bit checksum that can detect and correct data corruption caused by disk surface errors, DMA and cache memory errors, data path errors, and even device driver bugs. This process also enables active "self-healing" of disk data. When an application tries to read a block of data and the checksum indicates invalid data, ZFS finds good copies of the block (on the same disk or on a mirror disk), returns good data to the application, and repairs or replaces the invalid data block.

ZFS improves on RAID-based disk arrays that can still silently lose or corrupt data if the parity block write fails because of a hardware failure or power outage. ZFS includes RAID-Z, similar to the popular RAID-5 that uses data striping across multiple disks along with parity check data. RAID-Z writes in checksummed variable-length stripe blocks that don't overwrite live data; an enhanced version, RAID-Z2, includes double-parity checking so that even two ZFS pool disks can fail without loss of data.

Once you create a ZFS pool, you manage the total storage pool space with a few simple commands, as you'll see in the next section. You can easily set file system and user directory characteristics such as quotas or data compression. You manage *space*, not disks or partitions. ZFS lets you create file system snapshots and clones that you can use to back up and restore data; OpenSolaris uses these ZFS features to manage multiple boot images and updates. The Time Slider file manager tool uses automatic ZFS file system snapshots that let you retrieve deleted files. In short, ZFS is the foundation for allocating and managing OpenSolaris disk space for system administration and for end users. Let's see how this all works.

> **Note** At the time of publication of this book, there was no ZFS GUI distributed with OpenSolaris. Sun Microsystems has one for Solaris 10 that might become available for OpenSolaris, and there are community projects under development such as the EasyTools project at `http://opensolaris.org/os/project/phpEasyTools/`.

Creating and Managing ZFS Storage Pools

There are two general tasks you must perform when managing storage with ZFS: the first is creating a pool and setting its characteristics using the `/usr/sbin/zpool` command, and the second is creating and configuring file systems on the pool using the `/usr/bin/zfs` command. A ZFS pool is an aggregate of storage locations, called *virtual devices* (hard disks, flash memory, USB memory sticks, or even preallocated files) that provides space for ZFS datasets; all datasets within the pool share the same total space. Virtual device options are categorized according to their performance and data integrity features. Table 6-2 shows the options for storage locations.

Table 6-2. *ZFS Virtual Devices*

Device Type	Description
disk	A disk block device or partition; using an entire disk is recommended
file	A file; intended for temporary or experimental work
mirror	A replicate of a virtual device; data is copied identically to a device and its mirror
raidz, raidz1, raidz2	A virtual device with striping and parity features
spare	A virtual device to be used if an allocated device fails
log	A virtual device for temporarily stacking multiple ZFS write requests
cache	A virtual device for intermediate caching of ZFS data; typically set to flash memory or solid state disks for performance enhancement

Creating a ZFS Pool

The zpool command has several key options, shown in Table 6-3.

Table 6-3. *Pool Management Options for the zpool Command**

Option	Brief Description
create	Creates a new ZFS pool using the specified virtual devices and properties
destroy	Destroys a ZFS pool (removes all virtual devices from a pool); does not erase device data
add	Adds a virtual device to a pool
remove	Removes a virtual device from a pool; does not erase device data
list	Lists all defined pools
iostat	Lists I/O statistics for a pool including capacity, R/W operations, and effective bandwidth
status	Displays the state of a pool
online	Sets the pool state to online
offline	Sets the pool state to offline
attach	Attaches a new device to an existing pool
detach	Detaches a device from a pool
replace	Replaces a device in a pool with another device; equivalent to detach olddev followed by attach newdev
scrub	Verifies all pool checksums; repairs any bad data
history	Lists the history of all actions taken on a pool
get	Retrieves and lists the properties of a pool
set	Sets one or more properties of a pool

* *By default device names referenced by the zpool command are assumed to be in the /dev/dsk directory. Device name references to this directory can omit the directory name; otherwise, the full device path name is required. For example, you can use device name c0t0d0 for /dev/dsk/c0t0d0.*

Some Examples Using the zpool Command

In the following examples, we use the pseudo devices (files) mydisk01 through mydisk06 in the /dev/dsk directory. On your system, you can discover your system's device names by using the /usr/sbin/format command, which will list attached hardware device names and partitions as in Figure 6-2, which shows the device name of /dev/dsk/c3d0s0 for the primary system disk. If there were more disks available on the system, they would also be listed; the listed device names on your system will vary according to the number and type of disk drives installed. You must be aware of the available drives and partitions on your system before assigning them to a ZFS pool.

Figure 6-2. *Use the /usr/sbin/format command to list device names.*

Figure 6-3 shows a sequence of zpool commands. The first, zpool list, simply lists the existing ZFS pools on your system; there's only one, rpool (the root pool; you'll learn more about that one later).

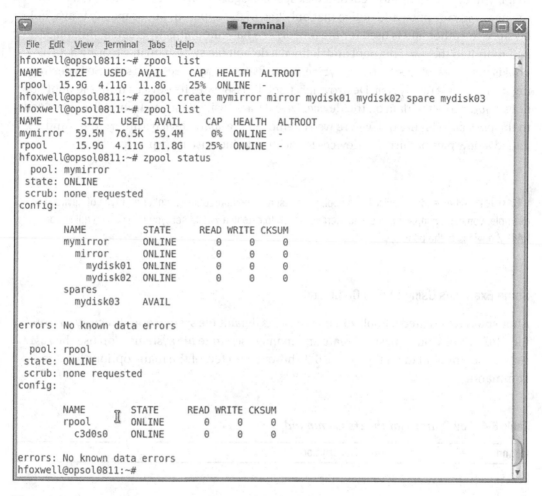

```
hfoxwell@opsol0811:~# zpool list
NAME   SIZE   USED  AVAIL    CAP  HEALTH  ALTROOT
rpool  15.9G  4.11G  11.8G    25%  ONLINE  -
hfoxwell@opsol0811:~# zpool create mymirror mirror mydisk01 mydisk02 spare mydisk03
hfoxwell@opsol0811:~# zpool list
NAME       SIZE   USED  AVAIL    CAP  HEALTH  ALTROOT
mymirror  59.5M  76.5K  59.4M     0%  ONLINE  -
rpool     15.9G  4.11G  11.8G    25%  ONLINE  -
hfoxwell@opsol0811:~# zpool status
  pool: mymirror
 state: ONLINE
 scrub: none requested
config:

        NAME          STATE     READ WRITE CKSUM
        mymirror      ONLINE       0     0     0
          mirror      ONLINE       0     0     0
            mydisk01  ONLINE       0     0     0
            mydisk02  ONLINE       0     0     0
        spares
          mydisk03    AVAIL

errors: No known data errors

  pool: rpool
 state: ONLINE
 scrub: none requested
config:

        NAME        STATE     READ WRITE CKSUM
        rpool       ONLINE       0     0     0
          c3d0s0    ONLINE       0     0     0

errors: No known data errors
hfoxwell@opsol0811:~#
```

Figure 6-3. *Creating a ZFS mirrored pool with a spare*

Next you create a mirrored pool named mymirror along with a spare disk:

```
zpool create mymirror mirror mydisk01 mydisk02 spare mydisk03
```

It's that simple; you've created a storage disk with a mirror, and you've created a spare that will be used automatically if half of the mirror pair fails. The subsequent `zpool list` and `zpool status` commands display and verify what you've created. Note that if you use `df -h` to show current disk space usage, you see the root pool along with the new `mymirror` pool, and notice that only half of the apparent pool capacity is available because the other half is used for the mirror; ZFS has automatically created, initialized, and mounted the `mymirror` pool and defined a default file system on it. Creating a RAID-Z pool is just as easy: `zpool create myriad raidz mydisk04 mydisk05 mydisk06`. So is destroying it: `zpool destroy myriad`. Destroying a pool disassociates its devices from the pool but does not destroy the data on the device. Devices are easily removed from a pool or added to the pool as in Figure 6-4, where we've removed the spare device from `mymirror` and added a new pair of mirrored devices to the pool to increase its capacity.

Caution When adding devices to a pool, you must add the appropriate number and type of device. For example, you can't simply add a single storage device to extend a `raidz` set; you must add a full set of RAID-Z devices to the pool.

Some Examples Using the zfs Command

After you have created a pool, you could use its default file system and directory to store files, but it's obviously best to create and manage separate file systems. You use the /usr/sbin/zfs command to do this. Table 6-4 shows only a few of the many options for this command.

Table 6-4. *Key Options for the zfs Command*

Option	Brief Description
create	Creates a file system
destroy	Destroys a file system
snapshot	Takes a snapshot of a file system
rollback	Restores a file system from a snapshot
clone	Makes a copy of a file system
promote	Creates a full file system from a clone
list	Lists the characteristics of a file system
set	Sets the value for a file system characteristic
get	Retrieves the value for a file system characteristic

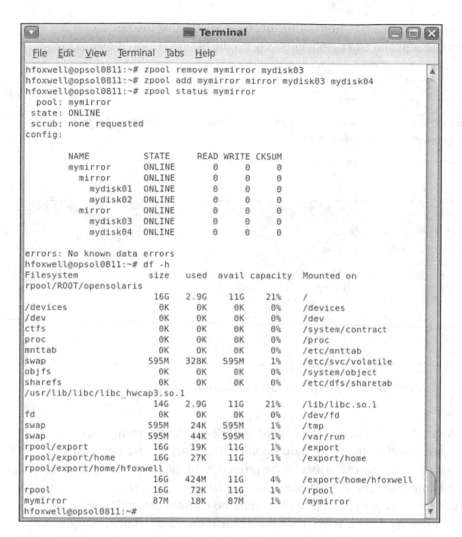

```
                                      Terminal
 File   Edit   View   Terminal   Tabs   Help
hfoxwell@opsol0811:~# zpool remove mymirror mydisk03
hfoxwell@opsol0811:~# zpool add mymirror mirror mydisk03 mydisk04
hfoxwell@opsol0811:~# zpool status mymirror
  pool: mymirror
 state: ONLINE
 scrub: none requested
config:

        NAME        STATE     READ WRITE CKSUM
        mymirror    ONLINE       0     0     0
          mirror    ONLINE       0     0     0
            mydisk01  ONLINE     0     0     0
            mydisk02  ONLINE     0     0     0
          mirror    ONLINE       0     0     0
            mydisk03  ONLINE     0     0     0
            mydisk04  ONLINE     0     0     0

errors: No known data errors
hfoxwell@opsol0811:~# df -h
Filesystem           size   used  avail capacity  Mounted on
rpool/ROOT/opensolaris
                      16G   2.9G    11G    21%    /
/devices              0K     0K     0K     0%    /devices
/dev                  0K     0K     0K     0%    /dev
ctfs                  0K     0K     0K     0%    /system/contract
proc                  0K     0K     0K     0%    /proc
mnttab                0K     0K     0K     0%    /etc/mnttab
swap                 595M   328K   595M     1%    /etc/svc/volatile
objfs                 0K     0K     0K     0%    /system/object
sharefs               0K     0K     0K     0%    /etc/dfs/sharetab
/usr/lib/libc/libc_hwcap3.so.1
                      14G   2.9G    11G    21%    /lib/libc.so.1
fd                    0K     0K     0K     0%    /dev/fd
swap                 595M    24K   595M     1%    /tmp
swap                 595M    44K   595M     1%    /var/run
rpool/export          16G    19K    11G     1%    /export
rpool/export/home     16G    27K    11G     1%    /export/home
rpool/export/home/hfoxwell
                      16G   424M    11G     4%    /export/home/hfoxwell
rpool                 16G    72K    11G     1%    /rpool
mymirror              87M    18K    87M     1%    /mymirror
hfoxwell@opsol0811:~#
```

Figure 6-4. *Removing and adding devices in a ZFS pool*

In Figure 6-5, we've created a home directory file system using the zfs create mymirror/homedirs command and then recursively list the file systems in the mymirror pool using zfs list -r mymirror.

■**Tip** When referring to a pool name with the zfs command, there is *no leading slash* for the pool name; you will probably frequently make this typing error!

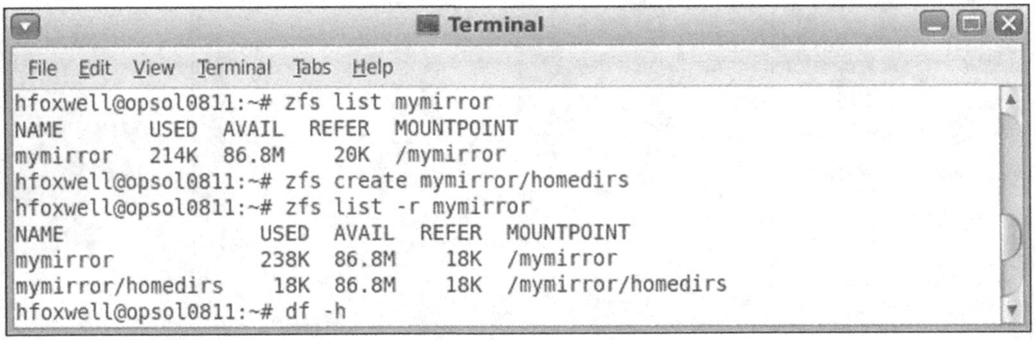

```
hfoxwell@opsol0811:~# zfs list mymirror
NAME       USED   AVAIL   REFER   MOUNTPOINT
mymirror   214K   86.8M    20K   /mymirror
hfoxwell@opsol0811:~# zfs create mymirror/homedirs
hfoxwell@opsol0811:~# zfs list -r mymirror
NAME               USED   AVAIL   REFER   MOUNTPOINT
mymirror           238K   86.8M    18K   /mymirror
mymirror/homedirs   18K   86.8M    18K   /mymirror/homedirs
hfoxwell@opsol0811:~# df -h
```

Figure 6-5. *Creating a ZFS file system using the zfs command*

ZFS file systems have a large number of configurable properties, including compression, user quotas and reservations, mountpoints, NFS sharing, case sensitivity, and writability, to name a few. Figure 6-6 lists all the properties of the mymirror/homedirs file system using the command zfs get all mymirror/homedirs.

To set any of these properties, use the zfs command with the set option. For example, zfs set compression=on mymirror/homedirs turns on transparent file system compression to save disk space; zfs set sharenfs=on mymirror/homedirs exports the homedirs file system for NFS sharing (note that you do *not* add NFS entries for ZFS file system sharing to the /etc/vfstab file). You can set a disk quota for user hfoxwell by specifying his home directory: zfs set quota=5g mymirror/homedirs/hfoxwell. Or, because file system properties are hierarchically *inherited*, you could set the quota for *all* users of the homedirs file system: zfs set quota=5g mymirror/homedirs.

If a user anticipates that she will need extra space for a project, you can preassign, or *reserve*, that space: zfs set reservation=10g mymirror/homedirs/chris. This ensures that other users of the file system can't exhaust the storage beyond what has been previously reserved for that user.

```
hfoxwell@opsol0811:~# zfs get all mymirror/homedirs
NAME                PROPERTY              VALUE                    SOURCE
mymirror/homedirs   type                 filesystem               -
mymirror/homedirs   creation             Tue Dec 30 19:02 2008    -
mymirror/homedirs   used                 18K                      -
mymirror/homedirs   available            86.8M                    -
mymirror/homedirs   referenced           18K                      -
mymirror/homedirs   compressratio        1.00x                    -
mymirror/homedirs   mounted              yes                      -
mymirror/homedirs   quota                none                     default
mymirror/homedirs   reservation          none                     default
mymirror/homedirs   recordsize           128K                     default
mymirror/homedirs   mountpoint           /mymirror/homedirs       default
mymirror/homedirs   sharenfs             off                      default
mymirror/homedirs   checksum             on                       default
mymirror/homedirs   compression          off                      default
mymirror/homedirs   atime                on                       default
mymirror/homedirs   devices              on                       default
mymirror/homedirs   exec                 on                       default
mymirror/homedirs   setuid               on                       default
mymirror/homedirs   readonly             off                      default
mymirror/homedirs   zoned                off                      default
mymirror/homedirs   snapdir              hidden                   default
mymirror/homedirs   aclmode              groupmask                default
mymirror/homedirs   aclinherit           restricted               default
mymirror/homedirs   canmount             on                       default
mymirror/homedirs   shareiscsi           off                      default
mymirror/homedirs   xattr                on                       default
mymirror/homedirs   copies               1                        default
mymirror/homedirs   version              3                        -
mymirror/homedirs   utf8only             off                      -
mymirror/homedirs   normalization        none                     -
mymirror/homedirs   casesensitivity      sensitive                -
mymirror/homedirs   vscan                off                      default
mymirror/homedirs   nbmand               off                      default
mymirror/homedirs   sharesmb             off                      default
mymirror/homedirs   refquota             none                     default
mymirror/homedirs   refreservation       none                     default
mymirror/homedirs   primarycache         all                      default
mymirror/homedirs   secondarycache       all                      default
mymirror/homedirs   usedbysnapshots      0                        -
mymirror/homedirs   usedbydataset        18K                      -
mymirror/homedirs   usedbychildren       0                        -
mymirror/homedirs   usedbyrefreservation 0                        -
hfoxwell@opsol0811:~#
```

Figure 6-6. *Properties of a ZFS file system*

Using ZFS

For all its special features, ZFS is "just a file system" for your OpenSolaris users and
applications. This means it functions like any other type of file system in that it provides
a place to store data in files and directories; applications do not need to "know" that their
files are being stored on ZFS. Standard read and write APIs are used. End users will not
see any difference in how they access their files and directories.

One question about ZFS that does come up, however, is about performance: how does ZFS performance compare to other file systems, particularly for databases?

ZFS has evolved significantly since its introduction in 2005. Its initial priorities were to provide an easily administered pooled storage model with virtually no size or scalability restrictions and near absolute data integrity. Performance was also a high priority, and ZFS continues to advance in that area; ZFS performance has been shown to be equal to or better than UFS and ext3 for many application types, although some tuning may be required. Performance will depend on the reads-to-writes ratio, sequential vs. random reads and writes, write block size, and the amount of memory in your system. Some early comparisons of ZFS performance on Solaris 10 are listed in Table 6-5. They confirm comparable or better ZFS performance in many cases when compared to ext3 and Veritas file systems, and significantly better when compared to NTFS.

Table 6-5. *Some ZFS Performance Reports*

Report	URL
ZFS vs. ext3	http://blogs.sun.com/Peerapong/resource/zfs_linux.pdf
ZFS vs. VxFS	http://blogs.sun.com/Peerapong/resource/zfs_veritas.pdf
ZFS vs. NTFS	http://blogs.sun.com/Peerapong/resource/zfs_msft.pdf

One interesting recent ZFS-related development is the availability of storage appliances based on OpenSolaris and ZFS. Such appliances consist of disks and controllers along with an OS modified to provide network file services. It turns out that OpenSolaris and ZFS are ideal for these devices, especially when they also exploit flash memory caches resulting in dramatic performance improvements. Commercial storage products based on OpenSolaris and ZFS are starting to appear on the market, such as Nexenta (http://www.nexenta.com) and Sun's Storage 7000 product line.

Note The *ZFS Best Practices Guide* (http://www.solarisinternals.com/wiki/index.php/ ZFS_Best_Practices_Guide) has extensive recommendations on deploying ZFS, and there is an active OpenSolaris ZFS community at http://opensolaris.org/os/community/zfs/.

Taking Snapshots

Probably one of the most important ZFS features is its ability to create nearly unlimited and instantaneous file system *snapshots*, which are effectively read-only copies of a ZFS file system at a selected point in time. Such snapshots are used to enhance OpenSolaris's boot environment management as well as to assist end users and administrators to back up and restore changeable file systems. A file system snapshot initially takes up no additional space in a pool; as the original active file system image changes, however, the snapshot grows to keep track of the changes. Creating a snapshot using the zfs command is trivially easy; just specify the full pool/file system name and a user-specified snapshot name:

```
zfs snapshot mymirror/homedirs/hfoxwell@daily
```

or

```
zfs snapshot mymirror/homedirs/hfoxwell@01Jan09
```

After taking your file system snapshot, continue working. If you decide later that you need to return to an earlier state of your file system or to recover an accidentally erased file, you can restore, or *roll back*, the file system to its earlier state. Let's see how this works. In Figure 6-7 we first created a file report.text, and then we took a snapshot named rpool/export/home/hfoxwell@thursday. Oops! Then we accidentally erased the file. But we can roll back the directory to its previous state, and the file is recovered.

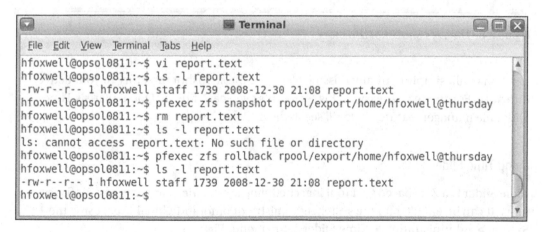

Figure 6-7. *Recovering a file by rolling back to a snapshot*

Where do these snapshots hide? In each file system directory, snapshots reside in a .zfs subdirectory (that's "dot zfs," a hidden directory).

Tip The ls command, even with the –a flag, will not list the .zfs directory. You need to use the zfs list –t snapshot command, which will list all snapshots including those created by Time Slider. Some users create links to their .zfs directories to access them more directly.

If you cd to that directory, as in Figure 6-8, you'll see the *read-only* copy of your file system (along with your missing report.text file!).

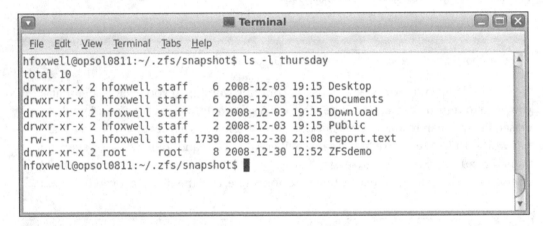

Figure 6-8. *The .zfs snapshot directory*

You could simply copy any missing files from the snapshot directory to your active directory. Fortunately, as easy as this seems, it's even easier using OpenSolaris's Time Slider file manager feature, as you'll see in the next section.

Using Time Slider

Time Slider is a ZFS-based GUI tool for scheduling automatic snapshots of your file systems. It can be enabled for the system administrator or for individual users using the System ➤ Administration ➤ Time Slider Setup menu (Figure 6-9).

The setup GUI lets you specify which file systems are to be regularly backed up using periodic ZFS snapshots. You can see and access these snapshots in your file system's .zfs directory, as shown in Figure 6-10.

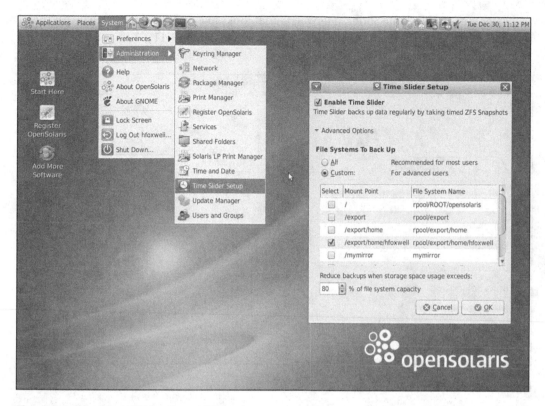

Figure 6-9. *The Time Slider Setup GUI*

```
hfoxwell@opsol0811:~/.zfs/snapshot$ ls
thursday                                  zfs-auto-snap:hourly-2008-12-24-04:00
zfs-auto-snap:daily-2008-12-14-15:24     zfs-auto-snap:hourly-2008-12-24-05:00
zfs-auto-snap:daily-2008-12-22-12:27     zfs-auto-snap:hourly-2008-12-24-06:00
zfs-auto-snap:daily-2008-12-23-00:00     zfs-auto-snap:hourly-2008-12-30-12:32
zfs-auto-snap:daily-2008-12-24-00:00     zfs-auto-snap:hourly-2008-12-30-13:00
zfs-auto-snap:daily-2008-12-30-12:32     zfs-auto-snap:hourly-2008-12-30-14:00
zfs-auto-snap:frequent-2008-12-30-22:45  zfs-auto-snap:hourly-2008-12-30-15:00
zfs-auto-snap:frequent-2008-12-30-23:00  zfs-auto-snap:hourly-2008-12-30-16:00
zfs-auto-snap:frequent-2008-12-30-23:15  zfs-auto-snap:hourly-2008-12-30-17:00
zfs-auto-snap:frequent-2008-12-30-23:30  zfs-auto-snap:hourly-2008-12-30-18:00
zfs-auto-snap:hourly-2008-12-23-19:00    zfs-auto-snap:hourly-2008-12-30-19:00
zfs-auto-snap:hourly-2008-12-23-20:00    zfs-auto-snap:hourly-2008-12-30-20:00
zfs-auto-snap:hourly-2008-12-23-21:00    zfs-auto-snap:hourly-2008-12-30-21:00
zfs-auto-snap:hourly-2008-12-23-22:00    zfs-auto-snap:hourly-2008-12-30-22:00
zfs-auto-snap:hourly-2008-12-23-23:00    zfs-auto-snap:hourly-2008-12-30-23:00
zfs-auto-snap:hourly-2008-12-24-00:00    zfs-auto-snap:weekly-2008-12-14-15:24
zfs-auto-snap:hourly-2008-12-24-01:00    zfs-auto-snap:weekly-2008-12-22-12:27
zfs-auto-snap:hourly-2008-12-24-02:00    zfs-auto-snap:weekly-2008-12-30-12:32
zfs-auto-snap:hourly-2008-12-24-03:00
hfoxwell@opsol0811:~/.zfs/snapshot$
```

Figure 6-10. *The periodic snapshots reside in your file system's* .zfs *directory.*

After you enable Time Slider, a new icon that looks like a small clock appears on the navigation bar of any file browser window, as shown in Figure 6-11.

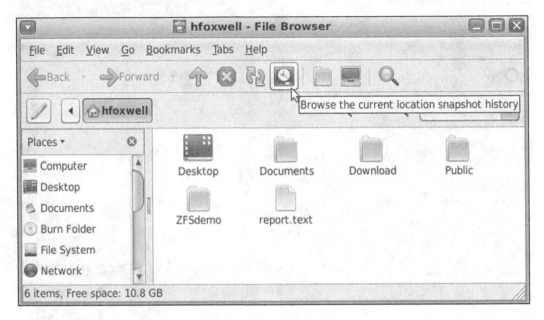

Figure 6-11. *The Time Slider icon*

Now suppose you remove the ZFSdemo directory and the `report.text` file shown in Figure 6-11 *and* even empty the `Trash` folder. Simply click the Time Slider icon, and you will see a slider bar with *Now* at the right end and Time Slider's start date and time at the left end (Figure 6-12).

Simply use the slider to move back through time to the snapshot that contains your erased files, as shown in Figure 6-13. Remember that snapshots are read-only, so you can simply read the erased file in place if that's all you need, or you can recover it back to your desktop with a simple drag and drop (note that our `ZFSdemo` directory and `report.text` file are now shown in the snapshot view).

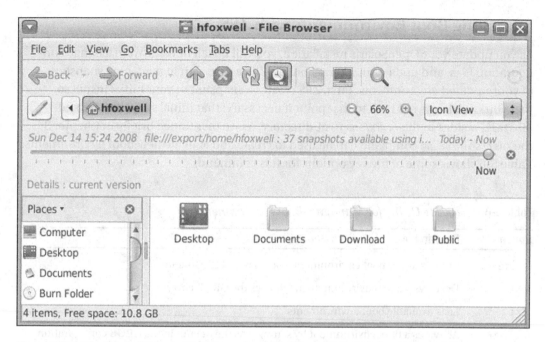

Figure 6-12. *The Time Slider's slider bar, showing Time Slider's start time and date, the name of your file system, and the number of available snapshots*

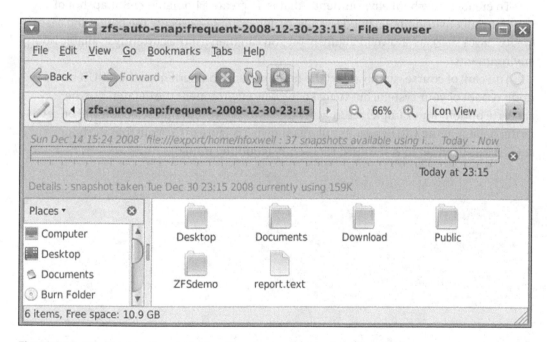

Figure 6-13. *Displaying the contents of past snapshots using Time Slider*

Managing Boot Environments with ZFS

As you update your OpenSolaris installation, you will install new software, change configuration files, and update your kernel builds. ZFS assists you in managing snapshots of your updated environments. First, ZFS creates a snapshot of your initial install so that you can always roll back to that point if necessary; that initial snapshot, named @install, resides in the /.zfs/snapshot directory. As we mentioned briefly in Chapter 3, the /usr/sbin/beadm command can be used to create and activate new boot environments. Table 6-6 shows some of the key options for this command.

Table 6-6. *The beadm Utility for Managing Boot Environments*

Option	Description
create	Creates a new boot environment snapshot and GRUB entry
destroy	Destroys a boot environment and deletes the GRUB entry
list	Lists available boot environments
activate	Activates a boot environment by setting it as the default in the GRUB configuration file, /rpool/grub/boot/menu.lst

To create a new boot environment—that is, to create a bootable ZFS snapshot of your current environment named Env01Jan09, for example—execute the command beadm create Env01Jan09, as shown in Figure 6-14. You can then list the currently available boot environments.

You can, of course, simply select the new boot environment from the GRUB menu upon reboot of your system, but to make the new environment the default, use the activate option (for example, beadm activate Env01Jan09), and that selection will be set as the default in the GRUB menu.lst file, as shown in Figure 6-15. Note that the boot default has been set to 2, the third title entry (counting from 0).

```
hfoxwell@opsol0811:~# cd -
/rpool/boot/grub
hfoxwell@opsol0811:/rpool/boot/grub# beadm create Env01Jan09
hfoxwell@opsol0811:/rpool/boot/grub# beadm list
BE          Active Mountpoint Space Policy Created
--          ------ ---------- ----- ------ -------
Env01Jan09  -      -          71.0K static 2008-12-31 01:24
opensolaris NR     /          3.13G static 2008-12-03 17:44
hfoxwell@opsol0811:/rpool/boot/grub# beadm activate Env01Jan09
hfoxwell@opsol0811:/rpool/boot/grub# cat menu.lst
splashimage /boot/grub/splash.xpm.gz
background 215ECA
timeout 30
default 2
#---------- ADDED BY BOOTADM - DO NOT EDIT ----------
title OpenSolaris 2008.11 snv_101b_rc2 X86
findroot (pool_rpool,0,a)
splashimage /boot/solaris.xpm
foreground d25f00
background 115d93
bootfs rpool/ROOT/opensolaris
kernel$ /platform/i86pc/kernel/$ISADIR/unix -B $ZFS-BOOTFS,console=graphics
module$ /platform/i86pc/$ISADIR/boot_archive
#--------------------END BOOTADM--------------------

title OpenSolaris 2008.11 snv_101b_rc2 X86 text boot
findroot (pool_rpool,0,a)
bootfs rpool/ROOT/opensolaris
kernel$ /platform/i86pc/kernel/$ISADIR/unix -B $ZFS-BOOTFS
module$ /platform/i86pc/$ISADIR/boot_archive

title Env01Jan09
findroot (pool_rpool,0,a)
splashimage /boot/solaris.xpm
foreground d25f00
background 115d93
bootfs rpool/ROOT/Env01Jan09
kernel$ /platform/i86pc/kernel/$ISADIR/unix -B $ZFS-BOOTFS,console=graphics
module$ /platform/i86pc/$ISADIR/boot_archive
#============ End of LIBBE entry =============
hfoxwell@opsol0811:/rpool/boot/grub#
```

Figure 6-14. *Creating and activating a new OpenSolaris boot environment using beadm*

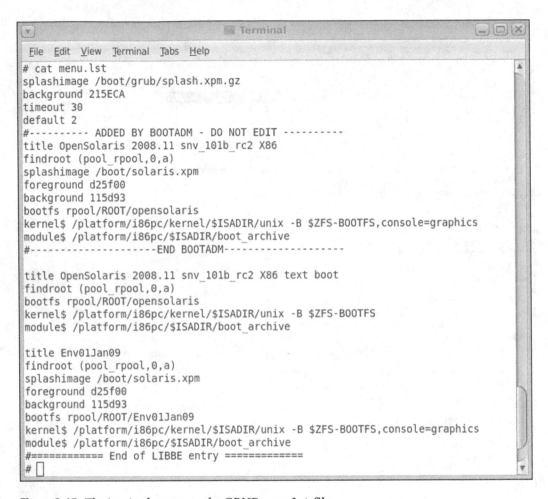

Figure 6-15. *The beadm changes to the GRUB* menu.lst *file*

Summary

In this chapter, we have only scratched the surface of how ZFS helps you manage your system's storage. It provides a simple view of any number of disk devices as a single block of available space that can be allocated as mirrored or RAID-Z storage. It lets users snapshot their file systems and revert to previous snapshots or recover individual files and directories using the Time Slider GUI. OpenSolaris boots from a ZFS file system and thus can be configured to boot from snapshots; this allows rollback to earlier boot environments after updates, patches, and software modifications. ZFS also helps support OpenSolaris's virtualization features described in the next chapter.

CHAPTER 7

■■■

OpenSolaris and Virtualization

If you can see it and it's there it's real; if you can't see it and it's there it's transparent;
if you can see it and it's not there it's virtual.

—Jeff Savit, Sun system engineer

Virtualization is a very broad and somewhat overused term that now encompasses a great number of different technologies. The basic ideas and implementations date back to the early days of mainframe computers in the 1960s when such systems were large, expensive, and scarce resources. In order to efficiently use these systems for multiple simultaneous computational tasks, techniques were developed to provide separate execution environments for individual workloads, including support for different operating systems. These execution environments provided performance and security boundaries through both hardware and software containment methods. To do this in software, indirect abstractions were created for access to system resources such as CPUs, memory, disks, and network interfaces. These abstractions are called *virtual* resources, which is where the term *virtualization* originates.

■**Note** Hardware partitioning techniques used on mainframe class systems are often referred to as forms of virtualization, but such partitioning does not always use virtualized system components. Such techniques are forms of the more general concept of *workload containment*. Hardware partitioning allocates real server resources to each operating system and generally requires specialized server hardware.

Unfortunately, computers have become much smaller, faster, and cheaper! Unfortunately, because this led to the practice of giving nearly every application its own hardware system, some large organizations now have thousands of individual hardware servers that use enormous amounts of space and electrical power and that require complex and expensive environmental cooling. Many of these servers are extremely overpowered for the applications they host; average utilization rates for most servers today are around 5 percent or even lower. And in many data centers today, more than half of the power consumption goes to cooling and infrastructure, not to computational power.

Fortunately, computers continue to grow smaller yet more powerful, and modern servers are capable of handling dozens or hundreds of simultaneous application workloads. That's where virtualization reappears, and there are now numerous community-developed and commercially developed virtualization solutions for nearly every operating system and processor family, including OpenSolaris on AMD, Intel, and SPARC. Virtualization technologies are a critical component of the new "Cloud Computing" products offered by Google, Amazon, Sun Microsystems, and others. These products provide computational, network, and storage services as *utilities*, much like the electric and water distribution companies.

A single operating system's primary tasks are to efficiently schedule user application work on available CPU and memory hardware and to efficiently handle and route interrupts for data I/O from disks, network interfaces, and other devices. Server virtualization techniques allow operating systems and their applications to share the underlying hardware in a way that gives each OS the impression that it is still running directly on the server hardware when in fact it is *sharing* it with other OS/application environments. Deploying applications in this manner allows IT architects and system administrators to do the following:

- Increase hardware utilization rates

- Reduce the total server hardware required to host multiple applications

- Provide greater flexibility for resource allocation among application environments

- Reduce electrical power, cooling, and physical space requirements in data centers

- Easily create test and development environments

- Preserve legacy OS environments

- Reduce system management costs

One important way to categorize virtualization techniques is according to the number of operating system kernels involved. Some techniques support multiple different *guest* operating system kernels running simultaneously on a hardware server, under the control of a program called a *hypervisor* or *virtual machine monitor*. Each guest OS and its applications can have the appearance of being an independent server.

Note Although you normally think of a "server" as a hardware system, all it really provides is a name for the host environment, an IP address for network access, and a restricted space in which to execute the OS and its assigned applications. This can be accomplished with hardware or, using virtualization, with software.

There are several kinds of virtualization to consider:

- *Hardware emulation*: Permits operating systems developed for one processor architecture to run on a different processor architecture.

- *Full or native OS virtualization*: Allows unmodified OS guests to run under a hypervisor.

- *Paravirtualization*: Guest operating systems run under a hypervisor and are modified to use virtualization APIs to assist performance.

- *OS virtualization* (sometimes called *lightweight virtualization* or *containers*): Presents to an application environment the *appearance* of running in a dedicated server and OS but without duplicating the entire kernel environment; in this case, your system's OS plays the role of the hypervisor.

- *Application virtualization*: Provides application portability across different operating systems and processor architectures; the Java Virtual Machine is the best-known example.

- *Resource virtualization*: I/O and network hardware can be separately virtualized to emulate other hardware or to partition such hardware into multiple virtual devices that can be dedicated to individual VMs or containers (see the Crossbow technology discussed at `http://opensolaris.org/os/project/crossbow/` for an example).

Table 7-1 summarizes just a few of the various virtualization technologies that are available.

Table 7-1. *Some Available Virtualization Technologies*

Technology	Type	Description	URL
User Mode Linux (UML)	Paravirtualization	Runs Linux VMs within Linux host	`http://user-mode-linux.sourceforge.net/`
KVM	Full and paravirtualization	In-kernel hypervisor for Linux; provides three execution modes: kernel, user, and guest	`http://kvm.qumranet.com/kvmwiki`
Xen	Full and paravirtualization	Multiplatform hypervisor	`http://xen.org/` and `http://xensource.com`
QEMU	Hardware emulation	Multiplatform processor emulator	`http://bellard.org/qemu/`
VirtualBox	Full	Desktop virtualization of OS guests	`http://www.virtualbox.org/`
VMware Server	Full	Fast server hypervisor	`http://www.vmware.com/`
V-Server	OS virtualization	Runs multiple Linux containers	`http://linux-vserver.org`
Zones	OS virtualization	Solaris and OpenSolaris containers	`http://www.sun.com/software/solaris/containers/` and `http://opensolaris.org/os/community/zones/`
Parallels	Full	Desktop virtualization for Mac, Windows, and other OSs	`http://www.parallels.com/`
xVM Server	Full and paravirtualization	Xen-based hypervisor	`http://www.sun.com/xvm`
xVM Hypervisor	Full and paravirtualization	Xen-based hypervisor	`http://opensolaris.org/os/community/xen/`
LDoms	Paravirtualization	Hypervisor for UltraSPARC Sun4v processors	`http://www.sun.com/ldoms`
Microsoft Hyper-V	Paravirtualization	Hypervisor for Windows Server 2008	`http://www.microsoft.com/virtualization`

Note Most current paravirtualization implementations on the x86 architecture now require processors that support Intel VT or AMD-V features, such as the Core 2 Duo or Opteron.

OpenSolaris can operate as a guest operating system, as we discussed in Chapter 3; platforms for this mode of operation include the following:

- VMware Workstation, Server, and ESX and VMware Fusion

- Xen 3 and Citrix XenServer

- Sun xVM Server and OpenSolaris xVM Hypervisor

- Parallels Workstation and Server

- Sun VirtualBox

- Microsoft Hyper-V and Virtual Server 2008

But OpenSolaris can be a host for a variety of virtual environments as well, and the criteria for choosing which type of virtualization solution you need depends on your performance requirements, the number and kind of guest operating systems you need to host, and the overall infrastructure of real and virtual systems you need to manage.

Figures 7-1 through 7-3 will help you visualize the differences among the virtualization technologies we've just outlined and how they are implemented with OpenSolaris.

Figure 7-1 shows how a Type 1 hypervisor, installed "natively" or on "bare metal," provides virtualization services to guest virtual machines. It generally uses a small, privileged kernel called the *control domain* or *Domain 0* that communicates with the hypervisor and manages the creation and resource allocations of guests. Generally used for server virtualization, it provides good performance especially when using paravirtualization and processor features such as Intel-VT or AMD-V.

Some discussions of Type 1 hypervisors classify them further into two types. *Thin* hypervisors, like the Xen kernel, contain only the minimum needed for booting and creating guest VMs; the remaining functionality, such as device drivers, is provided by a more traditional operating system kernel in the control domain. *Thick* hypervisor kernels, such as that used by VMware ESX, provide boot support, VM management tools, device drivers, and resource management.

Note that when using hypervisor-based virtualization each guest VM must be a fully installed, configured, and possibly licensed OS kernel, such as Windows, Linux, Solaris, or OpenSolaris. Sun's commercial xVM Server is an example of this virtualization architecture, as is the xVM Hypervisor implementation in OpenSolaris, both based on the work of the Xen community. You can see the details of this project at `http://opensolaris.org/os/community/xen/`.

Figure 7-2 shows a Type 2, or *hosted*, hypervisor, which is essentially just another application running in your OS. It still provides a control interface for creating and managing guest VMs, along with device virtualization services that link with the host OS's device drivers. Because of this extra level of indirection, performance of the guest VMs can suffer, but this architecture provides a convenient method for adding guest OS support to workstations or laptops. VirtualBox, VMware Workstation, and Parallels are examples of this type; VirtualBox is available for OpenSolaris, so it can serve as both a host for OpenSolaris and as a platform for hosting other operating systems on OpenSolaris. Note again that each guest is a fully installed OS kernel.

OS virtualization, shown in Figure 7-3, does *not* implement guests as full OS kernels and does *not* use a hypervisor. Rather, it provides performance, resource, and security boundaries around application process environments generally known as *containers*. Containers have the appearance of a full kernel but they more directly use the kernel resources and device drivers of the host OS. Because of this, they can be very fast and efficient; however, this approach limits the kinds of virtual guests that can be supported since guests are in a sense just subsets of the host OS environment. Solaris 10 and Open-Solaris have built-in support for container virtualization.

Let's start by exploring OpenSolaris containers, since we'll be using them in the next chapter to host web applications.

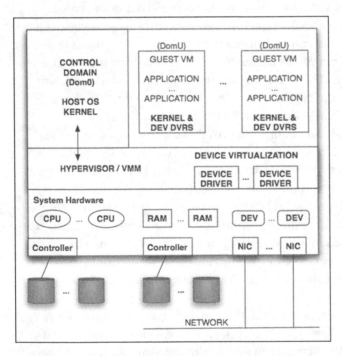

Figure 7-1. *The Type 1 hypervisor architecture*

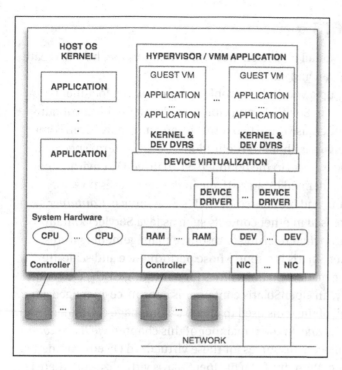

Figure 7-2. *The Type 2 hypervisor architecture*

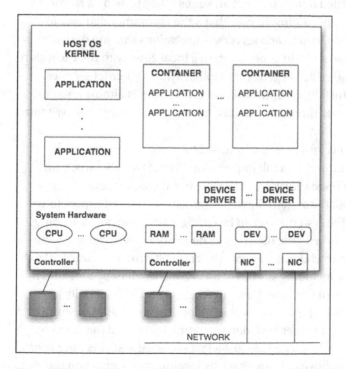

Figure 7-3. *The OS virtualization, or container architecture*

Zones and Containers

In this section, we'll present more detail on what zones and containers are, how to create and manage them, and what they can and can't do.

But before we start, let's clear up a vocabulary problem. Much of the documentation and articles about OS virtualization in Solaris 10 and OpenSolaris refer to both containers and zones, and many writers often use these two terms interchangeably. Even some of the Sun documentation is ambiguous about the definitions. *Zone* is a term specific to Solaris 10 and to OpenSolaris, and it refers to the bounded, virtualized OS environment created using the zonecfg program, defined by an XML file in the /etc/zones directory, managed with the zoneadm program, and monitored by SMF's zone service. *Container* is a more general term that is also used in other contexts such as Java Servlet Containers and in earlier versions of Solaris when referring to resource management features. A container in Solaris 10 or in OpenSolaris is a zone whose performance and scale are controlled using the OS's resource management facilities for allocating CPUs, execution threads, memory, and I/O. Briefly, an OpenSolaris container is a resource-managed zone. To add to the confusion, nearly all of the tools used to create and manage containers, and their documentation, use the term *zone*. In the remainder of this chapter, we'll use *zone* until we start discussing how to allocate resources for these virtualized OS environments.

A zone is *not* a virtual machine. With this form of OpenSolaris virtualization, there is only one OS kernel running; it's called the *global zone*. Virtualized OS environments created within the global zone are called *nonglobal* or *local* zones. They provide a restricted environment in which to deploy applications. In fact, that's the recommended way to host applications on Solaris 10 and OpenSolaris servers. Applications that are designed to run on Solaris 10 and on OpenSolaris will in general run in a local zone with the exception of programs and services that require privileged access to hardware or kernel services, such as firewalls or NFS servers. Installing applications in local zones is almost identical to installing them in the global zone, although you must create the zone with the writable directories expected by the application.

To end users, applications, developers, and administrators, the view from inside a local zone looks as if they are running on a full implementation of OpenSolaris, with some notable exceptions that we'll see shortly. A local zone has the equivalent of a host name, an IP address, and nearly all the system files an administrator would expect to see. Each local zone has its own root file system that can be configured to include read-only access to global zone file systems or writable file systems dedicated to that zone. A local zone has its own root administrator who can "reboot" the zone. Startup of a zone looks and acts similar to a boot process, including startup of local zone services by SMF and by rc scripts. But because a zone is *not* a full virtual machine kernel and is essentially just a collection of restricted processes and files, "rebooting" a local zone equates to shutting down those processes in an orderly manner and then restarting them, and that can happen *very* quickly; local zones can be "rebooted" in just a few seconds! Also, because zones are not full OS kernels, they are "lightweight" and have little additional impact on the global zone beyond the applications running in them. The theoretical maximum number of local zones on a single OpenSolaris instance is more than 8000, although you would certainly never attempt to configure that many. But modern x86 and SPARC servers can comfortably handle dozens or even hundreds of zones depending on the size of the system and the kind of applications being run within the zones.

Because a local zone is simply a bounded area within the global OpenSolaris OS, it can run only those applications compiled for that OS (there are a few exceptions such as Linux branded zones that we'll discuss later). So, unlike VMware or other hypervisor-based virtualization, you can't run Windows, Linux, or other virtualized OS kernels within a zone. Nevertheless, you can still do a lot of interesting things with this type of virtualization.

Figure 7-4 shows a sample scenario of an OpenSolaris server hosting three local zones.

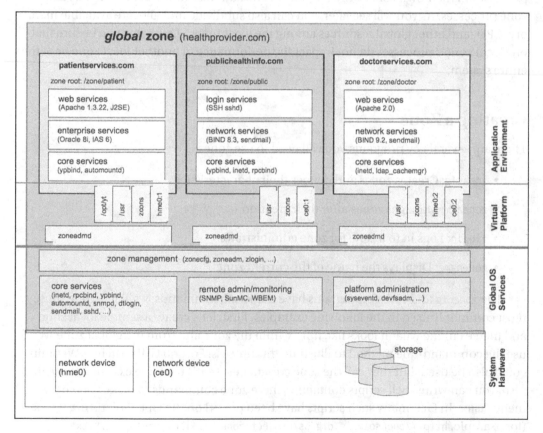

Figure 7-4. *Example configuration of OpenSolaris zones*

In this scenario, OpenSolaris is installed on a server providing web services for healthprovider.com. Three separate zones are configured for patients, doctors, and public health information. Each zone has its own authentication/login services and its own host name and IP address. Each can run different authentication services, net services, and application versions, and they can communicate only with each other using standard TCP/IP protocols.

Tip Zones on the same system communicate using TCP/IP, but intra-zone networking runs at memory bus speed, not Ethernet controller/wire speed. This means that you have very high bandwidth with low latency for network applications that can run in difference zones on the same server, such as an application server communicating with a database.

Users of one zone cannot see the processes of the other zones; they can only observe processes in their own zone. Only the global zone administrator can observe all local zone processes. As you will see later, you can also subdivide and allocate available memory, CPU, and other global resources among the local zones. This helps you ensure that one local zone's processes do not impact the performance of another local zone or of the entire system.

Creating a Zone

There are several key programs you will need to use zones:

- `zonecfg`: Creates zones and defines their characteristics

- `zoneadm`: Manages zones after their creation

- `zlogin`: Logs in to a zone for zone administrators

- `zonename`: Displays the name of the current zone

The `zonecfg` and `zoneadm` programs have many subcommands; we'll illustrate those most commonly used in the following examples. First, let's create a sample local zone and then examine what it looks like from within the zone and from the global zone. We'll use the command-line method to illustrate this process. Several GUIs, such as Webmin, could also be used, but they call the zone commands, so it's useful to examine these first. Also, you can write shell scripts containing these zone commands to make zone management easier. In fact, many such scripts have been posted on the OpenSolaris.org web site (for example, `http://opensolaris.org/os/project/zonemgr/files/zonemgr-1.8.txt`).

In Figure 7-5, we've become the `root` administrator and created a zone named *myfirstzone* using the `zonecfg` command.

```
000                    Terminal -- ssh -- 80×13
      ssh                   bash
/export: zonecfg -z myfirstzone
myfirstzone: No such zone configured
Use 'create' to begin configuring a new zone.
zonecfg:myfirstzone> create
zonecfg:myfirstzone> set zonepath=/export/myfirstzone
zonecfg:myfirstzone> add net
zonecfg:myfirstzone:net> set address=192.168.1.201
zonecfg:myfirstzone:net> set physical=e1000g0
zonecfg:myfirstzone:net> end
zonecfg:myfirstzone> verify
zonecfg:myfirstzone> commit
zonecfg:myfirstzone> exit
/export:
```

Figure 7-5. *Defining a zone using zonecfg*

Notice the syntax: zonecfg -z myfirstzone attempts to reference that zone name, but it's not defined yet, so zonecfg tells you to create it. Like a normal OS, a zone needs a root file system. In this example, we've specified a path for its directory, /export/myfirstzone. For now, ensure that /export has sufficient disk space for the zone's files, about 300MB. We've also specified an IP address for the zone along with the name of the physical network device we want the zone to use. Some systems will have multiple network interface cards (NICs), and their names might differ from the device name in this example (use the /usr/sbin/ifconfig -a command to display your system's NICs and addresses). The remaining zonecfg subcommands end the configuration subcommands, verify the syntax of the parameter definitions, commit the configuration to disk, and then exit the zonecfg program.

All that has happened at this point is that zone myfirstzone has been defined. Its configuration file, as are those of all local zones you will define on your system, is an XML file in the /etc/zones directory. Let's examine the contents of that directory and the myfirstzone.xml file (Figure 7-6).

```
000                    Terminal — ssh — 79×16
      ssh                   ssh
/: cd /etc/zones
/etc/zones: ls
index           SUNWblank.xml     SUNWipkg.xml
myfirstzone.xml  SUNWdefault.xml   SUNWlx.xml
/etc/zones: cat myfirstzone.xml
<?xml version="1.0" encoding="UTF-8"?>
<!DOCTYPE zone PUBLIC "-//Sun Microsystems Inc//DTD Zones//EN" "file:///usr/sha
re/lib/xml/dtd/zonecfg.dtd.1">
<!--
    DO NOT EDIT THIS FILE.  Use zonecfg(1M) instead.
-->
<zone name="myfirstzone" zonepath="/export/myfirstzone" autoboot="false" brand=
"ipkg">
  <network address="192.168.1.201" physical="e1000g0"/>
</zone>
/etc/zones:
```

Figure 7-6. *The zone configuration files directory, /etc/zones*

The directory has several default definition files (SUNWblank.xml and SUNWdefault.xml, for example) that you can copy and use as templates when you create new zones; you can preconfigure devices, IP addresses, zone paths, and other parameters in your template file using the syntax zonecfg -z zonename -f zonetemplatefile. The XML Document Type Definition (DTD) file is referenced in the first two lines of each zone file.

Note Heed the "DO NOT EDIT THIS FILE" warnings in this and other OpenSolaris configuration files; use the recommended program! If you introduce errors by directly editing such files (as many UNIX/Linux admins are inclined to do), unpredictable erroneous behaviors can occur.

The myfirstzone.xml file that was created by zonecfg contains the parameter definitions shown in Table 7-2.

Table 7-2. *Configuration Parameters in File /etc/zones/myfirstzone.xml*

Parameter	Description
name="myfirstzone"	The name of the zone, not the zone's host name, although many users make them the same.
zonepath="/export/myfirstzone"	The directory of the zone's root file system.
autoboot="false"	Set this to true if you want the zone to boot when the global zone boots.
brand="ipkg"	There are several "brands" of zones: native, ipkg, lx (Linux), s8 (Solaris 8 on SPARC), and s9 (Solaris 9 on SPARC).
address="192.168.1.201"	The zone's IP address. Currently must be set as a static address.
physical="e1000g0"	The physical NIC used by the zone; can be dedicated or shared.

You can use the zoneadm program to list the zones that are available on your system (Figure 7-7). The -cv flag shows a listing of all configured zones in verbose mode.

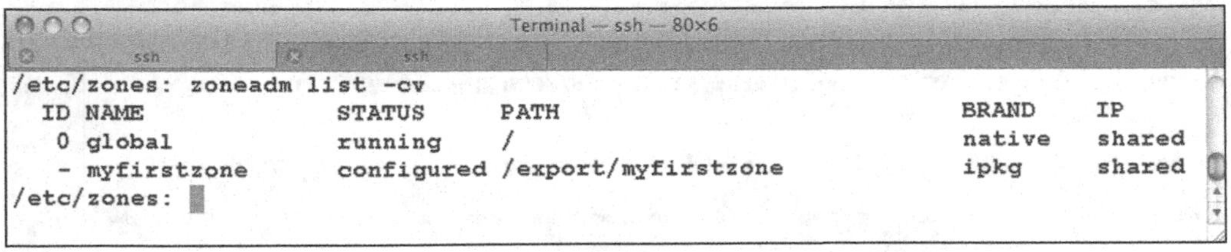

Figure 7-7. *Listing the zones on your system*

Zones can have several states, as listed in Table 7-3. Notice in Figure 7-7 that the global zone's state is `running` (of course!) and that myfirstzone is only `configured`.

Table 7-3. *Possible Zone States*

State	Description
`configured`	The zone has been defined; it has a configuration file in `/etc/zones`.
`installed`	The zone's root file system (`zonepath`) has been copied and the zone registered with the global zone.
`incomplete`	The zone is in the process of being installed or uninstalled and its files are being copied or deleted.
`ready`	The zone is properly configured and installed, but no zone processes are running (the zone has not been "booted").
`running`	The zone has successfully "booted" and its processes are running.
`shutting down`	The zone is in the process of being halted.
`down`	The zone is not running and is stuck possibly because the failure of one of its applications to properly shut down.

The next step is to install your zone (Figure 7-8). Depending on the speed of your system, this process will take several minutes; this example took less than two minutes. Take special note of the output: a ZFS file system was created for the zone; we will take advantage of that later. Note also that necessary packages were downloaded from the OpenSolaris `release` repository.

```
Terminal — ssh — 80x25
/: zoneadm -z myfirstzone install
A ZFS file system has been created for this zone.
  Authority: Using http://pkg.opensolaris.org/release/.
      Image: Preparing at /export/myfirstzone/root ... done.
      Cache: Using /var/pkg/download.
 Installing: (output follows)
DOWNLOAD                                    PKGS       FILES     XFER (MB)
Completed                                  52/52   7862/7862   72.41/72.41

PHASE                                        ACTIONS
Install Phase                            12939/12939
PHASE                                          ITEMS
Reading Existing Index                           9/9
Indexing Packages                              52/52

       Note: Man pages can be obtained by installing SUNWman
Postinstall: Copying SMF seed repository ... done.
Postinstall: Working around http://defect.opensolaris.org/bz/show_bug.cgi?id=741
       Done: Installation completed in 93.632 seconds.

 Next Steps: Boot the zone, then log into the zone console
             (zlogin -C) to complete the configuration process
/:
```

Figure 7-8. *Installing a zone*

Following the directions given by zoneadm when it's finished installing your zone, you're ready to boot the zone:

```
# zoneadm -z myfirstzone boot
```

Then log into the zone console using the password you assigned earlier:

```
# zlogin -C myfirstzone
```

The first time you log in to a zone console after its creation and first boot, you will see a series of instructions similar to those for installing a full OpenSolaris operating system. You will be asked to select a terminal type to use; select xterm, VT100, or whatever type you prefer depending on what terminal program you are running (the default terminal type setting when you open a terminal session in OpenSolaris is VT100).

Note Your keyboard's function keys will almost certainly *not* work during this final configuration process; the installation terminal will emulate those keys with ESC-#, where # is the number of your function key (so ESC-2 emulates the F2 key).

The zone configuration process will next ask you to assign a host name, which could be the same as the zone name but that's not required. Next you'll be asked whether you want to enable Kerberos, what name service you want to use (NIS, DNS, LDAP, none), what time zone you want to use (which can be different from that of the global zone!), and finally the root password for the zone. After all of this you can log in to your zone.

Global and Local Zone Environments

At this point, it's important for you to understand the difference between the global zone administrator environment and that for a local zone, especially if you are simultaneously logged in as root on both types of zones.

Caution It's a good idea to set your shell prompt in your login profile for both global and local zone work to include the zone name to help you recall which zone you're working in. Executing the reboot command in a local zone will simply reboot that zone in a few seconds. Mistakenly executing reboot in the global zone will reboot the entire system and terminate any user processes running in local zones.

For the bash shell in each zone, the following will set your prompt to include both the zone name and your current working directory:

```
export 'PS1=$(zonename):${PWD}:'
```

System administrators are familiar with several tools to monitor the state of their system and the processes running on it; Linux users will often use the top command. OpenSolaris 2008.11 includes top (Figure 7-9).

```
● ○ ○                        Terminal — ssh — 80×24
last pid: 20327;  load avg:  0.18,  0.17,  0.16;  up 22+05:40:03       17:09:46
276 processes: 275 sleeping, 1 on cpu
CPU states: 91.7% idle,  7.3% user,  1.0% kernel,  0.0% iowait,  0.0% swap
Kernel: 1093 ctxsw, 10 trap, 415 intr, 2700 syscall, 8 flt
Memory: 2031M phys mem, 78M free mem, 1015M total swap, 731M free swap

   PID USERNAME NLWP PRI NICE   SIZE   RES STATE    TIME    CPU COMMAND
 29854 hfoxwell    9  59    0   267M  124M sleep   26:27  7.35% firefox-bin
 20628 root        1  59    0    89M   46M sleep   13:45  0.26% Xorg
 20327 root        1  59    0 6088K 4116K cpu/1    0:00  0.15% top
 18281 hfoxwell    2  59    0   131M   51M sleep    0:42  0.04% gnome-netstatus
 23489 hfoxwell    1  59    0    97M   14M sleep    3:46  0.03% mixer_applet2
 18282 root        1  59    0 1632K 1068K sleep    0:28  0.02% gnome-netstatus
 20095 lp          1  59    0 6836K 2496K sleep    0:00  0.02% httpd
 20038 lp          1  59    0 6852K 2512K sleep    0:00  0.02% httpd
 23485 hfoxwell    1  59    0 8252K 3748K sleep    2:13  0.01% gvfsd-trash
 22882 root       12  59    0 8536K 3792K sleep    0:17  0.01% svc.configd
 23433 hfoxwell    2  59    0 9508K 4612K sleep    1:28  0.01% bonobo-activati
 23431 hfoxwell    1  49    0   128M   42M sleep    1:43  0.01% nautilus
 18310 hfoxwell    2  49    0   124M   40M sleep    0:31  0.01% gnome-terminal
 23425 hfoxwell    2  59    0    95M   12M sleep    1:20  0.01% gnome-settings-
 23430 hfoxwell    1  59    0   110M   21M sleep    1:27  0.01% gnome-panel
 23421 hfoxwell    1  59    0    10M 5052K sleep    0:08  0.01% gconfd-2
 23250 root       22  59    0 5404K 2260K sleep    0:08  0.01% nscd
```

Figure 7-9. *Running top on OpenSolaris*

However, the top program for OpenSolaris has not yet been modified to work in a local zone or to identify local zone–related processes when called from the global zone. Instead, use the prstat command, which has been enhanced with two extra flags, -z and -Z. The prstat command alone will report data on all processes regardless of which zone they run in, sorted by descending CPU usage. That's somewhat useful for the global zone administrator, but prstat -Z, run from the global zone, will report additional data on local zones (Figure 7-10).

■**Tip** You will notice several services, such as sendmail, are configured by default to start in local zones. You should disable unnecessary services using the svcadm command from within the local zone.

```
000                    Terminal — ssh — 80×24
  PID USERNAME   SIZE   RSS STATE   PRI NICE      TIME  CPU PROCESS/NLWP
29854 hfoxwell   266M  123M sleep    59    0   0:30:57 8.2% firefox-bin/10
20375 root      7028K 3292K cpu1     59    0   0:00:08 1.0% prstat/1
20628 root        89M   46M sleep    59    0   0:13:55 0.4% Xorg/1
20376 hfoxwell    78M   17M sleep    59    0   0:00:00 0.0% xscreensaver-lo/1
18281 hfoxwell   131M   52M sleep    59    0   0:00:44 0.0% gnome-netstatus/2
23468 hfoxwell    10M 5036K sleep    59    0   0:00:07 0.0% xscreensaver/1
23489 hfoxwell    97M   14M sleep    59    0   0:03:47 0.0% mixer_applet2/1
18282 root      1632K 1068K sleep    59    0   0:00:29 0.0% gnome-netstatus/1
18310 hfoxwell   124M   40M sleep    49    0   0:00:32 0.0% gnome-terminal/2
23485 hfoxwell  8252K 3748K sleep    59    0   0:02:14 0.0% gvfsd-trash/1
23421 hfoxwell    10M 5052K sleep    59    0   0:00:08 0.0% gconfd-2/1
23433 hfoxwell  9508K 4612K sleep    59    0   0:01:28 0.0% bonobo-activati/2
23487 hfoxwell    80M   14M sleep    59    0   0:01:16 0.0% clock-applet/1
23431 hfoxwell   128M   42M sleep    49    0   0:01:43 0.0% nautilus/1
23430 hfoxwell   110M   21M sleep    59    0   0:01:27 0.0% gnome-panel/1
ZONEID   NPROC  SWAP   RSS MEMORY      TIME  CPU ZONE
     0     260  774M  499M    25%   1:15:43 9.7% global
     2      18   21M   13M   0.6%   0:00:30 0.0% myfirstzone


Total: 278 processes, 613 lwps, load averages: 0.22, 0.20, 0.18
```

Figure 7-10. *prstat running in the global zone*

Local zone administrators can run ps or prstat, but they will only get details on processes running in their own zone; *they cannot see any process information for other zones or the global zone.* The global zone administrator can view process details for specific zones using the -z flag with ps or with prstat, giving the desired zone name. For example, the command prstat -z myfirstzone displays process data for the myfirstzone zone (Figure 7-11).

```
000                    Terminal — ssh — 80×24
  PID USERNAME   SIZE   RSS STATE   PRI NICE      TIME  CPU PROCESS/NLWP
23228 root      2732K  948K sleep    59    0   0:00:00 0.0% automountd/4
22866 root      2664K  620K sleep    59    0   0:00:00 0.0% init/1
22838 root         0K    0K sleep    60    -   0:00:00 0.0% zsched/1
22882 root      8536K 3792K sleep    59    0   0:00:17 0.0% svc.configd/12
23264 root      4020K 1304K sleep    59    0   0:00:00 0.0% syslogd/11
22880 root      8324K 2516K sleep    59    0   0:00:05 0.0% svc.startd/12
23277 root      4284K  904K sleep    59    0   0:00:00 0.0% sshd/1
23256 root      2468K 1024K sleep    59    0   0:00:00 0.0% sac/1
23250 root      5404K 2260K sleep    59    0   0:00:08 0.0% nscd/22
23073 daemon    1884K  788K sleep    59    0   0:00:00 0.0% kcfd/2
22885 root      3756K 1064K sleep    59    0   0:00:00 0.0% svc-dlmgmtd/1
23263 root      2480K 1032K sleep    59    0   0:00:00 0.0% ttymon/1
18426 root      3384K 2144K sleep    59    0   0:00:00 0.0% bash/1
23259 root      1636K  812K sleep    59    0   0:00:00 0.0% utmpd/1
23106 root      1840K 1004K sleep    59    0   0:00:00 0.0% cron/1
23220 daemon    3184K  848K sleep    59    0   0:00:00 0.0% rpcbind/1
23225 root      2660K  868K sleep    59    0   0:00:00 0.0% automountd/2
23262 root      4284K 1040K sleep    59    0   0:00:00 0.0% inetd/3



Total: 18 processes, 78 lwps, load averages: 0.17, 0.17, 0.17
```

Figure 7-11. *prstat -z myfirstzone running in the global zone*

The global zone administrator can monitor local zone activity using a variety of tools; some of these are familiar programs that have been modified to understand zones. Table 7-4 describes these tools.

Table 7-4. *Tools for Monitoring Local Zone Resources from the Global Zone**

Command	Description
ps -eZ	Lists every running process in all local zones and global zone
ps -ez *zonename*	Lists every running process in the specified zone name
prstat -Z	Monitors all process activity in all zones
prstat -z *zonename*	Monitors all process activity in the specified zone name
pgrep -z *zonename pname*	Finds the pid (the process ID) of process *pname* in the specified zone name
ptree -z *zonename pid*	Lists the process tree for *pid* in the specified zone name
zlogin *zonename* vmstat|iostat|mpstat	Runs vmstat|iostat|mpstat in the specified zone name and displays the output on the global zone

* Other commonly used option flags can still be used with these programs.

Caution Interpreting statistics such as CPU utilization, I/O data, and memory usage for processes running in local zones can be a bit difficult. Traditional tools such as vmstat and iostat were not originally designed for virtualized environments. Fortunately, the OpenSolaris developer community is starting to contribute solutions to this problem; for example, the zonestat tool for developing a better understanding of resource consumption and resource controls of zones and their workloads. Read about this project at http://opensolaris.org/os/project/zonestat/.

Cloning a Zone

Before we go further, let's create another zone. Here's where ZFS again helps us; it takes a snapshot of the source zone's root file system and uses it for the new zone, saving the time of creating and copying the zone files. The source zone must be halted before it can be cloned, however. Figure 7-12 shows the sequence of commands needed to clone myfirstzone. First the source zone is halted; then zoneconfig exports the myfirstzone configuration into a temporary work file. You must then edit that file to specify a new zone path and IP address for the new zone (since two zones can't share the same zone path or IP address). You then use zonecfg to configure the new zone using the modified file, and finally you use zoneadm to create the clone. When it's all finished, zoneadm list -cv confirms that the new zone is ready to go; use the same initial boot procedure you did for myfirstzone.

```
000                    Terminal — ssh — 80×20
global:/: zoneadm -z myfirstzone halt
global:/: zonecfg -z myfirstzone export -f /tmp/myfirstzone.cfg
global:/: zonecfg -z mysecondzone -f /tmp/myfirstzone.cfg
global:/: zoneadm -z mysecondzone clone myfirstzone
sys-unconfig started Wed Jan 21 20:16:34 2009
sys-unconfig completed Wed Jan 21 20:16:35 2009
global:/: zoneadm list -cv
  ID NAME            STATUS     PATH                     BRAND    IP
   0 global          running    /                        native   shared
   - myfirstzone     installed  /export/myfirstzone      ipkg     shared
   - mysecondzone    installed  /export/mysecondzone     ipkg     shared
global:/: zoneadm -z myfirstzone boot
global:/: zoneadm -z mysecondzone boot
global:/: zoneadm list -cv
  ID NAME            STATUS     PATH                     BRAND    IP
   0 global          running    /                        native   shared
   4 myfirstzone     running    /export/myfirstzone      ipkg     shared
   5 mysecondzone    running    /export/mysecondzone     ipkg     shared
global:/:
```

Figure 7-12. *Cloning a zone*

Managing Zones

If all this seems like a lot of command line work, you can again rely on OpenSolaris
community software for help; zone management scripts are available such as the `zonemgr`
tool at `http://opensolaris.org/os/project/zonemgr/`. Or, you can use the browser-based
Webmin tool discussed in Chapter 5; it has a basic Zone Management GUI that lets you
create and configure zones on your system from anywhere on your network (Figure 7-13).

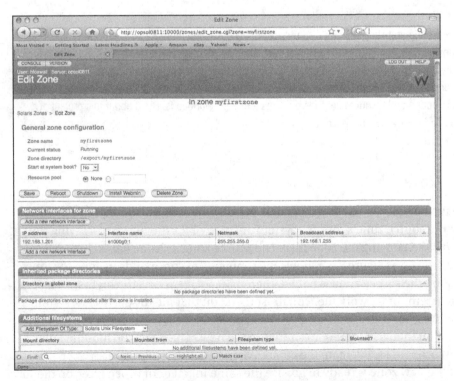

Figure 7-13. *The Webmin zone management GUI*

Using the Zone

Okay, you've got zones! Now what? Recall that a local zone is very much like a server implemented in software: it has a host name and an IP address, and you can communicate with it using standard TCP/IP programs and protocols just as you do with traditional hardware servers. From the point of view of end users, application developers, and system administrators, working in a local zone is similar to working in an independent OS environment running on a hardware server, but with some very important restrictions. From inside a local zone, you can't "see out" into the global zone or see anything belonging to other local zones, even if you are the local zone root user. Also, you don't have direct access to system hardware; only the global zone administrator can configure hardware resources such as file system disks and network interfaces. And in general, user applications that are designed to run on Solaris and OpenSolaris in the global zone will run fine in a properly configured local zone. However, some programs or services that need privileged access to hardware or to kernel services, such as NFS servers (disks) or NTP servers (system clock), can be run from only the global zone.

■Note There are numerous detailed answers about how OpenSolaris zones work (and their limitations) in the Zones and Containers FAQ at `http://opensolaris.org/os/community/zones/faq`.

One of the most common use cases for local zone deployment is for hosting web servers. In general, applications such as Apache are not resource intensive, and you can therefore host a large number of web servers on a single hardware server running Open-Solaris using zones virtualization. Because each zone has its own IP stack, address, and port list, web servers running in local zones look the same to the outside world as those running on separate hardware servers. Moreover, you can configure your system to restrict access to your web content by placing the content files in a zone writable only by global zone users while mounting the content directories in read-only mode for access by the web server. In this way, you can prevent defacement of your web site content even if the web server software is compromised (see "Eliminating Web Page Hijacking" at `http://www.sun.com/software/solaris/howtoguides/s10securityhowto.jsp` for details). You can of course run multiple web servers on your system, each in their own protected local zone. You could also use Apache's Virtual Hosts to do this, but confining each web server to a local zone allows you to better allocate system resources to it, and if a local zone is compromised, the other zones are still protected.

Installing the web server software in a local zone uses the command-line interface to the Image Packaging System described in previous chapters. Using the Package Manager GUI from your global zone desktop, you search for and find that the necessary package for the Apache 2 web server is called SUNWapch22. Then, from a terminal command line in the local zone, install Apache using this command: `pfexec pkg install SUNWapch22`. IPS will install Apache; you then enable it with SMF using `svcadm enable apache22`, and you're ready to access web content by pointing your browser to the host name or IP address of the local zone.

Tip On OpenSolaris, Apache's `httpd.conf` configuration file resides in the `/etc/apache2/2.2` directory; the default `index.html` and web content files reside in the `/var/apache2/2.2/htdocs` directory.

In the next chapter, you'll learn more about deploying the OpenSolaris web stack in zones.

Managing Zone Resources

One of the concerns about hosting multiple virtual environments on a single server is competition among the environments for resources. This is true for hypervisor-based virtualization (Xen, VMware, Microsoft Hyper-V) as well as for OS virtualization models such as OpenSolaris zones. Virtualization models must not only provide security boundaries for their environments but must also provide configurable resource allocation for them.

Operating systems can allocate resources to applications using different process scheduling algorithms (rules) depending on how you want processes to be prioritized. OpenSolaris can use any of the following scheduling classes:

- `RT`, the real-time class, for predictable latency environments

- `TS`, the time-sharing class, for guaranteeing all threads some CPU time

- `IA`, the interactive class, which prioritizes active window processes

- `FX`, the fixed-priority class, for scheduled batch processes

- `FSS`, the fair-share class, which allocates CPU time according to assigned shares

By default, the OpenSolaris global zone uses the TS and IA classes. You can change the default on your server to be the FSS class so that you can later reserve a specified proportion of CPU resources to each local zone. To enable the FSS scheduling class, use the `dispadmin` program:

```
# dispadmin -d FSS
```

This sets the default scheduler class listed in the `/etc/dispadm.conf` file to FSS; you must reboot your global zone for this change to take effect. After you have made this change, you need to decide how to allocate shares to each local zone.

Tip It's best to test your zone configuration first under the default TS class and observe how it performs; OpenSolaris is already pretty good at allocating resources to processes and to local zones. If you later observe the need to give more resources to a local zone (for example, one running a database), you can enable FSS and adjust that zone's relative resource allocation.

Shares are an arbitrary number that can be divided into whatever proportions you want to assign to each local zone. You can assign 40 shares to local zone myfirstzone and 10 shares to mysecondzone, and these zones will get 80 percent and 20 percent, respectively, of available CPU time from the process scheduler. Or you can assign four shares and one share to each and get the same result. The proportion of the total shares assigned is used; the total number of shares is irrelevant.

To assign shares to each of your local zones, use the zoneadm command as follows:

```
# zonecfg -z myfirstzone
zonecfg: myfirstzone> add rctl
zonecfg: myfirstzone:rctl> set name=zone.cpu-shares
zonecfg: myfirstzone:rctl> add value (priv=privileged, limit=40, action=none)
zonecfg: myfirstzone:rctl> end
zonecfg: myfirstzone> exit
#
# zonecfg -z mysecondzone
zonecfg: mysecondzone> add rctl
zonecfg: mysecondzone:rctl> set name=zone.cpu-shares
zonecfg: mysecondzone:rctl> add value (priv=privileged, limit=10, action=deny)
zonecfg: mysecondzone:rctl> end
zonecfg: mysecondzone> exit
#
```

This sequence sets the relative shares for each of these local zones. The action parameter specifies what is to be done if the zone requests more resources than have been allocated; deny indicates that no additional resources are to be allocated even if available. In this way, an application environment running in a local zone can be limited.

In some cases, it's advisable to also limit hardware resources used by local zones, either for performance purposes or for software licensing requirements. On a multicore or multi-CPU system, you can confine a local zone to run on a restricted number of CPUs. To do this, you need create a resource pool consisting of a set of CPUs (a processor set, or *pset*) and then assign the zone to use that pool.

First, enable resource pools using the pooladm command:

```
# pooladm -e
```

Assuming you have multiple CPUs available on your system, you create a processor set of some number of CPUs using the `poolcfg` command, for example:

```
# poolcfg -c 'create pset myfirstzone-pset (uint pset.min=1;uint pset.max=4)'
# poolcfg -c 'create pool myfirstzone-pool'
# poolcfg -c 'associate pool myfirstzone-pool (pset myfirstzone-pset)'
# pooladm -c
```

This sequence of commands creates a processor set named `myfirstzone-pset` with a minimum of one CPU and a maximum of four CPUs, creates a resource pool named `myfirstzone-pool` linked to the processor set, and then activates the new configuration and updates the `/etc/pooladm.conf` configuration file. Lastly, you need to tell the zone to use your newly created resource pool:

```
# zonecfg -z myfirstzone
zonecfg:myfirstzone> set pool=myfirstzone-pool
zonecfg:myfirstzone> verify
zonecfg:myfirstzone> commit
zonecfg:myfirstzone> exit
```

You now have your local zone bound to a maximum of four CPUs on your system; it cannot use more than you have allocated.

Note Depending on the processor family you are using, OpenSolaris will recognize hardware threads or cores as individual CPUs. A quad-core Intel Xeon processor will present as 4 CPUs; an 8-core CMT SPARC processor will present as 64 CPUs.

Remember, the term *container* is used when you constrain and control a zone's resources. So, in the previous discussion, it's now more appropriate to call myfirstzone and mysecondzone OpenSolaris *containers*. In addition to shares and pool CPUs we just discussed, there are additional system resources that you can allocate to local zones, as shown in Table 7-5. See the man page for `resource_controls` for additional details.

The reason for using such configurable zone resource controls is to contain applications running in local zones so that they do not interfere with other zones. A runaway process in one local zone can consume global system resources needed by the other local zones. Limiting a local zone's resources can prevent problems such as memory leaks or network based denial-of-service attacks from spreading outside the zone. You can find more details on zone/container resource allocation at http://www.solarisinternals.com/wiki/index.php/Zones_Resource_Controls and http://opensolaris.org/os/community/zones/faq/#rm.

Table 7-5. *Configurable Zone Resources*

Resource	Description
zone.cpu-cap	Maximum CPU time allowed for the zone
zone.cpu-shares	Number of FSS shares allocated to the zone
zone.max-locked-memory	Maximum physical memory allowed for the zone
zone.max-lwps	Maximum number of lightweight processes (roughly, kernel threads)
zone.max-shm-memory	Maximum shared memory segment for the zone
zone.max-swap	Maximum swap space allocated to the zone

More OpenSolaris Virtualization

OS virtualization in the form of OpenSolaris zones is just one method of virtualized environment containment. Although zones are very efficient and easy to create, they are limited in the type of application environments they can provide. Table 7-6 shows other OpenSolaris virtualization projects and features.

Table 7-6. *OpenSolaris Virtualization Technologies*

Technology	Description	URL
VirtualBox	An open source Type 2 virtualization application. Runs on OpenSolaris on Intel and on AMD systems and supports a variety of guest operating systems including Solaris, Linux distributions, OpenSolaris, and Windows.	http://www.virtualbox.org/
xVM	A Type 1 hypervisor based on the work of the Xen community; will be productized by Sun as xVM Server, a virtualization appliance and available as an OpenSolaris community project.	http://www.sun.com/software/products/xvmserver/index.xml and http://opensolaris.org/os/community/xen/
BrandZ	Also called Solaris Containers for Linux Applications; allows Linux binary applications to run in a Solaris 10 for x86 zone; does *not* require a full Linux kernel, so it is *not* a full Linux VM.	http://wikis.sun.com/display/chosug/Installing+a+Linux+Zone and http://www.sun.com/software/solaris/scla.jsp
LDoms Logical Domains	Chip-based virtualization for Sun's UltraSPARC CMT/CMP processors. SPARC support for OpenSolaris will start to appear in the 2009.06 release.	http://www.sun.com/servers/coolthreads/ldoms/index.jsp and http://opensolaris.org/os/community/ldoms/

VirtualBox

If you want to use OpenSolaris as a base OS for running guest operating systems, VirtualBox is a good candidate. Since it was acquired in 2008 by Sun Microsystems, it's been offered both in a commercially supported Enterprise Subscription edition and as a GPL-licensed OpenSource Edition; no cost binary copies are downloadable at `http://dlc.sun.com/virtualbox/vboxdownload.html`, along with a platform-independent Software Development Kit (SDK) of APIs and command-line tools that let you create scripts and services to manage VMs. VirtualBox supports dozens of different operating systems, although not all features work for some VMs; a list of OSs and their support/bug status is at `http://www.virtualbox.org/wiki/Guest_OSes`.

Download a copy of VirtualBox for your system, but carefully note whether your system's processor is 32-bit or 64-bit, because 64-bit guest VMs will not work on 32-bit OpenSolaris systems. You can check your processor's instruction set and type using the `isainfo` and `psrinfo` commands, as shown in the example output in Figure 7-14.

```
/: isainfo -v
64-bit amd64 applications
        ssse3 cx16 mon sse3 sse2 sse fxsr mmx cmov amd_sysc cx8 tsc fpu
32-bit i386 applications
        ssse3 ahf cx16 mon sse3 sse2 sse fxsr mmx cmov sep cx8 tsc fpu
/: psrinfo -v
Status of virtual processor 0 as of: 01/24/2009 15:28:22
  on-line since 01/24/2009 09:44:03.
  The i386 processor operates at 2000 MHz,
        and has an i387 compatible floating point processor.
Status of virtual processor 1 as of: 01/24/2009 15:28:22
  on-line since 01/24/2009 09:44:07.
  The i386 processor operates at 2000 MHz,
        and has an i387 compatible floating point processor.
/:
```

Figure 7-14. *Checking your processor capabilities using* `isainfo` *and* `psrinfo`

The VirtualBox executable and support files for OpenSolaris download is a gzipped tar file that you unzip and unarchive into any directory of your choice. Note that this is an application not installed using IPS. After installing VirtualBox, download the `.iso` image of your preferred guest OS (or obtain a CD/DVD). When you start up VirtualBox (located in `/usr/bin/VirtualBox`), you can choose to add new guests as in Figure 7-15, selecting the name, OS type, and version.

After selecting the OS type and version, specify the memory and file sizes you need for your VM. Select the CD/DVD-ROM item from the GUI, and mount either the physical CD or the `.iso` boot file for your VM, as in Figure 7-16.

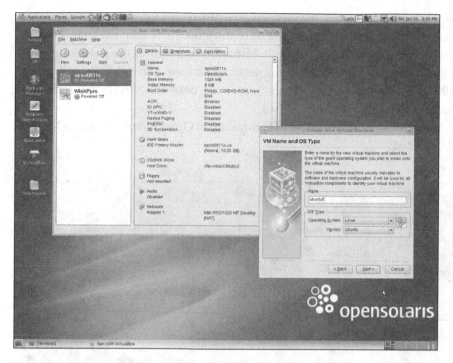

Figure 7-15. *Installing a new guest VM in VirtualBox*

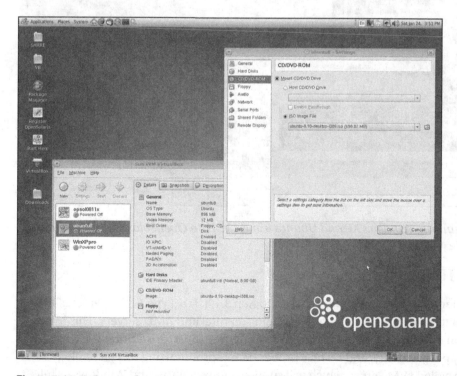

Figure 7-16. *Select and mount your guest VM's CD, DVD, or .iso file.*

At this point, you need to follow the installation instructions for your guest VM. After your guest(s) are installed, VirtualBox lets you start and stop them, take VM snapshots, and run guest-specific applications. By default, VirtualBox configures the guest's network interfaces using NAT so you will be able to connect to your local network from within the guests. VirtualBox also supports "not attached" mode (no network) and "host interface" mode (direct access to your host system's NIC).

Figure 7-17 shows two example guest VMs running on OpenSolaris, Windows XP Professional, and Ubuntu 8.

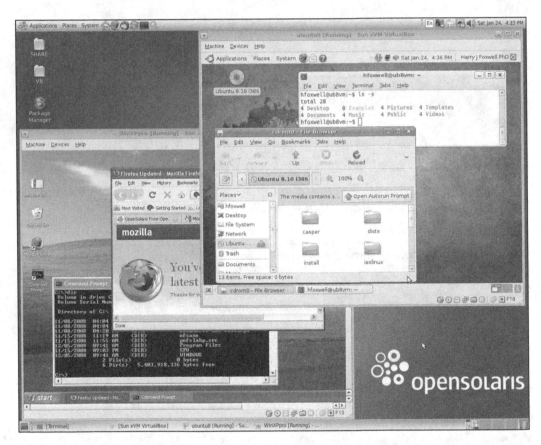

Figure 7-17. *Running Windows XP and Ubuntu 8 guest VMs on OpenSolaris using VirtualBox*

The xVM Hypervisor

The xVM hypervisor, based on OpenSolaris and Xen 3.1.4, is a Type 1 ("bare-metal") hypervisor that supports guest operating systems on Intel and AMD servers. This hypervisor has been enhanced with patches from Xen and from Sun for additional security, hardware support, stability, and DTrace probes. Sun is productizing this technology as an appliance called xVM Server, which will support Linux, Solaris, and Windows as full or paravirtualized guest VMs including support for hardware assisted virtualization. The xVM Server appliance product includes a browser-based user interface (BUI) for creating and managing guest VMs; the underlying OS and hypervisor will not be directly accessible. See `http://www.sun.com/software/products/xvmserver/index.xml` for the productized version that will include hardware and software support subscriptions, and see `http://www.sun.com/software/products/xvmserver/faqs.xml` for a comprehensive FAQ list about the product.

But there's a full community developed base for the OpenSolaris xVM hypervisor at `http://opensolaris.org/os/community/xen/`. It implements OpenSolaris as the privileged control domain, or Dom0, as the first VM booted by the hypervisor. You log into Dom0 to administer your virtualization environment. Commands issued from within Dom0 are used to create and manage guest operating system VMs known as *user domains*, or *DomUs*, which can be Linux, Windows, or UNIX kernels. Figure 7-18 shows the general layout of the Open-Solaris xVM environment.

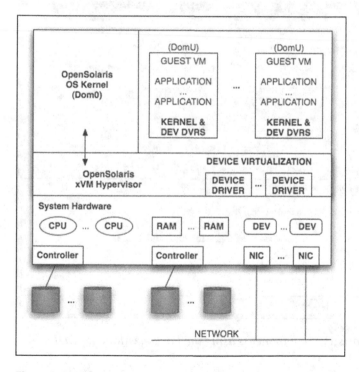

Figure 7-18. *The OpenSolaris xVM hypervisor*

Currently, installing and configuring the OpenSolaris xVM hypervisor is a somewhat tedious manual process; future releases of OpenSolaris are expected to include community-developed xVM Hypervisor setup and management tools similar to those planned for Sun's xVM Server product.

Installing the OpenSolaris 2008.11 xVM Hypervisor

Using the Package Manager, install the xVM virtualization files and drivers shown in Figure 7-19.

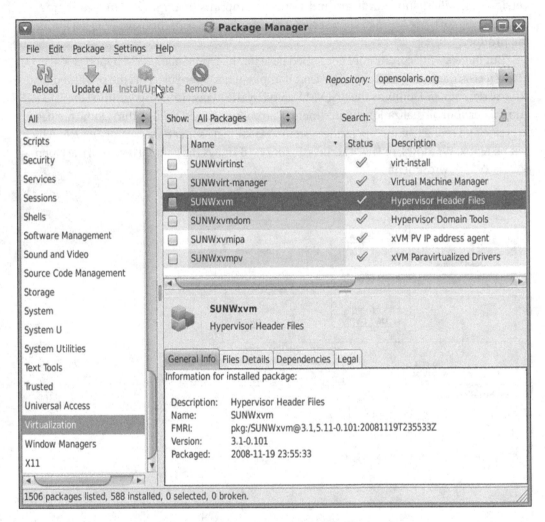

Figure 7-19. *Installing OpenSolaris xVM components using the Package Manager GUI*

Create a symbolic link from /rpool/boot/grub/menu.lst to /boot/grub/menu.lst:

```
# ln –s /rpool/boot/grub/menu.lst /boot/grub/menu.lst
```

then add the following to the end of the menu.lst file:

```
title OpenSolaris 2008.11 xVM
bootfs rpool/ROOT/opensolaris
kernel$ /boot/$ISADIR/xen.gz
module$ /platform/i86xpv/kernel/$ISADIR/unix /platform/i86xpv/kernel/$ISADIR/unix
-B $ZFS-BOOTFS
module$ /platform/i86pc/$ISADIR/boot_archive
```

Reboot your system, choosing the OpenSolaris 2008.11 xVM GRUB menu option. Log in again, and use the SMF svcadm command to enable the xVM services, as listed in Table 7-7.

Table 7-7. *SMF svcadm Commands to Enable xVM services*

Command	Meaning
svcadm enable store	Creates a database to store domain configuration data
svcadm enable xend	Daemon used by xVM admin tools to control hypervisor
svcadm enable console	Enables access to guest domain (DomU) consoles
svcadm enable domains	Starts/stops guest domain on boot/shutdown of Dom0
svcadm enable virtd	Daemon used by DomU guests to communicate with hypervisor

Verify that these services are running using the svcs command (Figure 7-20).

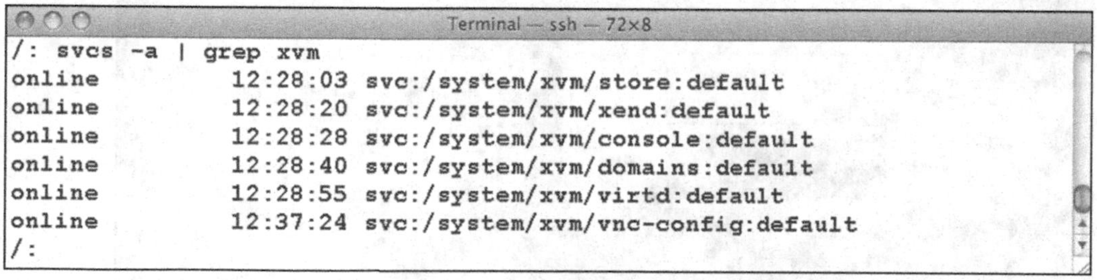

```
/: svcs -a | grep xvm
online          12:28:03  svc:/system/xvm/store:default
online          12:28:20  svc:/system/xvm/xend:default
online          12:28:28  svc:/system/xvm/console:default
online          12:28:40  svc:/system/xvm/domains:default
online          12:28:55  svc:/system/xvm/virtd:default
online          12:37:24  svc:/system/xvm/vnc-config:default
/:
```

Figure 7-20. *Verifying the OpenSolaris xVM services*

At this point, it becomes a bit easier, because you can now use the virt-manager GUI tool to create and manage guest VMs. This tool lets you monitor existing remote and local DomU VMs, including Dom0, and steps you through the process of creating new DomUs (Figures 7-21 and 7-22).

Figure 7-21. *Starting the virt-manager GUI*

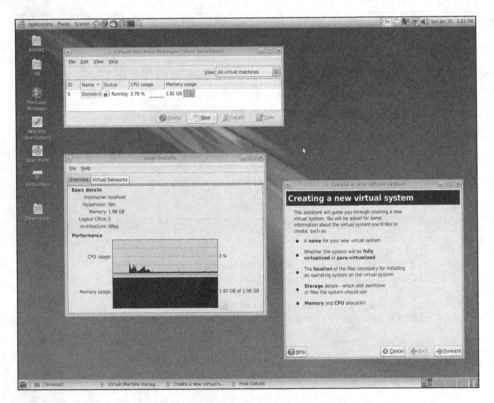

Figure 7-22. *The virt-manager GUI for creating and monitoring VMs*

The next series of figures outline the process for using virt-manager to add a new guest VM to the OpenSolaris Dom0.

In Figure 7-23, you select a name for your VM. Note that this name is used by the hypervisor to identify individual VMs; it is not necessarily the host name assigned to the VM, although you can use the same name if you want.

In Figure 7-24, you select a virtualization method. Currently, OpenSolaris is supported only as a paravirtualized guest.

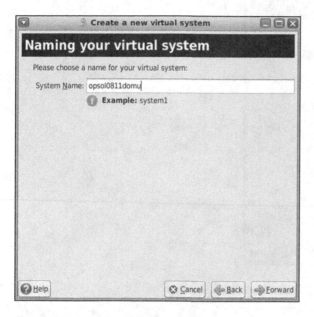

Figure 7-23. *Naming your virtual system*

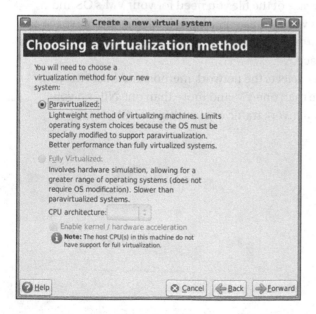

Figure 7-24. *Choosing a virtualization method*

Figure 7-25 shows how to indicate the location of your installation media. This location can be a locally mounted boot image or DVD (mounted in Dom0), or it can be a URL pointing to a boot image or to a kickstart file.

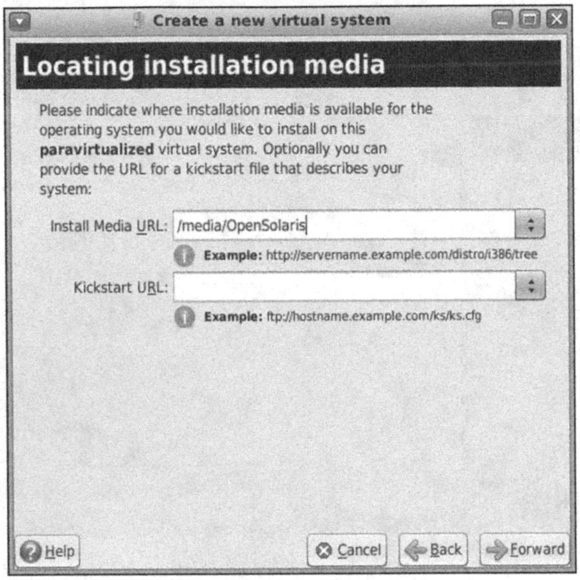

Figure 7-25. *Locating the install media*

You can choose to use either an existing disk partition or a disk image file as shown in Figure 7-26. You need to specify the size of the file you need for your VM's OS and applications. Note that it's a good idea while you are just experimenting to save space and don't allocate the entire virtual disk; later, when you have a better idea of your VM storage needs, you can preallocate needed space.

The next step shown in Figure 7-27 selects the network method and host NIC you want your VM to use. If you have more than one VM and more than one NIC on your system, it may be useful to spread VM network traffic over multiple NICs.

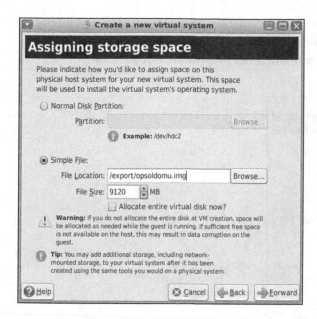

Figure 7-26. *Assigning storage space*

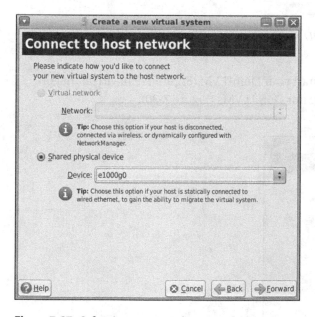

Figure 7-27. *Selecting your VM's network device*

In Figure 7-28 you allocate memory to your VM. Be sure to leave sufficient memory for your host domain (Dom0). If your host system has multiple CPUs (or cores), you can allocate multiple virtual CPUs for better multithread performance of your VM.

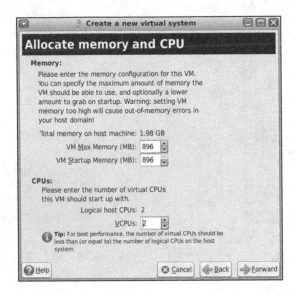

Figure 7-28. *Allocating memory and CPU*

You are now ready to install and start your DomU VM (Figure 7-29); virt-manager then allows you to start, stop, and monitor DomU VMs (Figure 7-30).

Figure 7-29. *Ready to begin DomU VM installation*

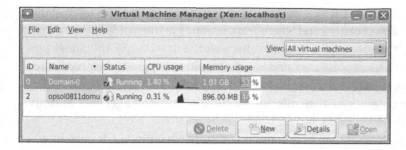

Figure 7-30. *Monitoring the new DomU with* **virt-manager**

At this point (Figure 7-29), you are ready to install the guest VM. The installation steps for the guest OS are the same as we discussed earlier, configuring the OS, host name, network address, user, and root accounts in the usual manner. The virt-manager tool then lets you start, stop, and monitor your newly installed VM.

BrandZ

Users of Solaris 10 and OpenSolaris often ask whether there's anything else besides Solaris environments that can be run in zones. Recalling that zones are *not* full virtual machine kernels and that they are really named and highly restricted containment areas for applications that merely look like VMs, it would appear at first that the answer is no. But it turns out that not all application environments need a full kernel to support them. They need system libraries and APIs that in theory can be provided by a different kernel than the application was compiled for. This is the basic idea behind *branded zones*, which allow non-native operating environments to run within an OpenSolaris zone. When an application in such a zone makes a system call, the call is intercepted and redirected to a user module from the foreign operating system. This avoids the requirement of a full VM environment to run the application.

Branded zones are now implemented in both the x86 and SPARC versions of Solaris 10. You can create a Linux, or *lx*, zone on x86 systems running Solaris 10 or OpenSolaris that lets you run many Linux binaries within that kind of zone. This can be useful for running applications compiled for Linux that have not yet been ported to run on Open-Solaris.

Note A Linux branded zone is *not* a full Linux kernel, so it cannot support Linux kernel modules, and it cannot create and use Linux-specific file systems or device drivers. This feature should be considered interesting but still experimental. Nevertheless, several useful Linux binaries have been successfully run on OpenSolaris lx zones, such as Maple and MATLAB. A list of runnable binaries that have been shown to work is here: http://opensolaris.org/os/community/brandz/applications/.

Another kind of branded zone, which we'll mention only briefly, is for Sun's UltraSPARC Sun4v processors. This allows Solaris 8 and Solaris 9 applications to run in a Solaris 10 zone and is called the Solaris 8 (or 9) Migration Assistant. Because the new UltraSPARC Sun4v processors run only Solaris 10, users of Solaris 8 and Solaris 9 could not upgrade their hardware to the new processor. So, Sun created a nominally temporary solution using branded zones, with the intent of helping users finish their migration to Solaris 10. But let's get back to Linux zones.

The OpenSolaris implementation of lx zones is still somewhat limited. It currently only supports the CentOS 3 Linux distribution in 32-bit mode; a copy of the required installation instructions and CentOS image is available on the OpenSolaris web site at http://wikis.sun.com/display/chosug/Installing+a+Linux+Zone. Creating an lx zone is similar to creating a native zone:

```
# pfexec zonecfg -z lzone1
lzone1: No such zone configured
Use 'create' to begin configuring a new zone.
zonecfg:lzone1> create -t SUNWlx
zonecfg:lzone1> set zonepath=/export/lzone1
zonecfg:lzone1> add net
zonecfg:lzone1:net> set address=192.168.1.205/24
zonecfg:lzone1:net> set physical=e1000g0
zonecfg:lzone1:net> end
zonecfg:lzone1> verify
zonecfg:lzone1> commit
zonecfg:lzone1> exit
#
```

Then download and install the CentOS image:

```
# cd /var/tmp
# wget http://dlc.sun.com/osol/brandz/downloads/centos_fs_image.tar.bz2
# pfexec zoneadm -z lzone1 install -d /var/tmp/centos_fs_image.tar.bz2
```

Boot the zone, and log in:

```
# pfexec zoneadm -z lzone1 boot
# pfexec zlogin lzone1
```

The results of this process are shown in Figure 7-31. You are now in a Linux zone, and you can load and run almost any user application that runs on CentOS 3.

```
$ pfexec zonecfg -z lzone1
lzone1: No such zone configured
Use 'create' to begin configuring a new zone.
$ pfexec zoneadm -z lzone1 install -d /var/tmp/centos_fs_image.tar.bz2
A ZFS file system has been created for this zone.
Installing zone 'lzone1' at root directory '/export/lzone1'
from archive '/var/tmp/centos_fs_image.tar.bz2'

This process may take several minutes.
...
Installation of zone 'lzone1' completed successfully.
Details saved to log file: "/export/lzone1/root/var/log/lzone1.install.654.log"

$ pfexec zoneadm -z lzone1 boot
$ zoneadm list -cv
  ID NAME            STATUS     PATH                          BRAND    IP
   0 global          running    /                             native   shared
   1 lzone1          running    /export/lzone1                lx       shared
   - myfirstzone     installed  /export/myfirstzone           ipkg     shared
   - mysecondzone    installed  /export/mysecondzone          ipkg     shared
$ pfexec pfexec zlogin lzone1
[Connected to zone 'lzone1' pts/4]
Welcome to your shiny new Linux zone.

       - The root password is 'root'.  Please change it immediately.
       - To enable networking goodness, see /etc/sysconfig/network.example.
       - This message is in /etc/motd.  Feel free to change it.

For anything more complicated, see:
       http://opensolaris.org/os/community/brandz/

You have mail.
-bash-2.05b#
-bash-2.05b# uname -a
Linux lzone1 2.4.21 BrandZ fake linux i686 i686 i386 GNU/Linux
-bash-2.05b#
```

Figure 7-31. *Installing a Linux (lx) zone on OpenSolaris*

One long-missing application from Solaris 10 and OpenSolaris for Intel/AMD is Adobe's PDF reader, acroread. A blog on Adobe's web site reported in March 2008 that the reader will be available for Solaris and OpenSolaris some time in 2009. It is available for Linux, however, and if you don't like running OpenSolaris's evince PDF reader, you can download acroread for Linux and run it in an lx-branded zone. Like any other zone, you access it with TCP/IP communication tools. In the previous example, you can log in to the zone (using its IP address, or using its host name if you've added it to your global hosts file) using ssh and X11 forwarding, as shown in Figure 7-32. Note that upon login to lzone1, we verified that we were in a Linux environment (using uname -a) and then ran the Linux version of acroread to view a local PDF file (opensolaris_datasheet.pdf). You can run other applications in this manner, including of course any of the X11 applications (such as xcalc in the example) on the installed version of Linux. Also note (in the smaller terminal window) that the global zone has access to the local zone's file system and that the global zone administrator *could* copy files into any local zone directory. This is not advisable, however, and a better practice is to create a sharable global zone file system that can be mounted by the local zone.

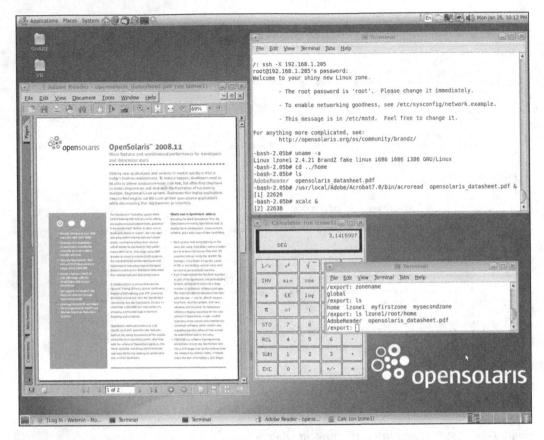

Figure 7-32. *Running the Linux versions of acroread and xcalc in an lx-branded zone and displaying on the global zone desktop using X11 forwarding*

LDoms

With the coming release of OpenSolaris 2009.06 you will begin to see support for Open-Solaris on SPARC processors. This will be a significant development when there is full support for the UltraSPARC Sun4v processor family. These processors have multiple CPU cores with multiple independently executable threads per core. For example, the Ultra-SPARC T2 processor chip (http://www.sun.com/processors/UltraSPARC-T2/) has 8 cores with 8 threads per core; Solaris 10 now and OpenSolaris in future releases see the equivalent of 64 CPUs when running on these chips. Sun has created a virtualization technology for these "CoolThreads" processors called *LDoms* (for logical domains). In brief, this includes a SPARC-based hypervisor, not unlike the Xen architecture, that allows Solaris or OpenSolaris VMs to be created on groups of processor threads.

There is already an active LDom developer community at http://opensolaris.org/os/community/ldoms/ that is studying and contributing to the open source LDoms code base for Solaris 10 (Figure 7-33). Watch this site for more news about LDoms support in Open-Solaris.

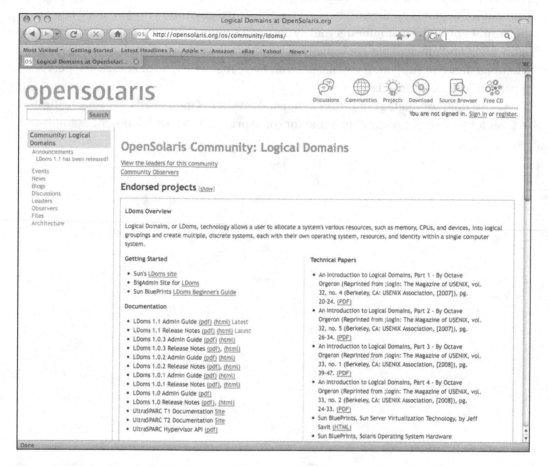

Figure 7-33. *The OpenSolaris LDoms community web site*

Summary

OpenSolaris provides a number of choices for virtualized environments, including zones, branded zones (Linux), desktop OS virtualization (VirtualBox), and server virtualization (xVM Hypervisor), with more to look forward to in future releases (LDoms for SPARC). Your choice depends on the number and type of virtual environments you need and on the number of such environments your system can support. OpenSolaris containers are lightweight and efficient but are somewhat limited in the variety of application/OS combinations they can support. If you need to run more than one type of kernel, a hypervisor approach is more appropriate.

We've now completed our introduction and review of OpenSolaris's special features. In Chapter 8, we'll put them all together for some practical web development examples.

PART 3

■ ■ ■

Exploiting OpenSolaris's Unique Features

Now that you have learned about SMF, ZFS, and zones, it's time to take advantage of these features for your applications. The final two chapters present practical examples and innovative OpenSolaris technologies that enhance and extend your development environment and show you where to learn more about this innovative operating system.

## CHAPTER 8

A Development Environment on OpenSolaris

Developer, n: an organism that turns coffee into software.

—Author Unknown

Not terribly long ago, if a developer had wanted to load a development environment on her laptop, she could count on spending half a day building the operating system and another half a day getting and loading her tools, compilers, scripting languages, and database. If she were a casual tinkerer or a beginner, add another day for figuring out where all the knobs are and reading the manuals. By the time she's ready to get down to business, her flash of inspiration may well have smoldered down to embers, or worse, the idea of having to go through with the build is so wearying that our budding developer chucks it all in disgust.

Tools that are accessible get used most often—in fact, that's the first rule of the wood shop. OpenSolaris has made itself extremely accessible to the developer, whether you are developing in C, developing in Java, or building web infrastructures and database applications. You can have a full-featured developer's "wood shop" in about 90 minutes.

Note It helps to provide a little perspective: we remember loading Solaris (the progenitor of OpenSolaris); b-splitting device drivers and schlepping them onto the hard drive via thumb drives; and downloading `gcc` and updated versions of Perl, `ssh`, and gtk+. All of that and more was done manually over a very long weekend. With OpenSolaris, there are fewer war stories.

Introducing the Web Stack and AMP

Web development used to mean many things, from graphics design and layout to the actual coding of the engine behind the web page. The end result is a construct that follows this pattern: a browsable, interactive front end; a database back end to store the input; and a programming-logic middle to manage the data. For example, you might issue a database query for audio files that match a certain characteristic, sort them, generate a web page for them to appear on, and stream them in a certain format.

Regardless of the web application and other technology factors, anything that does something useful via a browser loosely follows this design pattern. In fact, web commerce in its heyday was described as using a three-tier architecture, and most web development was geared toward developing an e-commerce site. This design pattern is now more familiarly known as the *web stack*.

The web stack comprises three parts: the web server front end, the programming-logic middle, and the database back end. The tools dominating each niche are Apache, Perl, PHP (or any other popular scripting language), and MySQL. Thus, it's called AMP—or LAMP if the operating system underneath it all is Linux. The web stack has undergone hybridization as it is being used; AMP is no longer strictly limited to its eponymous part. That is, PostgreSQL can stand in for MySQL, and Ruby can stand in for PHP; you may even have seen references to the LAMR stack.

Getting the AMP Stack

On your OpenSolaris desktop, open the Package Manager (IPS) GUI. The plain-vanilla AMP stack is called, not so surprisingly, amp. Your other choice is the amp-dev stack. Select the box next to the amp-dev package, and click the Install/Update icon; or, select Package ➤ Install/Update from the drop-down menu, as shown in Figure 8-1.

You will be asked to confirm this action, as shown in Figure 8-2.

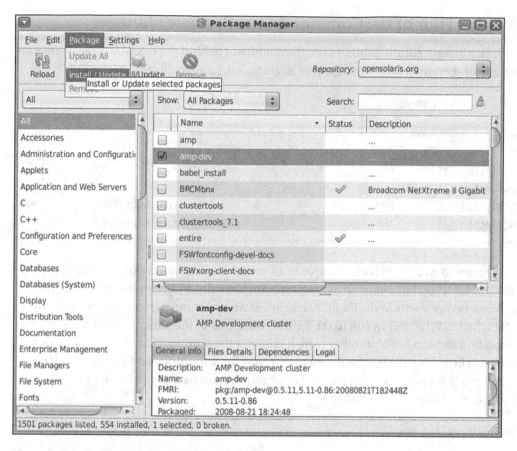

Figure 8-1. *Selecting the amp-dev package for installation*

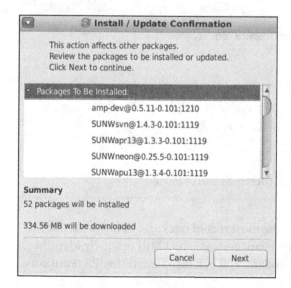

Figure 8-2. *Confirming installation of the amp-dev package*

Taking a Tour of the Command-Line Package Manager

For the inveterate command-line user, the command behind the IPS GUI is pkg. Here's an example of searching for a package from a remote image repository:

```
# pkg search -r amp
```

```
INDEX       ACTION    VALUE                 PACKAGE
description set       AMP                     description set       AMP
pkg:/amp@0.5.11-0.101
description set       AMP              pkg:/amp-dev@0.5.11-0.86
description set       AMP              pkg:/amp-dev@0.5.11-0.101
```

pkg:/amp@0.5.11-0.86 is an example of a Fault Management Resource Identifier (FMRI), which you encountered in Chapter 5. Incidentally, FMRI is also used to identify hardware components in the Fault Management Architecture, part of OpenSolaris. pkg is the scheme. What follows up to the @ sign is the name of the package and then the component version, build number (which matches the output of uname -r), and branch number. The last of these is the timestamp. You will see multiple, and seemingly identical, returns from pkg search; in fact, these are all different packages with their FMRIs abridged. For the full FMRI, run this:

```
# pkg info -r amp-dev
```

```
          Name: amp-dev
       Summary: AMP Development cluster
      Category: Development/Integrated Development Environments
         State: Installed
     Authority: opensolaris.org
       Version: 0.5.11
 Build Release: 5.11
        Branch: 0.101
Packaging Date: Wed Dec 10 00:46:05 2008
          Size: 0.00 B
          FMRI: pkg:/amp-dev@0.5.11,5.11-0.101:20081210T004605Z
```

The package version returned is always the most recent package. You should not have to interpret what these numbers really mean, because the FMRI uniquely identifies the package for the purposes of repair and update. You can also search the IPS repository at http://pkg.opensolaris.org.

You may be curious as to what the difference is between the two packages amp and amp-dev. They are both *metapackages*, or package clusters. This means they contain only other packages. Installing a metapackage installs the packages on which they depend. You can leverage this knowledge and look at their dependencies to see which other packages constitute amp and amp-dev. Here are the amp-dev contents:

```
# pkg contents -m amp-dev
```

```
depend fmri=SUNWsvn@1.4.3-0.101 type=require
depend fmri=SUNWmysql5@5.0.67-0.101 type=require
depend fmri=netbeans type=require
depend fmri=SUNWapch22@2.2.9-0.101 type=require
depend fmri=SUNWmercurial@1.0.2-0.101 type=require
depend fmri=SUNWPython@2.4.4-0.101 type=require
depend fmri=SUNWphp52d@5.2.6-0.101 type=require
depend fmri=SUNWapch22m-jk@1.2.25-0.101 type=require
depend fmri=SUNWapch22d@2.2.9-0.101 type=require
depend fmri=SUNWapch22m-security@2.1.5-0.101 type=require
depend fmri=SUNWcvs@1.12.13-0.101 type=require
depend fmri=SUNWapch22m-php52@5.2.6-0.101 type=require
depend fmri=SUNWphp52-pgsql@5.2.6-0.101 type=require
depend fmri=SUNWtcat@5.5.27-0.101 type=require
depend fmri=SUNWpython-twisted@0.5.11-0.101 type=require
depend fmri=SUNWsquid@2.6.17-0.101 type=require
depend fmri=SUNWphp52@5.2.6-0.101 type=require
depend fmri=SUNWmemcached@1.2.5-0.101 type=require
depend fmri=SUNWapch22m-fcgid@2.2-0.101 type=require
depend fmri=SUNWapch22m-dtrace@0.3.1-0.101 type=require
depend fmri=SUNWphp52-mysql@5.2.6-0.101 type=require
depend fmri=webstackui@0.5.11-0.101 type=require
```

Running the same command for the amp package shows that it has only the basic Apache, MySQL, and PHP packages, with a few Apache plug-ins. amp-dev provides all of this, as well as Tomcat, NetBeans, the Squid proxy, CVS, Mercurial version control, and much more.

The CLI command equal to the action you've taken with the Package Manager GUI is as follows:

```
# pkg install amp-dev
```

Next, you need to initialize your web stack for your workspace. You are logged in as the RBAC profile Primary Administrator, and you have assigned root as a role. You must modify some root-owned files' attributes to enable you to work with them. The RBAC profiles and authorization tokens for these new services also have to be added. The initialization also adds items under the Developer Tools ➤ Web Stack Admin menu drop-down. You can see this in Figure 8-3.

Figure 8-3. *Initializing the web stack*

You will see the web stack initialization in a terminal window, as shown in Figure 8-4. Figure 8-5 shows the new menu after initialization.

Note   ZFS implements extended ACL, sometimes called NFSv4-style ACL but more precisely described as ACL based on the Posix-draft specification. getfacl(1) does not work; you need ls -v to view extended ACL. Be careful, and check your path. If you take the default login environment without making any modifications, most likely /usr/gnu/bin will be ahead of /usr/bin and you are using GNU ls. The GNU ls -v switch does something entirely different from the Solaris ls -v switch, which is located in /usr/bin.

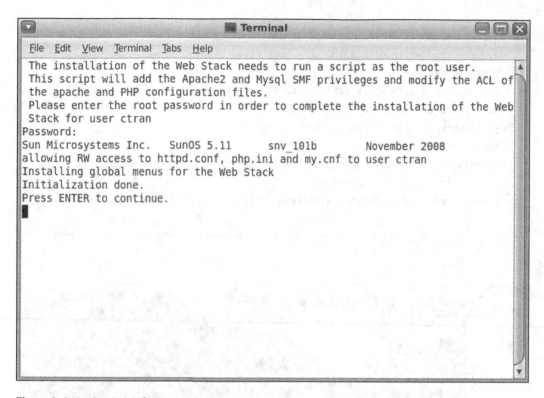

Figure 8-4. *Script initializing web stack*

You can see the difference in the following example:

```
ctran@ender:/etc/apache2/2.2$ cd /etc/apache2/2.2
ctran@ender:/etc/apache2/2.2$ ls -v httpd.conf
```

```
httpd.conf
```

```
ctran@ender:/etc/apache2/2.2$ which ls
```

```
/usr/gnu/bin/ls
```

```
ctran@ender:/etc/apache2/2.2$ /usr/bin/ls -v httpd.conf
```

```
-rw-r--r--+ 1 root      bin        13335 Jan 25 00:05 httpd.conf
    0:user:ctran:write_data:allow  <-- user ctran allowed to write to file
    1:owner@:execute:deny
    2:owner@:read_data/write_data/append_data/write_xattr/write_attributes
        /write_acl/write_owner:allow
    3:group@:write_data/append_data/execute:deny
    4:group@:read_data:allow
    5:everyone@:write_data/append_data/write_xattr/execute/write_attributes
        /write_acl/write_owner:deny
    6:everyone@:read_data/read_xattr/read_attributes/read_acl/synchronize
        :allow
```

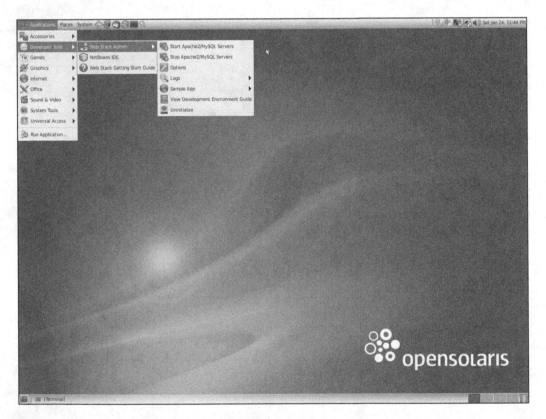

Figure 8-5. *New menus after web stack initialization*

■ **Note** You are installing a development environment, which is quite different from a production environment in aspects of security, manageability, customization, and so on. Typically, production-environment
Apache runs as the UNIX user webadmin or webservd group, and MySQL runs as the UNIX user mysql. It
has not been good practice to run these services as root for a long time. You will need to develop your own
method for deploying your newly minted web application onto a production server. For a production server,
we do not advise you to use chmod httpd.conf to give a number of users rights to modify it, as our example
here showed.

At this point, you can start up your Apache and MySQL servers by selecting from the
drop-down menu. Alternatively, you can issue the following commands:

```
# svcadm enable apache22
# svcadm enable mysql
```

Even though the full FMRI is svc:/network/http:apache22 and svc:/application/
database/mysql:version_50, SMF operates on the first unique match principle, so apache22
and mysql are OK (however, http is not, because there is an instance of http:squid).

You can view the process ID (PID) and contract ID (CTID) of these services by
running this:

```
# svcs -pv apache22
```

STATE	NSTATE	STIME	CTID	FMRI
online	-	1:03:06	153	svc:/network/http:apache22
	1:03:06	4463	httpd	
	1:03:07	4476	httpd	
	1:03:08	4477	httpd	
	1:03:08	4478	httpd	
	1:03:08	4479	httpd	
	1:03:08	4480	httpd	
	1:03:08	4481	httpd	

```
# svcs -pv mysql
```

STATE	NSTATE	STIME	CTID	FMRI
online	-	1:03:06	154	
	svc:/application/database/mysql:version_50			
	1:03:06	4472	mysqld	

At this point, you have a vanilla AMP environment on which you can begin building your web app. Beginners and tinkerers can choose to create and load a very simple AMP example, built with PHP, jMaki, and MySQL, under the Sample App menu.

Making a Case for Containers

Before you open the valves and steam full-speed ahead with the AMP stack you've just loaded, perhaps you want to build your application inside an OpenSolaris container. You can refer to Chapter 7 for discussions on zones and virtualization. Here are the reasons why you should consider running your application inside a zone:

- *Fault and resource isolation*: Zones are designed to be logically isolated from other zones, and software faults in one zone have no impact on any other zone. If you impose zone resource control, you also limit the impact of a resource-hogging application on other applications. You can also allocate separate storage space to each zone and not worry about which application is overusing its allotment.

- *Security isolation*: Zones are execution environments bounded by a reduced set of privileges. A process executing in a zone cannot escalate its privileges to access data in any other zone. For example, say a security vulnerability is discovered in an application. If the application is run in the global zone, the exploit will affect the entire system. If the application is run in a nonglobal zone, any effect from the exploit is limited to the nonglobal zone only.

■**Caution** There are cases when a zone is delegated an entire physical device such as tape, disk, or CD-ROM drive, as opposed to giving the zone limited access to an LOFS file system. This will present opportunities for faults incurred by the device to affect the entire platform. In general, we don't recommend this practice. We prefer delegating file systems instead of raw devices. If you've ever wondered what the zone configuration directive `add options [rw,nodevices]` is for, the mount option `nodevices` stops the zone from opening any device node present on the mount.

- *Delegation*: You can delegate the administrative and management function of an application running in a zone to a set of administrators with superuser privileges in the zone but not the entire system.

- *Scalability*: While you're building your application on a desktop or laptop platform, you may not yet be thinking of the day when your brainchild becomes a breakaway success and it's no longer feasible to run everything on a single platform. If you compartmentalize your web stack and build within a container, you will be able to horizontally scale your application. Anywhere you are able to deploy a zone, you will be able to run your application. Recently, a federated database model, sometimes referred to as *data sharding*, has been employed with some success. The idea behind data sharding is to separate, or "shard," the data into many parallel databases, called *silos*. Each connection will be directed to the silo containing the data it needs, instead of to a single database server or a number of replicated database servers containing all data. A zone is a very good solution for this architecture without incurring an additional hardware cost.

- *Portability*: Zones can be quickly built and torn down without much administrative overhead. If you take steps to ensure your web stack can run within a zone, your application will run anywhere you can export or rebuild the zone. NAS and SAN storage have been used creatively to provision zones and applications on the fly. For example, build a zone on a NAS or SAN that is accessible by multiple hosts. The zone can be detached from one host and attached to another, and within minutes the application can be provisioned on a different host. For the same reason, zones make efficient test and staging environments to pilot new applications or test code changes.

Building Applications for a Container Environment

We said that zones are virtual OS instances with a reduced set of privileges. For this reason, some actions possible in the global zone will not be permitted in a nonglobal zone. Let's examine how this works to come to a better understanding about why things behave the way they do in a zone.

Introducing Zones and Discrete Privileges

The OpenSolaris access control model differs from traditional Solaris (up to SunOS 5.9) in that Solaris used the UID to determine who has the privilege to do what. Processes running with UID 0 have unlimited privileges to the system. Processes running with UID not equal to 0 have privileges to their own files and directories, as well as files and directories accessible by their GIDs. This was the reason why the SUID bit was so dangerous. OpenSolaris breaks the omnipotent root powers down to 74 discrete privileges, enforceable by the kernel at runtime. Formally, this is referred to as *process rights management*. Note the word *process*. The privileges are enforced not at the user level but at the process level. We'll talk more about this in the "Installing Tomcat in a Container" section.

You can read the privileges(5) man page for the description of all the available privileges. Take, for example, the privilege PRIV_FILE_DAC_READ. A process running with this privilege is able to read directories and files it doesn't own; more precisely, a user running a process with PRIV_FILE_DAC_READ can read files that user doesn't own. Enforcement on reading files is no longer "Is UID == 0?" Rather, it is "Does the process have the correct privilege?"

You can view all available privileges with this:

```
# ppriv -l
```

To view privileges in a zone, log in to the zone, and run this:

```
# ppriv -l zone
```

To view the description of a privilege, such as `proc_clock_highres`, run this:

```
# ppriv -lv proc_clock_highres
```

```
proc_clock_highres
        Allows a process to use high resolution timers.
```

Note the difference between the number of privileges between the global zone and the nonglobal zone. Privileges for nonglobal zones—more precisely, privileges for processes running in a nonglobal zone—are restricted to maintain isolation between zones as well as to prevent an action in a zone from having a system-wide impact. An upper limit is set for these privileges to prevent zones from escalating their own privileges.

You will read about DTrace in the next chapter, but for now, notice that no DTrace privileges appear in the zone list of privileges. By default, you cannot use DTrace in a zone; however, you can change this provided you add a couple of privileges. They are `PRIV_DTRACE_PROC` and `PRIV_DTRACE_USER`. Add the following to the zone using `zonecfg`, and reboot the zone:

```
# zonecfg -z myzone set limitpriv=default,dtrace_proc,dtrace_user
```

It's not just a matter of picking out privileges to grant to a zone, cafeteria-style. There are privileges that a zone will never be able to assert, such as `PRIV_DTRACE_KERNEL`. A zone that can read kernel-level data would violate every principle of containment and isolation.

Qualifying Your Application for Zones

So, what does all this mean for the web app you're building? There are things that your application should take care not to do. At one time, there was a dependable list of privileges not available in a nonglobal zone, such as `PRIV_NET_RAWACCESS`, which allows a zone to directly access the network layer. That limitation went away when a zone of ip-type "exclusive" was integrated. At one time it was not possible for a zone to assert `PRIV_SYS_TIME` to change the system clock; now it's a usage example in the OpenSolaris documentation. With future versions of OpenSolaris, even more restrictions may be lifted, with caveats. Although there is no hard rule about this, here are a couple of things to keep in mind:

- Unless your zone is of ip-type "exclusive," you cannot access the raw network device, plumb interfaces, modify routing tables, use snoop, or modify attributes of /dev/ip.

- Zones can't access /dev/kmem or load or unload kernel modules.

- Zones can't modify processor sets, create device special files, or manipulate platform configuration.

- A global zone and a nonglobal zone on the same system may not be the NFS client of the same NFS server.

This is a swiftly moving area, and the thing to keep in mind is this: will the action of my application have an unexpected and deleterious effect on another nonglobal zone or the system? When in doubt, be conservative.

A tool called srcheck can help you determine whether what you want to run in a zone will work. It scans the source code for API calls that are not permitted in a zone. This tool is somewhat dated, and given how quickly things can change on OpenSolaris, use it with caution.

You can get the Solaris Ready Test Suite 1.2 here:

```
https://cds.sun.com/is-bin/INTERSHOP.enfinity/WFS/CDS-CDS_Developer-Site➥
/en_US/-/USD/ViewProductDetail-Start?ProductRef=srcheck1.2-G-F@CDS-CDS_Developer
```

You will find a guide for srcheck and examples at http://developers.sun.com/solaris/articles/zone_app_qualif.html.

Installing Tomcat in a Container

Create and install a zone. Refer to Chapter 7 for how to do this. Remember that OpenSolaris implements ZFS for the root file system, so create a ZFS file system for the zone first:

```
# zfs create rpool/zones
# zonecfg -z web
...
# zoneadm -z web install
```

```
A ZFS file system has been created for this zone.
   Authority: Using http://pkg.opensolaris.org/release/.
       Image: Preparing at /zones/web/root ... done.
       Cache: Using /var/pkg/download.
 Installing: (output follows)
DOWNLOAD                               PKGS      FILES     XFER (MB)
SUNWipkg                               7/52    2406/7862 10.87/72.41 Installed
Completed                             52/52    7862/7862   72.41/72.41
PHASE                                         ACTIONS
Install Phase                         12939/12939
PHASE                                          ITEMS
Reading Existing Index                          9/9
Indexing Packages                             52/52
```

Note If you're familiar with zones on Solaris 10, you may notice that the zone brand is not type `native` and that the zone installation actually pulls packages from `http://pkg.opensolaris.org` instead of copying them locally. `ipkg`-branded zones are independent of the global zone, and packages you've pulled for the global zone will not be installed in `ipkg`-branded zones. This is why, if you've already installed `amp-dev` into your global zone, it will not be automatically installed in any nonglobal zone you create.

For identification purposes, we're installing Tomcat into a zone called web. Log in, and install the IPS package SUNWtcat. You may have to tweak the network configuration inside the zone; for example, modify /etc/nsswitch.conf and /etc/resolv.conf to add name service for your network. Needless to say, the network connection inside your zone must be a working one so you can access the OpenSolaris package repository.

```
# zlogin web
root@web:~# pkg info -r SUNWtcat
```

```
        Name: SUNWtcat
     Summary: Tomcat Servlet/JSP Container
    Category: Web Services/Application and Web Servers
       State: Not installed
   Authority: opensolaris.org
     Version: 5.5.27
Build Release: 5.11
      Branch: 0.101
Packaging Date: Wed Nov 19 23:03:01 2008
        Size: 24.56 MB
        FMRI: pkg:/SUNWtcat@5.5.27,5.11-0.101:20081119T230301Z
```

```
root@web:~# pkg install SUNWtcat
```

```
Refreshing Catalog 1/1 opensolaris.org
DOWNLOAD                              PKGS       FILES     XFER (MB)
SUNWtcat                             0/1      900/2382    7.55/10.72
Completed                            1/1     2382/2382   10.72/10.72
```

Tomcat 5.5.27 runs on J2SE 5.0 or newer. If you just want to run Tomcat, you need only the JRE. If you plan on developing with Java, you'll want to install the entire JDK. A search of the package repository turns up only SUNWj6rt, so we'll install that along with SUNWtcat.

There exists a reserved UID:GID, webservd:webservd, traditionally used to run Apache. You can run Tomcat under this UID. If you are concerned about the separation of administrative functions in case you want to run another instance of Apache, create another user to run Tomcat. We like to keep a tidy passwd file, so we use the existing account webservd and change the home directory to /var/apache. Then we need to set some Tomcat environment variables.

```
root@web:~# usermod -d /var/apache -s /usr/bin/bash webservd
```

```
root@web:/var/apache# cat .bash_profile
```

```
# .bash_profile
if [ -f ~/.bashrc ]; then
   source ~/.bashrc
fi
```

```
root@web:/var/apache# cat .bashrc
```

```
PS1='$PWD:'
CATALINA_HOME=/usr/apache/tomcat
CATALINA_BASE=/var/apache/tomcat
JAVA_HOME=/usr/jdk/jdk1.6.0_10
export CATALINA_HOME CATALINA_BASE JAVA_HOME
PATH=$PATH:$JAVA_HOME/bin:$CATALINA_HOME/bin
```

If you have worked with Tomcat in a single directory hierarchy such as /opt/apache/tomcat, you will find that the Tomcat version distributed by Sun follows the Filesystem

Hierarchy Standard (which can be found at http://www.pathname.com/fhs/). SUNWtcat splits the bin and conf directories under /usr/apache/tomcat/bin and /var/apache/tomcat/conf.

Note Shells and UNIX flavors are funny things. Sometimes a big headache can be relieved (or be brought on) by a subtle distinction. The UNIX user webservd account is marked as *LK* in /etc/shadow. If you want this user to be able to run cron jobs, change *LK* to NP. .bash_profile is sourced for login shells, while .bashrc is sourced for nonlogin shells. You need .bashrc because Tomcat will be started from a nonlogin shell by SMF, not a login shell. This will apply only if you are using bash; if you're using another shell, know how that shell sources profiles and sets environment variables.

You may want to enable SSL for Tomcat. This process is similar to how it's done on other UNIX platforms. If you have elected to use a directory such as /var/apache or /usr/apache as the home for the user webservd, you need to modify the directory to enable webservd and put a .keystore file there.

```
root@web:~# chmod -R A+user:webservd:add_file/write_data/execute:allow /var/apache
root@web:~# $JAVA_HOME/bin/keytool -genkey -alias tomcat -keyalg RSA
```

```
Enter keystore password:  changeit
Re-enter new password: changeit
What is your first and last name?
  [Unknown]:  Christine Tran
What is the name of your organizational unit?
  [Unknown]:  Sandwich Ninja
What is the name of your organization?
  [Unknown]:  Apress Books
What is the name of your City or Locality?
  [Unknown]:  Washington
What is the name of your State or Province?
  [Unknown]:  DC
What is the two-letter country code for this unit?
  [Unknown]:  US
Is CN=Christine Tran, OU=Sandwich Ninja, O=Apress Books, L=Washington,
ST=DC, C=US correct?
  [no]:  yes
Enter key password for <tomcat>
        (RETURN if same as keystore password):  [RETURN]
```

Modify /var/apache/tomcat/conf/server.xml to uncomment the SLL connector port. You can add an ACL for webservd to be able to modify server.xml if you are editing files as webservd. You can comment out the non-SSL connector on port 8080 if you want.

```
root@web:~# vi /var/apache/tomcat/conf/server.xml
```

```
<!-- Define a SSL HTTP/1.1 Connector on port 8443 -->
<Connector port="8443" maxHttpHeaderSize="8192"
           maxThreads="150" minSpareThreads="25" maxSpareThreads="75"
           enableLookups="false" disableUploadTimeout="true"
           acceptCount="100" scheme="https" secure="true"
           clientAuth="false" sslProtocol="TLS" />
```

If you want to start Tomcat as user webservd, you need to do this:

```
# usermod -K defaultpriv=basic,net_privaddr webservd
```

Referring to the discussion on privileges (in the "Introducing Zones and Discrete Privileges" section), you are assigning an additional privilege to user webservd, named net_privaddr. You can see this change in /etc/user_attr. To get a description of the privilege netprivaddr, run:

```
# ppriv -lv net_privaddr
```

```
net_privaddr
        Allows a process to bind to a privileged port number. The privilege port
numbers are 1-1023 (the traditional UNIX privileged ports) as well as those
ports marked as "udp/tcp_extra_priv_ports" with the exception of the ports
reserved for use by NFS.
```

Although we have configured Tomcat to listen on 8080 and 8443 for non-SSL and SSL connections, respectively, it's a good idea to give this privilege to webservd in case you decide to add other web server instances or user different ports later. It will save head scratching should you decide to fire up an instance of Apache 2 on port 80.

Note Although we add or take away privileges from the user, they are enforced on the process. This is a subtle but important distinction. The user does not have privileges; the processes the user starts inherit their privileges from their privilege profile. You can also add or take away privileges from a process itself, but this method is only good for that process and for the duration of that process.

At the time of this writing, SUNWtcat does not come with an SMF manifest. You can find a basic Tomcat manifest, `tomcat5.xml`, along with all the source code on this book's page on the Apress web site (`http://www.apress.com`). A few things from that file deserve more attention.

Typically, HTTP services put their manifests in `/var/svc/manifest/network`, and their service names are under the network functional category. For example:

```
# svcs -a|grep http
```

```
disabled       Jan_19    svc:/network/http:squid
online         Jan_25    svc:/network/http:apache22
```

The Apress manifest puts the service into `/var/svc/manifest/site`, and the name of the service will be `svc:/site/http:tomcat5`. This is done with this line in the file:

```
name='site/http'
```

We do this to prevent the possible collision of the manifest with future manifests for Tomcat 5, should the OpenSolaris community decide to bundle one with the next version of the SUNWtcat package.

The start method includes a block to add the `net_privaddr` privilege, but not the stop method. That's because when Tomcat shuts down, it does not need to bind to a privileged port. SMF starts Tomcat as the user `webservd`; but with privileges explicitly assigned, you can run as `root` if you want. Still, if the sight of a slew of `httpd` processes running as `root` gives you heart palpitations before remembering that it's all done with discrete privileges now, run as `webservd` to be consistent with current practices. The following code snippet shows the start and stop methods for Tomcat 5:

```
<exec_method
    type='method'
    name='start'
    exec='/opt/apache/tomcat/bin/startup.sh'
    timeout_seconds='60' >
    <method_context>
    <method_credential user='webservd' privileges='basic,net_privaddr'/>
    </method_context>
</exec_method>
```

Every time a spawned `httpd` process exits, `SIGCHILD` is sent to the parent process. SMF interprets any external signal sent to a service as an error and restarts the service.

Likewise, if a process core dumps, SMF will restart the service. The following snippet tells SMF to ignore these conditions and not to restart Tomcat:

```
<property_group name='startd' type='framework'>
<propval name='ignore_error' type='astring'
    value='core,signal' />
</property_group>
```

Before importing your SMF manifest, you should start Tomcat manually to ensure that it works on its own before sending it off to SMF. Start it as the user webservd, and also remember that webservd will need permission to write into /var/apache to create and write logs. You can do this with ZFS ACL. If you've gone through the key-generating step, you've done this already.

```
root@web# su - webservd
```

```
Sun Microsystems Inc.    SunOS 5.11    snv_101b    November 2008
```

```
webservd@web$ /usr/apache/tomcat/bin/startup.sh
```

```
Using CATALINA_BASE:   /var/apache/tomcat
Using CATALINA_HOME:   /usr/apache/tomcat
Using CATALINA_TMPDIR: /var/apache/tomcat/temp
Using JRE_HOME:        /usr/jdk/jdk1.6.0_10
```

There should be a process listening on port 8080:

```
webservd@web$ netstat -an|grep 8080
```

```
   *.8080            *.*            0    0 49152    0 LISTEN
```

Now, from another computer (which could even be the global zone), open a browser and point to http://web:8080. You should be greeted with the Apache Tomcat/5.5.27 welcome page. Success!

Get the tomcat5.xml file from this book's home page on the Apress web site. Put it in the /var/svc/manifest/site directory, and import it. Before working with this manifest, remember to manually shut down the Tomcat process you just started. You will have to do the following as root, in the zone web:

```
root@web# svccfg import tomcat5.xml
```

Now you have an imported service in the disabled state:

```
root@web# svcs -v tomcat5
```

STATE	NSTATE	STIME	CTID	FMRI
disabled	-	15:43:15	-	svc:/site/http:tomcat5

Enable the service, and the -pv switch shows the contract ID as well as the process ID of any process running within the service. Here, the PID 12301 is the Java process running under the Tomcat service:

```
root@web# svcadm enable tomcat5
root@web# svcs -pv tomcat5
```

STATE	NSTATE	STIME	CTID	FMRI
online	-	15:43:29	475	svc:/site/http:tomcat5
		15:43:29	**12301 java**	

Installing MySQL

MySQL installs in /usr/mysql and /var/mysql. You'll find sample config files and my.cnf in /etc/mysql. The user and group mysql:mysql have already been created and own the data directory in /var/mysql. It installs with an SMF manifest and method. This must come as a refreshing breath of fresh air to DBAs turned reluctant systems administrators who have had to install MySQL, make the data directories, modify config files, add users, and grant privileges—and that's before any real database administration!

Still, there are a few things to be done. The default my.cnf is copied from my-small-cnf.cnf. You'll need to change this if your database is large and your system memory allows for more than 64MB.

Common and accepted practice suggests that you have created the data, administration, binary log, and backup directory. Some directories are implicit. For example, the data directory for this installation is /var/mysql/5.0/data, but the variable datadir is not set in my.cnf. We make it a habit to spell out everything, even when unnecessary. The variables serve as comments in the config file and save us time in hunting down the location of our directories. Add the following lines to my.cnf, under the MySQL server block:

```
# The MySQL server
[mysqld]
...
basedir=/usr/mysql/5.0 # Where MySQL is installed
datadir=/var/mysql/5.0/data # data directory were user mysql has write access
log-error=/var/mysql/5.0/data/errors/mysql5.0.err # MySQL error
log-bin=/var/mysql/5.0/data/dbbinlog/mysql-bin # MySQL binary log
log=/var/mysql/5.0/data/querylog $ MySQL query log
```

You need to create the errors and dbbinlog directories. The query log is optional. Use caution when you turn query logging on; it's not recommended for a production environment. Logs grow without bounds unless you explicitly tell MySQL to stop logging queries. If you forget to turn this off on an active database server, you can run out of disk space and into trouble very quickly.

■**Note** Runtime options to mysqld invoked at start time override the variables set in my.cnf. For example, had you set pid-file=/var/tmp/foo.pid, it would not have taken effect, because the MySQL method invokes mysqld with --pid-file=${PIDFILE}, where ${PIDFILE} happens to be /var/mysql/5.0/data/$hostname.pid.

Enable MySQL. The SMF manifest starts mysqld as the user and group mysql:mysql. Check that the database is functioning and answering queries:

```
root@ender:# svcadm enable mysql
root@ender: # su - mysql
mysql@ender$ /usr/mysql/bin/mysqladmin status
```

```
Uptime: 1154  Threads: 1  Questions: 2  Slow queries: 0  Opens:
12  Flush tables: 1  Open tables: 3  Queries per second avg: 0.002
```

Set a password for mysqld. Here we are setting the password for the user root at localhost:

```
root@ender:# /usr/mysql/bin/mysqladmin -u root password 'mysql'
```

Alternatively, you can run this:

```
root@ender:# /usr/mysql/bin/mysql_secure_installation
```

[Output has been truncated for brevity.]

To log into MySQL to secure it, you'll need the current password for the root user. If you've just installed MySQL and you haven't set the root password yet, the password will be blank, so you should just press Enter here:

```
Enter current password for root (enter for none): mysql
```

Setting the root password ensures that nobody can act as the MySQL root user without the proper authorization.

You already have a root password set, so you can safely answer with an n.

```
Change the root password? [Y/n] n
Remove anonymous users? [Y/n] Y
Disallow root login remotely? [Y/n] Y
Remove test database and access to it? [Y/n] Y
Reload privilege tables now? [Y/n] Y
Cleaning up...
```

All done! If you've completed all the previous steps, your MySQL installation should now be secure.

To see the current user list for MySQL, run this:

```
mysql@ender$ /usr/mysql/bin/mysql -u root -p
```

```
Enter password: mysql
Welcome to the MySQL monitor.  Commands end with ; or \g.
Your MySQL connection id is 19
Server version: 5.0.67-log Source distribution
mysql> select User,Host,Password from mysql.user;
+------+-----------+-------------------------------------------+
| User | Host      | Password                                  |
+------+-----------+-------------------------------------------+
| root | localhost | *E74858DB86EBA20BC33D0AECAE8A8108C56B17FA |
+------+-----------+-------------------------------------------+
1 row in set (0.00 sec)
mysql> exit;
```

In the previous example, you are UNIX user `mysql`, connecting to the database as user root. The -p prompts you for a password. Checking the user list, you can see that the only user allowed access to the database is user root at localhost. You can commence adding users and adding tables to the database, either by using SQL or by using the Java Database Connector (JDBC) driver Connector/J. The Connector/J driver sits between a Java application and MySQL database and provides the API for the application to manipulate the database.

Taking a Quick Tour of NetBeans IDE

The NetBeans integrated development environment (IDE) installs as part of the `amp-dev` package. Open it by selecting Applications ➤ Developer Tools ➤ NetBeans IDE. You can see the start screen of NetBeans in Figure 8-6.

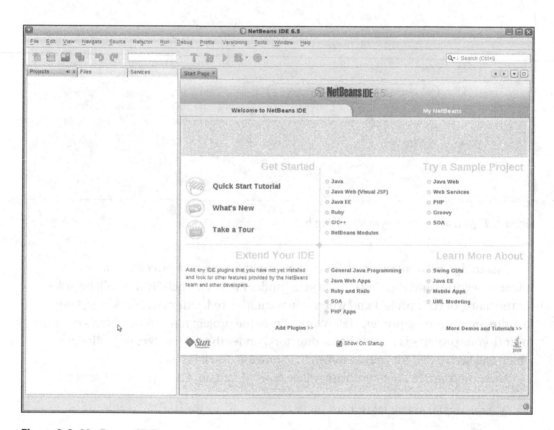

Figure 8-6. *NetBeans IDE start screen*

Clicking the Quick Start Tutorial link launches a Firefox browser with `http://www.netbeans.org/kb/docs/java/quickstart.html` loaded. The Projects tab on the left should be empty. To start a new project, select File ➤ New Project. You'll see a dialog box like the one shown in Figure 8-7.

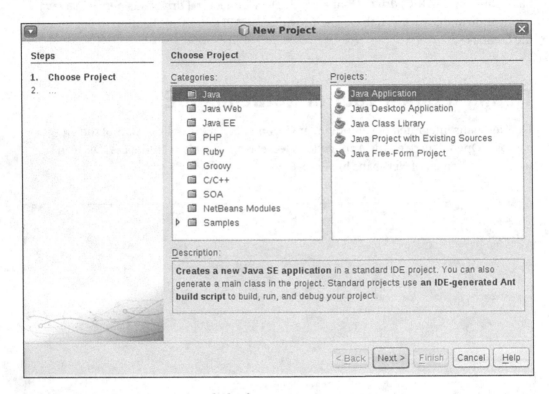

Figure 8-7. *NetBeans New Project dialog box*

Assuming you want to test-drive NetBeans with a new Java project, choose Java under Categories and then Java Application under Projects. Click Next. You'll be asked for the name of your project and where you want it stored. Our example is everybody's favorite programming primer, HelloWorld. Enter the project name. The default location to store your projects is in your home directory, under the `NetBeansProjects` directory, which will be created for you, as shown in Figure 8-8. Click Finish.

A new Java application template will be created for you. Change the following:

```
//TODO code application logic here
```

to this:

```
System.out.println("Hello World!");
```

Figure 8-9 shows you the code body from your HelloWorld project.

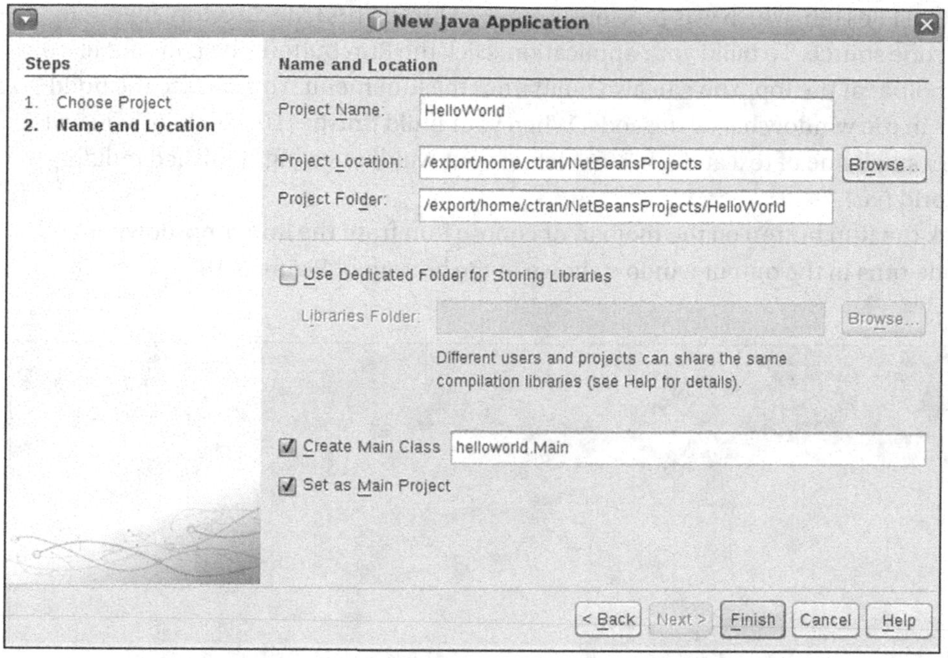

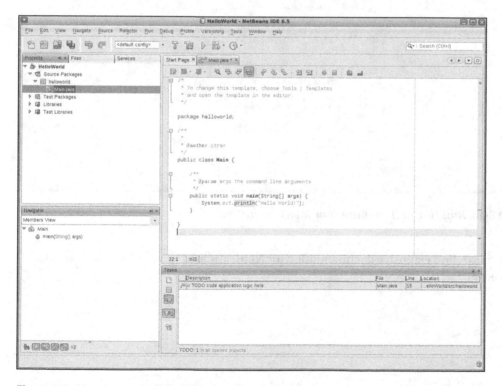

Figure 8-8. *NetBeans new Java project screen*

Figure 8-9. *New Java application template and code*

On the Files tab, which was previously empty, you will find the directory hierarchy of your code source. To build your application, click the Run button (the hammer icon) on the toolbar at the top. You can also build from the Run menu. You can see the build progress in the window below the code. When your build finishes successfully, you will also see a small line of text at the bottom left of your window saying "Finished building HelloWorld (jar)."

Click the Run button on the toolbar, or choose Run from the Run drop-down menu. Your code runs in the output window shown at the bottom of Figure 8-10.

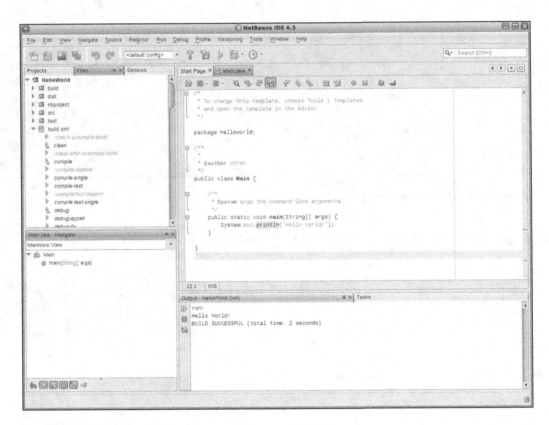

Figure 8-10. *Building and running your Java application*

You can find extensive documentation for NetBeans at http://www.netbeans.org/kb/index.html.

Using Subversion

Subversion is a version manager; it manages the recording, storing, cataloging, and retrieving of different versions of a file. If you are a developer, version control is essential to managing source code, scripts, and whatever else a developer needs to build. It enables many developers to access and modify one file, and it manages the storing of that file so all the modifications to the files are tracked and committed.

amp-dev includes the SUNWsvn package, which is Subversion 1.4.3. You need to set up Subversion first, before NetBeans can integrate with it. Specifically, you need to set up the repository, import your working files, and manage the access method.

Creating the Repository and Managing Files

To set up the repository, run this:

```
root@ender:# mkdir /opt/svn
root@ender:# svnadmin create --fs-type fsfs /opt/svn/repo
```

FSFS is a file system implementation from the folks who created Subversion. It is the alternative to storing your information in the BerkeleyDB database format. We use FSFS for small to medium-size projects. To read about the pros and cons of FSFS, see http://svn.collab.net/repos/svn/trunk/notes/fsfs.

You need to create the Subversion group and add any users who would need access to the repository to that group:

```
root@ender:# groupadd -g 99 svngrp
```

vi the /etc/group file, and add your user to the group. Or make the group the default group for the user.

Modify the ACL to allow group svngrp access to /opt/svn:

```
root@ender:# /usr/bin/chmod -R \n
A+group:svngrp:add_file/write_data/add_subdirectory/append_data:allow /opt/svn
```

You probably have some files that you'd like to put under Subversion control. For our example, we'll use files under the directory /var/tmp/project:

```
root@ender:# ls -l /var/tmp/project
```

```
total 3
-rw-r--r-- 1 root root 0 2009-01-30 23:32 bread.jar
-rw-r--r-- 1 root root 0 2009-01-30 23:32 ham.jar
-rw-r--r-- 1 root root 0 2009-01-30 23:32 lettuce.jar
-rw-r--r-- 1 root root 0 2009-01-30 23:32 mayo.jar
-rw-r--r-- 1 root root 0 2009-01-30 23:32 tomato.jar
```

Import your files into the repository. In this example, we are importing the files from
/var/tmp/project into a folder called hamsandwich:

```
root@ender:# svn import /var/tmp/project file:///opt/svn/repo/hamsandwich \n
-m "First import of Ham Sandwich project"
```

```
Adding          /var/tmp/project/lettuce.jar
Adding          /var/tmp/project/ham.jar
Adding          /var/tmp/project/mayo.jar
Adding          /var/tmp/project/bread.jar
Adding          /var/tmp/project/tomato.jar

Committed revision 1.
```

Show what's in the repository:

```
root@ender:# svn list file:///opt/svn/repo
```

```
hamsandwich/
```

```
root@ender:# svn list file:///opt/svn/repo/hamsandwich
```

```
bread.jar
ham.jar
lettuce.jar
mayo.jar
tomato.jar
```

checkout means make your own workspace a copy of what's currently in the repository. Note that we're doing this now as a non-root user. checkout makes a directory in our
current directory called hamsandwich, mirroring what's in the repository:

```
ctran@ender:$ svn checkout file:///opt/svn/repo/hamsandwich
```

```
A    hamsandwich/ham.jar
A    hamsandwich/lettuce.jar
A    hamsandwich/mayo.jar
A    hamsandwich/bread.jar
A    hamsandwich/tomato.jar
Checked out revision 1.
```

```
ctran@ender:$ ls ~/hamsandwich
```

```
bread.jar  lettuce.jar  ham.jar  mayo.jar  tomato.jar
```

Start working in your workspace. Using svn delete and svn add signals Subversion that you want these files deleted and added from the repository itself, when you commit the changes:

```
ctran@ender:~/hamsandwich$ svn delete mayo.jar
```

```
D        mayo.jar
```

```
ctran@ender:~/hamsandwich$ vi pesto.jar
```

Modify and save your pesto.jar.

```
ctran@ender:~/hamsandwich$ svn add pesto.jar
A        pesto.jar
```

This is the same as an svn move. We'll use ham.jar and prosciutto.jar as an example:

```
ctran@ender:~/hamsandwich$ svn move ham.jar prosciutto.jar
```

```
A        prosciutto.jar
D        ham.jar
```

```
ctran@ender:~/hamsandwich$ svn status
```

```
D     ham.jar
D     mayo.jar
A  +  prosciutto.jar
A     pesto.jar
```

The plus sign in the status output indicates that the item isn't merely scheduled for addition but scheduled for addition "with history."

You can show the difference between the working and base copies using svn diff:

```
ctran@ender:~/hamsandwich$ svn diff
```

```
Index: pesto.jar
```

svn update checks your current workspace against the latest revision in the repository. If other people have committed new changes to the repository since you checked out your files, you will be notified that a conflict has occurred. This is so that you do not overwrite other people's recent changes by committing your changes wholesale. In this example, there are no conflicts. Subversion is telling you that you are at revision 1, like the repository:

```
ctran@ender:~/hamsandwich$ svn update
```

```
At revision 1.
```

Committing your changes updates the repository and imprints a +1 revision number:

```
ctran@ender:~/hamsandwich$ svn commit -m "Italian style"
```

```
Deleting      ham.jar
Deleting      mayo.jar
Adding        prosciutto.jar
Adding        pesto.jar
Transmitting file data .
Committed revision 2.
```

If you get this message, check that the user who is doing the svn commit has access permission to the repository:

```
svn: Commit failed (details follow):
svn: Can't create directory '/opt/svn/repo/db/transactions/1-1.txn':
Permission denied
```

Using the Manage Access Control Method

We will now show how to set up a Subversion server that provides access to the repository over TCP/IP. This is the svn:// scheme. You can also tunnel svn under ssh, which is the
svn+ssh:// scheme for better security, if you have an environment where you need to enable
developers' laptops to connect to the Subversion server from the Internet, for example.

Simple svn Remote Access

Starting the Subversion server is very simple:

```
root@ender:# svnserve -d -r /opt/svn/repo
```

The -d switch tells svnserve to run as a daemon, and the -r switch specifies the full
path to the repository. svnserve runs on port 3690. You can see this by running pfiles on
the process svnserve; look at the sockets it has opened and the port number in the following code snippet:

```
root@ender:~# pfiles `pgrep svnserve`
```

```
3283:    svnserve -d -r /opt/svn/repo
  Current rlimit: 256 file descriptors
   0: S_IFCHR mode:0666 dev:291,0 ino:6815752 uid:0 gid:3 rdev:13,2
      O_RDONLY|O_LARGEFILE
      /devices/pseudo/mm@0:null
   1: S_IFCHR mode:0666 dev:291,0 ino:6815752 uid:0 gid:3 rdev:13,2
      O_WRONLY|O_CREAT|O_TRUNC|O_LARGEFILE
      /devices/pseudo/mm@0:null
   2: S_IFCHR mode:0666 dev:291,0 ino:6815752 uid:0 gid:3 rdev:13,2
      O_WRONLY|O_CREAT|O_TRUNC|O_LARGEFILE
      /devices/pseudo/mm@0:null
   3: S_IFSOCK mode:0666 dev:300,0 ino:55708 uid:0 gid:0 size:0
      O_RDWR
        SOCK_STREAM
        SO_REUSEADDR,SO_SNDBUF(49152),SO_RCVBUF(49152)
        sockname: AF_INET6 ::  port: 3690
```

To set Subversion for simple `svn` client remote access, modify the file `/opt/svn/repo/conf/svnserve.conf`.

Anonymous users get no access, and authenticated users get read/write access (read is implicit when you grant write). This is further refined to who can write to which directory in the file `/opt/svn/repo/conf/authz`:

```
anon-access = none
auth-access = write
```

Uncomment the following two lines:

```
password-db = passwd
authz-db = authz
```

Modify the file `/opt/svn/repo/conf/passwd`. This is where you set up users to access the repository:

```
[users]
ctran = toasted
trainee = grilled
```

Keep in mind that this user and password roster pertains to Subversion only. This is not the UNIX user `ctran` or user `trainee` in the `/etc/passwd` file. In fact, there is no such UNIX user `trainee` on the system.

Modify the file `/opt/svn/repo/conf/authz`. This is where you set up fine-grained privileges of who can read and write to which directory under the repository. This is called *path-based authorization*, and you can opt to skip this step if your development group is small or if you trust all authorized users to know what they are doing and not commit changes where they ought not.

```
[groups]
dev1 = ctran
intern = trainee
[/]
@dev1 = rw
* = r
```

In the previous code snippet, the `[groups]` code block says to create two groups, `dev1` and `intern`, and assign users to each group. In the next block, the directory location `[/]` (the root of the repository, not the root directory of the system) is readable and writable by group `dev1`; everybody else gets read-only access. As projects grow, you can grant read and write permissions to other groups, such as other directories, for example:

```
[/hamsandwich/experimental]
@intern = rw
```

This is all you need for simple svn access. From another host, you can check out a workspace, make modifications, and publish your changes. In the following example, UNIX user root from host dojo is checking out a workspace as Subversion user trainee. root is prompted for a password, which is grilled, which was what we set for user trainee in /opt/svn/repo/conf/passwd.

```
root@dojo:#svn --username trainee checkout svn://ender/hamsandwich
```

```
Authentication realm: <svn://ender:3690> 1c392b9b-7528-4ab7-f512-fb19ff8457c0
Password for 'trainee': grilled
A    hamsandwich/lettuce.jar
A    hamsandwich/pesto.jar
A    hamsandwich/prosciutto.jar
A    hamsandwich/bread.jar
A    hamsandwich/tomato.jar
Checked out revision 2.
```

The previous actions will allow you to access your Subversion repository remotely, as long as you are working in a private and safe network environment. If you are working remotely, you will need to set up your Subversion server to use svn+ssh.

Note Make sure the firewall protecting your Subversion server allows ssh access.

More Secure svn+ssh Access

The simple svn access depends on an svnserve server listening for connections from the svn client and authenticating using a user and password file defined in svnserve.conf. The svn+ssh scheme does not use svnserve at all; authentication is done by ssh. A remote user accesses the repository with her own UNIX credential, over the SSH connection. What is actually happening is that the user is spawning her own svnserve process, more precisely, svnserve -t for tunnel mode. This process is created and terminated for every invocation of svn+ssh:// Access control is via the permission on the repository. It is as if a user on the Subversion server is reading files locally.

To minimize having to create 20 different UNIX users on the Subversion server, you can create a single svn user and use that as a shared account for all remote users. You may wonder whether this will make it seem like every commit to the repository looks like it comes from user svn. The answer is, yes, it will, but there's a trick around that. Read on.

First, create the svn user on the Subversion server, which is host ender in our case:

```
root@ender:# useradd -u 102 -g 99 -m -d /export/home/svn -s \n
/usr/bin/bash -c "Subversion User" svn
```

From a remote server, access the repository. In our example, we are logged in on host dojo as UNIX user mysql. We use user mysql to avoid any confusion about SSH and root privileges:

```
root@dojo:# su - mysql
mysql@dojo$ id
```

```
uid=300(mysql) gid=300(mysql)
```

```
mysql@dojo$ svn list svn+ssh://svn@ender/opt/svn/repo/hamsandwich
```

```
Password: <password for svn on ender>
bread.jar
lettuce.jar
pesto.jar
prosciutto.jar
tomato.jar
```

You should note a few things about the previous command. The UNIX user mysql on host dojo is accessing the repository on host ender as user svn. Nothing special needs to be done on host ender, except to make sure that svn has a valid password and has read access to the repository on /opt/svn. All that user mysql needs is the svn password. Pay attention to the two slashes (//) and svn@ender, because frequent mistakes are forgetting the two forward slashes and forgetting to put in the user@host notation. You access the repository with the absolute path, not the relative path starting from the repository.

Every time you invoke svn+ssh://, you will be prompted for a password. Actually, every time the svn client makes a connection to the sunserve daemon, there is an authentication challenge. You don't notice this, because the client caches the password for you. With ssh, there is no caching going on.

To get around this problem, set up public/private keys for user svn to be automatically authenticated.

Note The following section is a short detour into the murky waters of SSH key generation. There are many vendor implementations of SSH on the market, each of them slightly different. There are SSHv1, SSHv2, RSA1, RSA, DSA keys. Putting them together in the right combination could possibly cause a normal person to tear his hair out. We'll describe the method to generate keys between two Solaris servers. If you are using a non-SUN platform for your svn remote client, read that vendor's SSH documentation carefully, and *make sure you understand it* before embarking.

Generating the Public/Private Key Pair

Our remote client is dojo. Our Subversion server is ender. We need to generate keys for user ctran@dojo, keep the private key in ~ctran/.ssh/id_dsa, and give the public key ~ctran/.ssh/ id_dsa.pub to svn@ender. Here's how we do that.

Generate the private and public key pair, and put them into the files id_dsa and id_dsa.pub in your home's .ssh directory:

```
ctran@dojo$ cd ~/.ssh
ctran@dojo$ ssh-keygen -t dsa
```

```
Generating public/private dsa key pair.
Enter file in which to save the key (/export/home/ctran/.ssh/id_dsa): [RETURN]
Enter passphrase (empty for no passphrase): <do not leave empty>
Enter same passphrase again: <do not leave empty>
Your identification has been saved in /export/home/ctran/.ssh/id_dsa.
Your public key has been saved in /export/home/ctran/.ssh/id_dsa.pub.
The key fingerprint is:
0a:52:de:ed:77:d3:3d:3a:fd:a7:b9:90:a2:3c:e2:bc ctran@dojo
```

You may have read elsewhere that in order to have a challenge-free login, you should use an empty passphrase. That's because you will be prompted for your passphrase (not your login password) when you initiate an SSH connection. An empty passphrase is an invitation for trouble. Go the extra step and do it right. We will show you another trick to overcome the passphrase challenge.

Keep the private key safe. Copy the public key to svn's .ssh directory on ender.

```
ctran@dojo$ scp id_dsa.pub svn@ender:/export/home/svn/.ssh/authorized_keys
```

```
Password: <password for svn on ender>
```

Now, try to ssh from dojo to ender and log in as user svn:

```
ctran@dojo$ ssh -l svn ender
```

```
Enter passphrase for key '/export/home/ctran/.ssh/id_dsa': <enter passphrase>
Last login: Sun Feb  1 00:42:27 2009 from dojo
svn@ender:~$
```

You are prompted for the passphrase you entered when you made the keys. Note that the passphrase is not the same thing as your UNIX password. To bypass this step, start a shell with ssh-agent, and use ssh-add to add the key to ssh-agent. You will be prompted for a passphrase only once.

```
ctran@dojo$ ssh-agent sh -c 'ssh-add < /dev/null && /usr/bin/bash'
```

```
Enter passphrase for /export/home/ctran/.ssh/id_dsa: <enter passphrase>
Identity added: /export/home/ctran/.ssh/id_dsa (/export/home/ctran/.ssh/id_dsa)
bash-3.00$
```

From the bash shell, from now on everything is smooth sailing. Notice you get no challenge of any kind:

```
bash-3.00$ ssh -l svn ender
```

```
Last login: Sun Feb  1 00:44:01 2009 from dojo
svn@ender:~$
```

Log out of ender. Try it with svn+ssh:

```
bash-3.00$ svn checkout svn+ssh://svn@ender/opt/svn/repo/hamsandwich
```

```
A    hamsandwich/lettuce.jar
A    hamsandwich/pesto.jar
A    hamsandwich/prosciutto.jar
A    hamsandwich/bread.jar
A    hamsandwich/tomato.jar
Checked out revision 2.
```

Modifying files, updating from the repository, and publishing and committing changes at this point are the same as with the simple svn remote client, except that you are tunneled under the safety of SSH.

But wait, did we not say there was a trick so not every commit looks like it came from user svn? Yes. And you implement that trick by making one more change to svn's .ssh/authorized_keys file. Right now, the content of that file looks like this:

```
ssh-dss [very long key] ctran@dojo.
```

Modify this line to look like this:

```
command="/usr/bin/svnserve -t --tunnel-user=ctran" ssh-dss \n
[very long key] ctran@dojo
```

The command directive tells ssh to run what's in the double quotes, instead of defaulting to svnserve -t. The --tunnel-user switch tells svnserve to take action as the named user, instead of user svn. Do not be mistaken—you are not connecting with the daemon svnserve. You are actually launching your own svnserve in tunnel mode. So, svn's .ssh/authorized_keys file could look like this:

```
command="/usr/bin/svnserve -t --tunnel-user=ctran" ssh-dss \n
[ctran's public key] ctran@dojo
command="/usr/bin/svnserve -t --tunnel-user=hfoxwell" ssh-dss \n
[hfoxwell's public key] harry@opsol01
```

Of course, user hfoxwell and everyone else who wants to use this method must generate their own public/private key pair, and the authorized_keys file has to include a line to identify the user and their public key.

■Caution You've modified the authorized_keys files for user svn to start svnserve every time ssh authenticates you. This will impair your ability to ssh into host ender as user svn normally. You won't be able to launch a shell; instead, you'll be greeted with something like this:

```
bash-3.00$ ssh -l svn ender
```

(success (1 2 (ANONYMOUS EXTERNAL) (edit-pipeline svndiff1 absent-entries)))

You are seeing the output from svnserve. In fact, you would see the same text if you open your browser to http://ender:3690 if the svnserve daemon were running and accepting connections on 3690. So, don't ssh -l svn to do any shell work.

Note When working with SSH, it helps to have logging turned on. `sshd` logging is not on by default. You need to modify your `/etc/syslog.conf` to add this line:

```
auth.info        ifdef(`LOGHOST', /var/log/authlog, @loghost)
```

Be careful editing this file. Tabs and whitespace matter:

```
auth.info<tab><tab><tab>ifdef(`LOGHOST', /var/log/authlog, @loghost)
```

Restart `syslog`:

```
root@ender:# svcadm restart system-log
```

`sshd` logs to `/var/log/authlog`. You might need the package SUNWspnego to resolve the problem you will see in `/var/log/authlog`. Basically, `sshd` is complaining that it's missing a GSS-API library, as you see from the following snippet from `authlog`:

```
Jan 31 21:45:41 ender sshd[4158]: [ID 800047 auth.info] Accepted publickey for
ctran from 192.168.0.5 port 33011 ssh2
Jan 31 22:05:23 ender sshd[4239]: [ID 685508 auth.info] libgss dlopen(/usr/lib/
gss/mech_spnego.so.1): ld.so.1: sshd: fatal: /usr/lib/gss/mech_spnego.so.1: ope
n failed: No such file or directory
```

You will find a Subversion SMF manifest, `subversion.xml`, along with all the source code on this book's page on the Apress web site. Put the manifest in `/var/svc/manifest/site`, import it, and start it. The following code block shows how to import the Subversion manifest, enable Subversion (make Subversion run as a daemon), and check the Subversion process ID and contract ID:

```
root@ender:# pwd
/var/svc/manifest/site
root@ender:# ls
```

```
subversion.xml  tomcat5.xml
```

```
root@ender:# svccfg import subversion.xml
root@ender:# svcs subversion
```

```
STATE          STIME    FMRI
disabled       17:25:34 svc:/site/subversion:default
```

```
root@ender:# svcadm enable subversion
root@ender:# svcs -pv subversion
```

```
STATE          NSTATE        STIME    CTID  FMRI
online         -             17:25:42   218 svc:/site/subversion:default
               17:25:42    4475 svnserve
```

This was by no means a comprehensive or advanced treatment of Subversion, which a rich and flexible tool that allows complex manipulation of the code base. You can find an excellent comprehensive guide, written by the Subversion developers and community, at http://svnbook.red-bean.com/.

Integrating NetBeans with Other Products

The following sections cover how to integrate NetBeans with Tomcat and Subversion.

Integrating with Tomcat

You may find it convenient to integrate your Tomcat server into the NetBeans IDE. This allows you to add Java application projects directly to Tomcat after debugging and running the project, in addition to stopping, starting, and debugging your Tomcat server from NetBeans.

In the example given in this chapter, you've configured Tomcat in a container. If you've followed the steps to start NetBeans on your desktop or laptop, your IDE is loaded in the global zone. As of this writing, there is no way to integrate NetBeans with a remote instance of Tomcat, running on a different server, even if that server is a nonglobal zone sharing the disk space with NetBeans. The reason for this is that the integration allows you to start and stop Tomcat from NetBeans; NetBeans runs in the global zone and will have no view into the process space of any other zone. Even if NetBeans can access the zone's /var/apache/tomcat and /usr/apache/tomcat directories, there's no way NetBeans can launch a process that belongs to the web zone itself. So, for the examples to follow, you will need to repeat the steps to start Tomcat in the global zone. That is, you'll need to modify the user profile for the user webserved and make sure that user has access permission to /var/apache and the right privilege. Then you'll need to modify server.xml, generate keys for SSL connection, and import the Tomcat manifest. You'll be working with the NetBeans IDE and Tomcat server running in the global zone.

Start the NetBeans IDE. On the left column, select the Services tab. Right-click the Server icon, and select Add Server from the drop-down menu. Choose the Tomcat 5.5 server, add a descriptive name, and click Next, as shown in Figure 8-11.

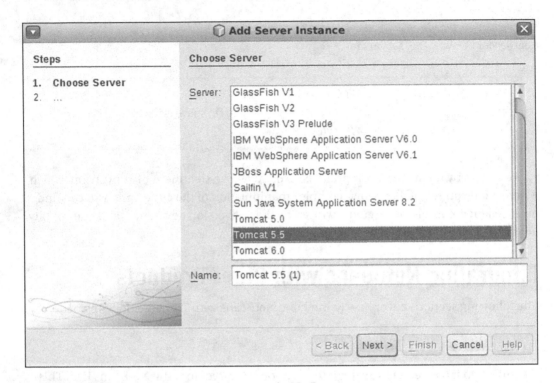

Figure 8-11. *Adding a Tomcat server instance in NetBeans*

Recall that the SUNWtcat package splits the bin and conf directories between /usr/apache/tomcat and /var/apache/tomcat. CATALINA_HOME is /usr/apache/tomcat, but NetBeans expects to be able to write into the conf directory as well. You need to make a symbolic link, linking the conf directory under CATALINA_HOME. You've already made everything under /var/apache/tomcat writable by webserved when you set up Tomcat:

```
root@ender:# ln -s /var/apache/tomcat/conf /usr/apache/tomcat/conf
```

Specify /usr/apache/tomcat as CATALINA_HOME. For CATALINA_BASE, any directory writable by NetBeans will do; we keep ours in our home directory. Select the box Create User If It Does Not Exist, as shown in Figure 8-12. Then click Finish. After this, you will see a Tomcat 5 instance on the left side of the IDE screen, under Server.

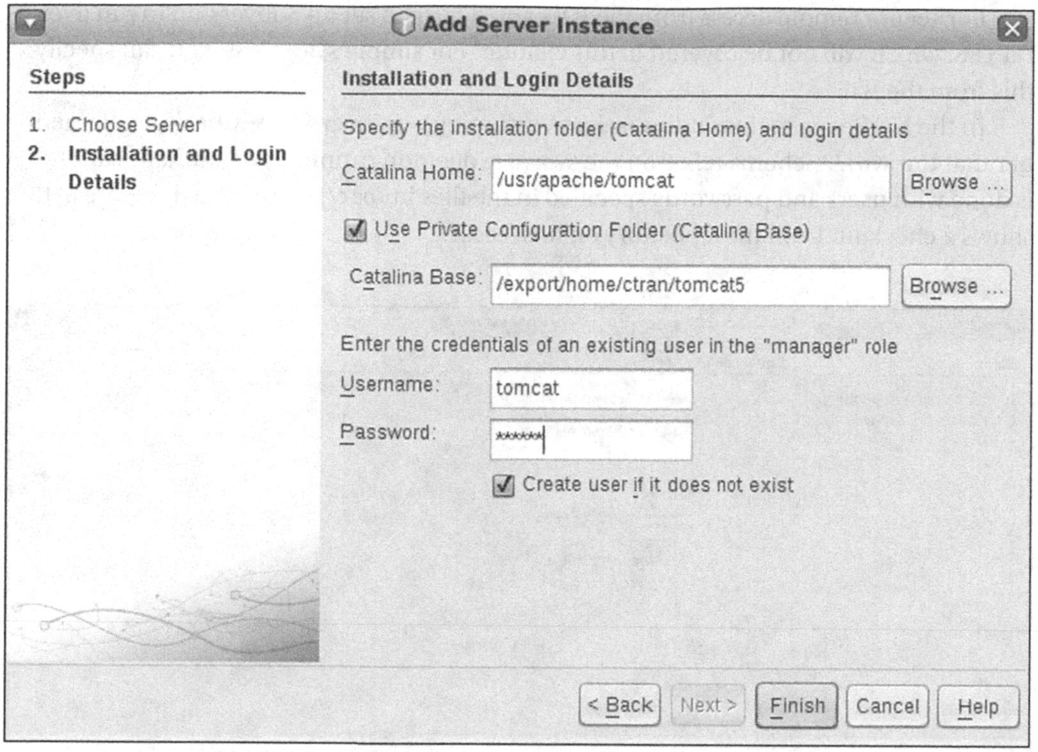

Figure 8-12. *Specifying Tomcat directory locations*

Integrating with Subversion

So, you've worked very hard to create a working Subversion repository, accessible with two schemas, `svn://` and `svn+ssh://`. You are tired from schlepping files back and forth. You'd rather check out and commit your code from within your IDE. The good news is you can do that, and it's a simple process. The bad news is that because of bug 6192335 (at the time of this writing), a file critical to the public/private key exchange for GUI tools is missing.

■**Note** You can view, and file, bugs against OpenSolaris at `http://defect.opensolaris.org`. Developers of OpenSolaris consider the OpenSolaris code base distinct from its predecessor, Solaris 10. Bugs against Solaris 10 can be viewed and filed at `http://bugs.opensolaris.org`. This bug is actually filed against the Solaris 10 code. It hasn't made it to the OpenSolaris defect tracker yet. You can see bug 6192335 at `http://bugs.opensolaris.org/bugdatabase/view_bug.do?bug_id=6192335`.

For secure remote access from the IDE, you'll have to set up Subversion to run over HTTPS, which will not be covered in this chapter. For simple svn access, you can specify this from the IDE.

In the NetBeans main window, select Versioning ➤ Subversion ➤ Checkout. Remember that the svn:// schema relies on the svnserve daemon running, and authentication is done with users and passwords specified in the files in /opt/svn/repo/conf. Figure 8-13 shows a checkout from the repository on host ender.

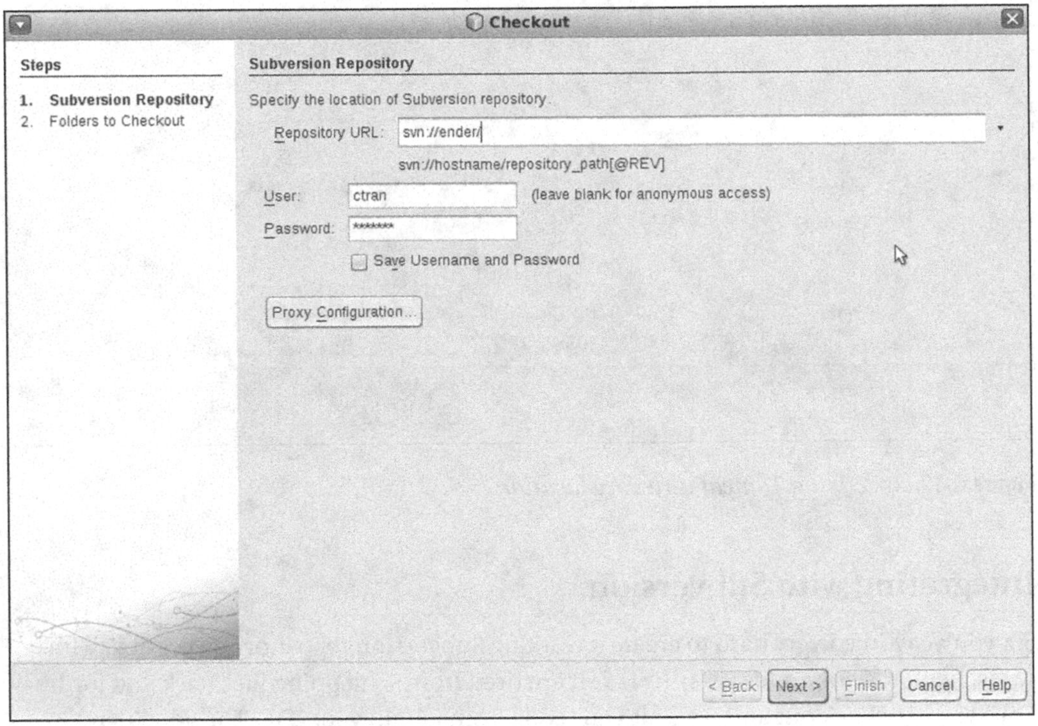

Figure 8-13. *Specifying the location of the Subversion repository and logging in*

You'll get a screen prompting you for the repository folder. Click the Browse button, and select hamsandwich. Figure 8-14 shows this. Click OK to return to the previous screen.

Choose the local folder where you want to put your new directory. In this example, hamsandwich will be created under the NetBeansProjects directory. Check the box Scan for NetBeans Project After Checkout, as shown in Figure 8-15, and then click Finish.

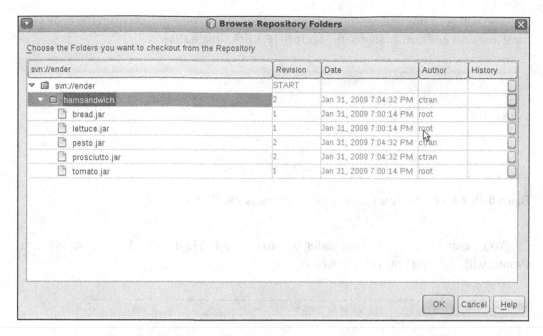

Figure 8-14. *Selecting the directory to check out*

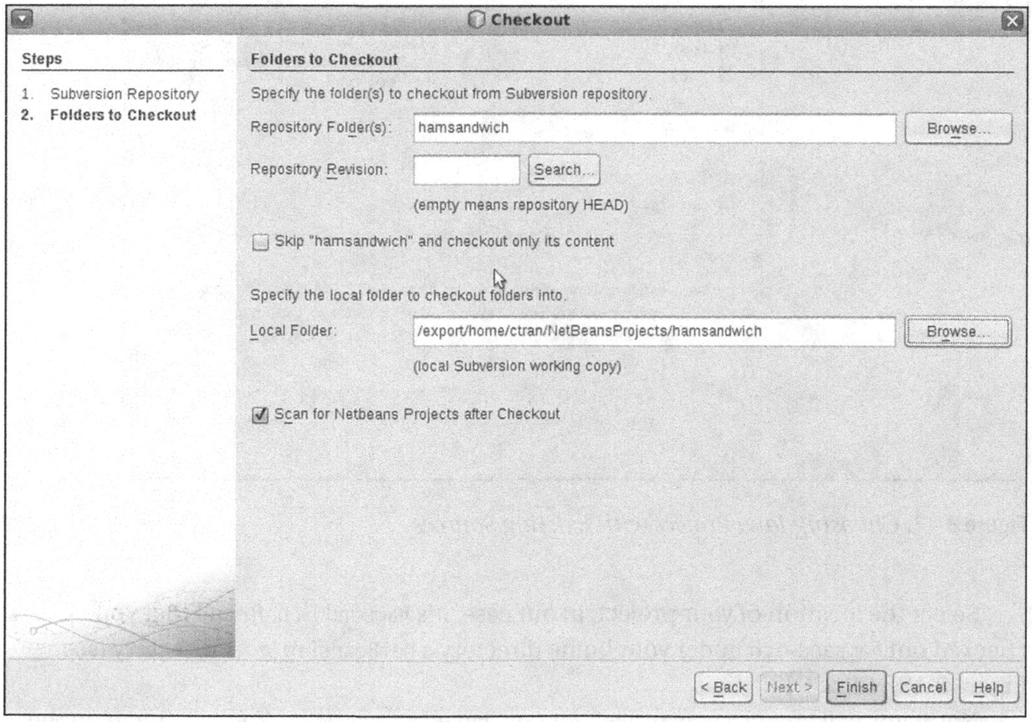

Figure 8-15. *Specifying the local directory and checking out*

You will get a box asking whether you want to create a new project from the code you have just checked out, as shown in Figure 8-16. Click Create Project.

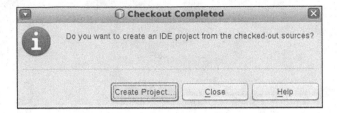

Figure 8-16. *Creating a new project from code you've checked out*

You'll come to a New Project dialog box, as shown in Figure 8-17. Select Java and Java Project with Existing Sources. Click Next.

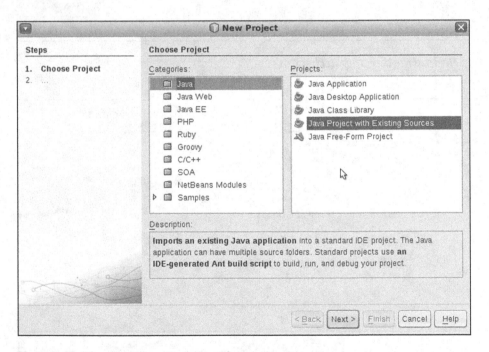

Figure 8-17. *Choosing Java Project with Existing Sources*

Select the location of your project; in our case, it's hamsandwich. Recall that you checked out hamsandwich under your home directory's NetBeansProjects directory (see Figure 8-18). Click OK.

NetBeans will create a new project for you, called hamsandwich. You will find it on the Projects tab. Now you can start working with your local copy of hamsandwich files inside NetBeans. You can see your new project and its files on the left side of Figure 8-19.

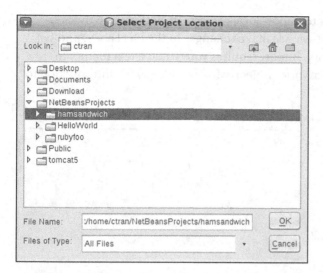

Figure 8-18. *Selecting the location of files for your new project*

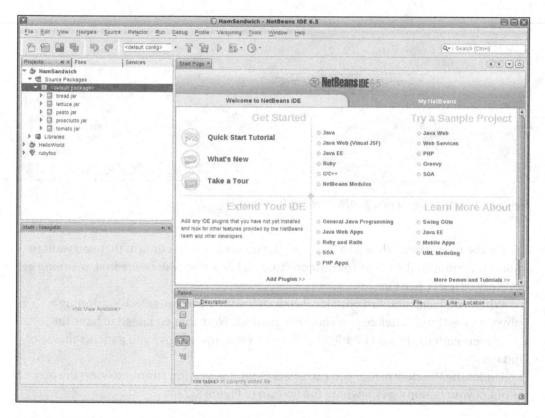

Figure 8-19. *Selecting the location of files for your new project*

You can go through similar steps to import local projects in NetBeans to the Subversion repository. Keep in mind that svn add makes changes to the local copy, and svn import makes changes to the repository. Import requires you to add a text memo. In Figure 8-20 we're importing our HelloWorld project, which I wrote in my introduction to NetBeans. Click Next.

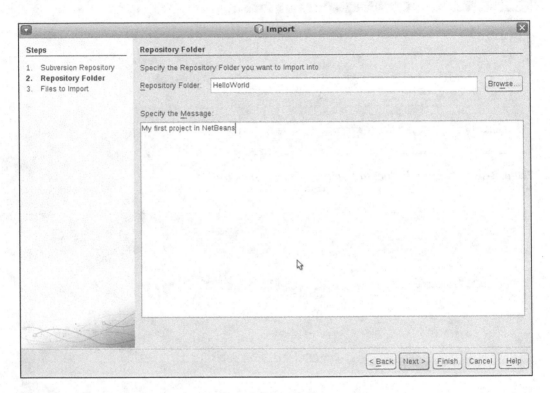

Figure 8-20. *Importing a new project into Subversion*

On the next screen, shown in Figure 8-21, you are asked to confirm that you want to import (or commit) these files to the repository and how they will be created, meaning as directory or text. Click Finish.

When you have modified your local copy of the files, you can select Versioning ➤ Subversion ➤ Update, before you choose to commit. Note that you need to have the files underneath the project highlighted, before NetBeans will give you a menu choice of Update.

Under the Window menu, you can select Output ➤ Version Output to view the text output of your actions, as shown on the bottom of Figure 8-22.

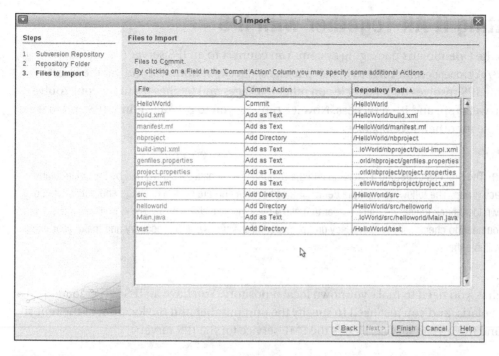

Figure 8-21. *Verifying the files you want to import*

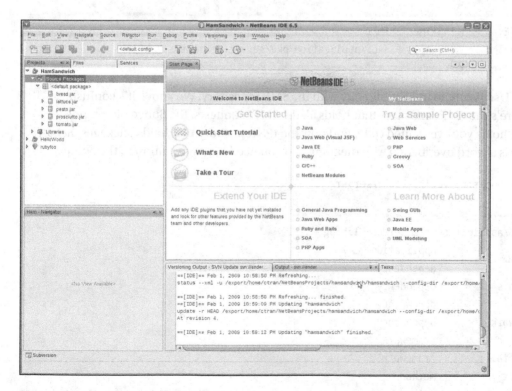

Figure 8-22. *Text in the output window*

Putting It All Together with IPS

IPS is the OpenSolaris packaging system. You connect to an IPS server (the default is
http://pkg.opensolaris.org) to install packages, check for updates, and get the latest
version. IPS resolves dependencies on other packages and fetches them for you. You've
built a web app, and it's a success. Now it's time for you to package it into IPS and make it
available for other developers.

> **Note** The process of getting a package into the OpenSolaris repository is governed by the OpenSolaris
> advocacy group. The following example demonstrates how to generate such a package and publish it into
> your own local package server. But in order to make a package available from http://pkg.opensolaris.
> org, you need to check with the advocacy group. You can run your own IPS repository and make your pack-
> age available there.

First, you need to make your own local repository. You have an IPS server loaded on
OpenSolaris, and you just need to specify the port number and the location of the repository and fire up the service. Here's the SMF service for the IPS server:

```
root@ender:# svcs pkg/server
```

```
STATE          STIME    FMRI
disabled       Jan_31   svc:/application/pkg/server:default
```

Use svccfg to interact directly with the SMF repository. We know, it's confusing.
There's the SMF repository that holds all the SMF manifests, the Subversion repository
that holds your versioned code, and now the IPS repository that holds packages. *Repository* is a word overloaded with meanings, so you need to pay attention to the context.

```
root@ender:# svccfg -s pkg/server
```

```
svc:/application/pkg/server> listpg
pkg            application
fs             dependency
autofs         dependency
ntp            dependency
network        dependency
startd         framework
general        framework
start          method
stop           method
```

```
tm_common_name   template
svc:/application/pkg/server> listprop pkg
svc:/application/pkg/server> setprop pkg/port = astring: "8000"
svc:/application/pkg/server> setprop pkg/inst_root = astring: /var/tmp/localrepo"
svc:/application/pkg/server> listprop pkg/*
pkg/content_root     astring   /usr/share/lib/pkg
pkg/log_access       astring   none
pkg/log_errors       astring   stderr
pkg/mirror           boolean   false
pkg/proxy_base       astring
pkg/readonly         boolean   false
pkg/socket_timeout   count     60
pkg/threads          count     10
pkg/port             astring   8000
pkg/inst_root        astring   /var/tmp/localrepo
svc:/application/pkg/server> exit
```

In the previous code snippet, listpg lists the property group, and the setprop commands set the port to 8000 and the location of the IPS repository to /var/tmp/localrepo.

Commit your changes, and start the IPS package server, as shown here:

```
root@ender:# svcadm refresh pkg/server
root@ender:# svcadm enable pkg/server
root@ender:# svcs -pv pkg/server
```

```
STATE       NSTATE        STIME    CTID    FMRI
online      -             11:50:11         213 svc:/application/pkg/server:default
            11:50:11      3855 pkg.depotd
```

Start a package:

```
ctran@ender:~/NetBeansProjects$ pkgsend -s http://localhost:8000 open ham_pkg@1
```

```
export PKG_TRANS_ID=1233598199_pkg%3A%2Fham_pkg%401%2C5.11%3A20090202T180959Z
```

```
ctran@ender:~/NetBeansProjects$ pkgsend -s http://localhost:8000 \n
add dir mode=0555 owner=root group=bin path=hamsandwich
```

```
pkgsend: No transaction ID specified in $PKG_TRANS_ID
```

You are getting the pkgsend error because the pkgsend open command gets back a variable, $PKG_TRANSACTION_ID. You need to include this ID with the rest of the add dir and add file commands to tell the repository that you mean to add it to a package you've just opened, identified by the publication transaction ID $PKG_TRANSACTION_ID. The way to do this is with the built-in shell command eval. Note the backticks.

```
ctran@ender:~/NetBeansProjects$ eval `pkgsend -s http://localhost:8000 \n
open ham_pkg@1`
```

Now, add files. Note that the path value is relative to your current path:

```
ctran@ender:~/NetBeansProjects$ pkgsend -s http://localhost:8000 \n
add dir mode=0555 owner=root group=bin path=hamsandwich
ctran@ender:~/NetBeansProjects$ pkgsend -s http://localhost:8000 \n
add file hamsandwich/bread.jar mode=0555 owner=root group=bin \n
 path=hamsandwich/bread.jar
ctran@ender:~/NetBeansProjects$ pkgsend -s http://localhost:8000 \n
add file hamsandwich/lettuce.jar mode=0555 owner=root group=bin \n
path=hamsandwich/lettuce.jar
ctran@ender:~/NetBeansProjects$ pkgsend -s http://localhost:8000 \n
add file hamsandwich/pesto.jar mode=0555 owner=root group=bin \n
path=hamsandwich/pesto.jar
ctran@ender:~/NetBeansProjects$ pkgsend -s http://localhost:8000 \n
add file hamsandwich/prosciutto.jar mode=0555 owner=root group=bin \n
path=hamsandwich/prosciutto.jar
ctran@ender:~/NetBeansProjects$ pkgsend -s http://localhost:8000 \n
add file hamsandwich/tomato.jar mode=0555 owner=root group=bin \n
path=hamsandwich/tomato.jar
```

Add a description and close the package:

```
ctran@ender:~/NetBeansProjects/hamsandwich$ pkgsend -s http://localhost:8000 \n
add set name=description value="Hamsandwich Example"
ctran@ender:~/NetBeansProjects/hamsandwich$ pkgsend -s http://localhost:8000 close
```

```
PUBLISHED
pkg:/ham_pkg@1,5.11:20090202T182929Z
```

You can see the packages you've published to your local repository by opening your browser to http://localhost:8000, as shown in Figure 8-23.

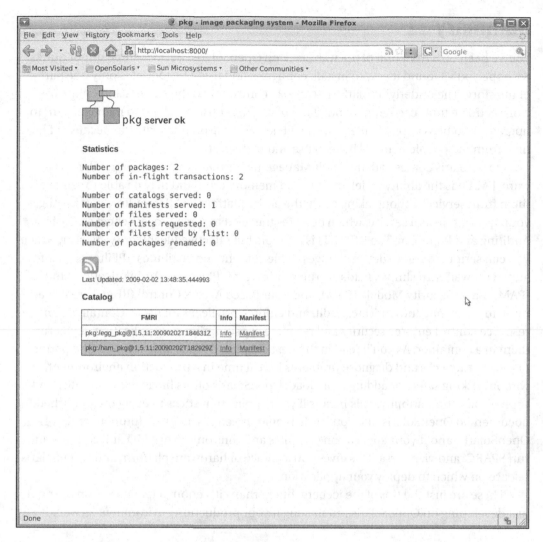

Figure 8-23. *Viewing the IPS packages you've just published*

But now you've made a mistake, and you want to modify or delete one of the packages you've recently published to your local IPS server. Unfortunately, there are no tools to do that as yet. If you want, you can muck around in the repository, /var/tmp/localrepo as we've specified it. You'll have to edit the catalog and index files, plus everything else that's been written there. This area is not well documented, so play here with caution. The tools to better manage your package are coming soon in a future release of OpenSolaris, or so we're told. Watch the IPS development space at http://opensolaris.org/os/project/pkg.

Summary

You've been on a brief tour of the web stack on OpenSolaris. Besides some minor quirks, we hope you've found it easy to install, configure, and use. The toolset is only one part of the story. The underlying platform can also contribute to the success and failure of a project. The tools can be good, but if the platform is unstable, hard to manage, hard to upgrade, and hard to patch, the project will not last long on that platform because of hostility from the people who will have to use and manage it.

OpenSolaris comes with the Fault Management Architecture. On particular hardware, FMA has the ability to detect CPU and memory error and may be able to remove them from service without taking down the entire platform. SMF monitors and manages your application as a service, which obviates the need to run a process checker. Basic Auditing and Reporting Tools (BART) is a simple but effective file integrity checker, which you can script around to detect changes in file content and attributes. IPFilter is an integrated firewall with simple, readable rules in `ipf.conf`. Pluggable Authentication Module (PAM), Basic Security Module (PAM), and Role-Based Access Control (RBAC) are three more toolsets that authenticate, audit, and enforce privileges for users. Containers and resource control enforce security and resource consumption per application, if you run them in a container. As you'll read in the next chapter, DTrace allows you to find performance bottlenecks and diagnose problems in real time in a production environment, without risking safety or adding more load. OpenSolaris offers binary compatibility and source code compatibility. This means if your application sticks to using the published, documented OpenSolaris API, your code is guaranteed to run on all future releases of OpenSolaris; and if your application compiles and runs on x86 or AMD, it'll compile and run SPARC, and vice versa. This gives you a choice of hardware platform and OpenSolaris release on which to deploy your application.

These are just the tips of the iceberg, but perhaps it's enough for you to consider not just developing on OpenSolaris but making it your production environment as well.

## CHAPTER 9

Innovative OpenSolaris Features

Code that has been honed sharp with decades of diligence by scientists and engineers will now be open to both industry and individuals...Open to the teacher. Open to the student. Every serious scientist or engineer will want to stand on the shoulder of this giant. OpenSolaris is the cure for the common computer.

—Dennis Clarke, Director, Blastwave

In the previous chapters, we covered much of the basics of installing and configuring OpenSolaris and using its unique features to develop AMP stack–based web applications. But there is so much more to explore. In this chapter, we'll introduce you to the DTrace observability tool for monitoring and discovering application and OS behavior. Then we'll wrap up with a look at a selection of other OpenSolaris features such as the Distribution Constructor, Tracker, Device Driver Utility, SongBird, and some key educational resources.

DTrace

DTrace (for Dynamic Trace) is perhaps one of the most prominent and talked-about features of Solaris 10 and OpenSolaris. It was introduced in Solaris 10 and was the first OS component to be released under an open source license in the OpenSolaris project in 2005. It's now an integral part of other operating systems as well, notably Apple's OS X Leopard (10.5) release. Because of its great utility and extensibility, DTrace has been extended to support development tools such as Java, Ruby, Python, and Perl, and database programs such as PostgreSQL and MySQL. This section gives you very brief overview of DTrace, with just enough to get you started. But remember that DTrace is only one tool for discovering and diagnosing system problems; you should still familiarize yourself, if you're not already, with more traditional tools such as `prstat`, `vmstat`, and `iostat`. The *Solaris Performance and Tools* book by McDougall, Mauro, and Gregg listed in

Appendix A is a great reference for this. These tools help you identify a general problem area; DTrace then helps you to quickly narrow and identify the specific issue.

DTrace refers to both the observability hooks in the OpenSolaris kernel and to the scripting language used to interface with those kernel hooks. The OS kernel must be instrumented for total observability, and there must be a programming interface to that instrumentation accessible to the system administrator. The goals of such a technology should include the following:

- Integration into the OS kernel, with no installation or activation required

- Real-time visibility of all OS actions, including application execution and hardware interface

- Usability on production systems without performance impact

- Safety when in use; no change of data and no risk of halting or crashing system

- No effect when not in use

In production server environments, diagnosing application or OS performance issues is often limited by a reluctance to interrupt processing. Administrators therefore resort to potentially incomplete or ineffective methods of discovering problems; Table 9-1 shows some of these methods and their drawbacks.

Table 9-1. *Diagnosing Problems on Production Systems*

Method	Drawbacks
Building a duplicate hardware/software environment to reproduce problem	Expensive, time-consuming, may not duplicate the problem
Installing a debug version of kernel or application	Requires processing interruption, potentially changes behavior of what's being observed
Monitoring OS or application directly with kernel or application debugger tool	Potential for corrupting data or crashing OS and/or application

Because DTrace is already integrated into your production OpenSolaris kernel, you don't have to install or change anything to use it.

The DTrace architecture consists of the DTrace Virtual Machine embedded within the OpenSolaris kernel; several sets of providers that make kernel probes and data available to the DTrace VM; and several consumers that collect, aggregate, and present data on kernel and application actions and events. Figure 9-1 shows the general structure of DTrace within the OpenSolaris kernel.

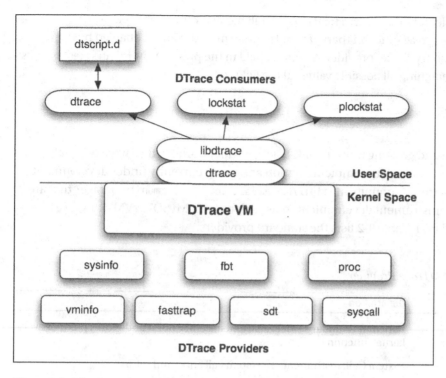

Figure 9-1. *The DTrace architecture*

You access data about your kernel and applications using a high-level, C-like scripting language called D (but commonly referred to as *DTrace*). This language lets you access the kernel variables made visible through the DTrace kernel probes; you can create your own user variables, define character strings, define and populate arrays, and summarize and aggregate probe data. In the later examples, you'll see how to use DTrace to characterize the behavior of your system.

Probes

A *probe* is a point of instrumentation in the kernel. OpenSolaris currently has more than 60,000 such points that are made available by the many providers (the command dtrace -l will list all probes for your system). Every probe has a four-part structured character string that indicates its provider, kernel module, functional purpose, and unique identifier (probes also have unique identifying numbers):

```
provider:module:function:name
```

For example, `fbt:ufs:ufs_read:entry` is the full name for the probe that instruments the entry into the `ufs_read` function (part of the `ufs` kernel module) and is enabled by the `fbt` (Function Boundary Trace) provider. An empty field in the probe, as in `fbt:ufs::entry`, acts as a wildcard matching all possible values of the field.

Providers

There is a large and growing number of DTrace providers—those that were originally included in the initial DTrace implementation and many currently under development by the OpenSolaris community at `http://opensolaris.org/os/community/dtrace/` that are being added to instrument development tools such as Java, MySQL, xVM, Ruby, TCP, JavaScript, and Perl. Table 9-2 lists the standard providers.

Table 9-2. *Some DTrace Providers*

Provider Name	Description
fbt	Function Boundary Trace, instruments entry point and return point of every kernel function
syscall	System Call, instruments all system call entry and return
profile	Instruments interrupts for collecting data over time intervals
vminfo	Instruments kernel memory actions
pid	Instruments application's function entry and return via its process ID
proc	Instruments process and LWP creation and termination
io	Instruments disk I/O events
sysinfo	Instruments kernel statistics
sched	Instruments CPU scheduling
plockstat	Instruments user synchronization events
lockstat	Instruments kernel synchronization events; used to monitor lock contention

DTrace Scripts

As you'll see later, you can activate full DTrace probes from the command line using a *single line* of DTrace interpreter code. But first let's look at the structure of typical DTrace scripts.

Note There is a collection of example DTrace scripts in the OpenSolaris /usr/demo/dtrace directory; these are the example scripts discussed in the Solaris Dynamic Tracing Guide at http://docs.sun.com/app/docs/doc/817-6223. Also note that DTrace is essentially the same on OpenSolaris as on Solaris 10, so the Solaris documentation is fully relevant.

Each DTrace script usually consists of the following:

- *DTrace interpreter path*: #!/usr/sbin/dtrace -s

- *pragma*: Used to control DTrace execution; for example, quieting unwanted output or controlling the script's output buffer size

- *probe name*: The name of the probe to activate

- *predicate*: Defines conditions for actions, such as specifying counter variable test values or selecting process IDs or process names

- *action*: If the predicate is satisfied, the probe collects and records monitored data in the consumer's buffer and then formats and reports output according to specified syntax.

Note DTrace is intended for use by the system administrator and by system performance professionals, not by unprivileged end users. As such, it requires root privileges (more specifically, it requires dtrace_kernel, dtrace_proc, and dtrace_user privileges). Also note that by default DTrace cannot be used in a local zone, even by root, unless these privileges are enabled. Even then DTrace's scope is limited to the local zone.

A Simple Example

Here's a simple example of a DTrace script, example1.d:

```
#!/usr/sbin/dtrace -s
/* this is example1.d */
fbt:zfs:zfs_write:entry
{
trace(execname);
}
```

Note the `.d` extension, which is not required but is helpful to indicate the nature of the file. This script accesses the `zfs_write` function call probe to list any processes that may be writing to the local ZFS file system during the execution of the script. Note the C syntax for the comment. When executed as shown in Figure 9-2, DTrace activates the probe and watches for any entries to the `zfs_write` function. For the first run (terminated with a ^C after waiting a few seconds), no such writes were reported. For the second run, in another terminal on the system we saved a file we were editing with `vim` and then copied it to another directory; the DTrace script reports that the probe has "fired" (that is, it detected an entry into the `zfs_write` function), and it lists the two program names (`execname`) that called `zfs_write`: `vim` and `cp`. Even such a simple script can be used to identify processes that periodically wake up and write data to the file system.

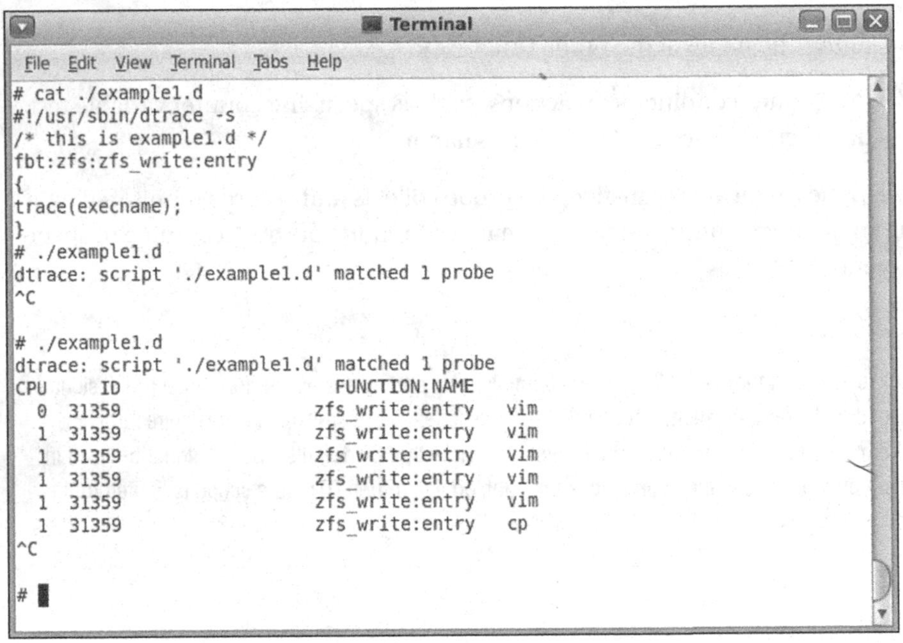

```
# cat ./example1.d
#!/usr/sbin/dtrace -s
/* this is example1.d */
fbt:zfs:zfs_write:entry
{
trace(execname);
}
# ./example1.d
dtrace: script './example1.d' matched 1 probe
^C

# ./example1.d
dtrace: script './example1.d' matched 1 probe
CPU     ID                    FUNCTION:NAME
  0   31359                   zfs_write:entry    vim
  1   31359                   zfs_write:entry    vim
  1   31359                   zfs_write:entry    vim
  1   31359                   zfs_write:entry    vim
  1   31359                   zfs_write:entry    vim
  1   31359                   zfs_write:entry    cp
^C

#
```

Figure 9-2. *A simple DTrace example*

DTrace Aggregations

DTrace includes language features for automatically creating and populating counter arrays, called *aggregations*. A simple example, `writesbycmd.d`, taken from the `/usr/demo/dtrace` directory, illustrates this:

```
syscall::write:entry
{
@counts[execname] = count();
}
```

This script watches all entries to the write system call, classifies and counts them according to the processes that made the calls, and accumulates the number of calls for each process in the counts array. Figure 9-3 shows the result of a sample run of this script over a period of a few seconds. It reveals the processes that write to the file system and how many times they've done so while the script was running (recall that you terminate this script with ^C at which point it outputs the formatted contents of the counts array).

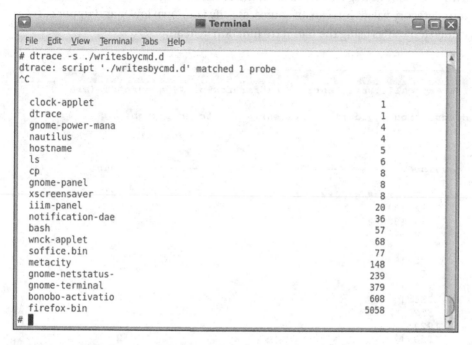

Figure 9-3. *A DTrace aggregation example*

Note that in this example the firefox executable is quite busy writing to the file system, presumably writing to its cache or downloading content. Such activity might be worth investigating further if your system or application is experiencing performance problems.

It's worth reviewing the other sample scripts in the demo directory; they illustrate how to get average, minimum, and maximum values for aggregations. When investigating system problems using these techniques, you need to watch for outliers or extreme behaviors of your OS or your applications such as excessive CPU usage, I/O activity, context switches, and so on.

Another use of DTrace's aggregation features uses its *quantize* function to create a frequency graph of the data collected (Figure 9-4). In this example, adapted from a DTrace one-liner, the sizes of the writes performed by firefox are tabulated. We see that during the brief few seconds during which we ran the script, firefox had quite a bit of write activity, including more than 100 4Kb writes and a similar number of 1-byte writes. It's worth asking what it's doing! Notice that this quantize tabulation automatically generates "power-of-two" frequency categories by default, where each category value is double that of the previous category value; you can, of course, specify your own lower and upper category range and step values using the lquantize function instead.

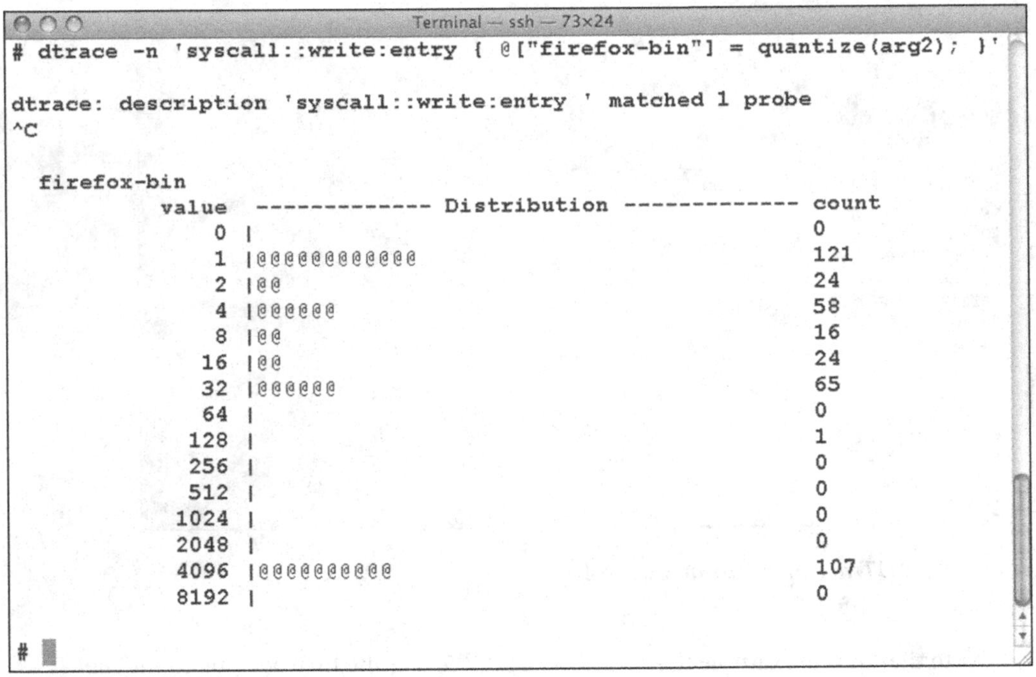

```
# dtrace -n 'syscall::write:entry { @["firefox-bin"] = quantize(arg2); }'

dtrace: description 'syscall::write:entry ' matched 1 probe
^C

  firefox-bin
           value  ------------- Distribution ------------- count
               0 |                                         0
               1 |@@@@@@@@@@@@                             121
               2 |@@                                       24
               4 |@@@@@@                                   58
               8 |@@                                       16
              16 |@@                                       24
              32 |@@@@@@                                   65
              64 |                                         0
             128 |                                         1
             256 |                                         0
             512 |                                         0
            1024 |                                         0
            2048 |                                         0
            4096 |@@@@@@@@@@                               107
            8192 |                                         0
#
```

Figure 9-4. *Using the DTrace* quantize *function*

DTrace Community Contributions

The OpenSolaris community, especially active developers such as Brendan Gregg (http://www.brendangregg.com/), has contributed a large collection of highly useful tools for exploiting DTrace. In particular, the DTrace Toolkit and the DTrace OneLiners (Figure 9-5, http://www.brendangregg.com/dtrace.html) provide great examples for both learning and day-to-day system monitoring.

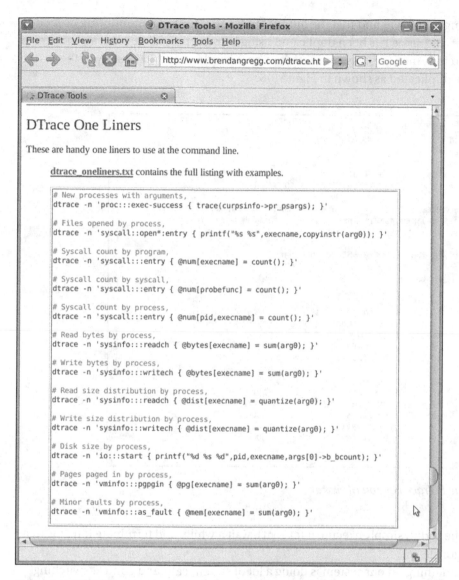

Figure 9-5. *The DTrace one-liner scripts*

The DTrace Toolkit, written by Brendan Gregg and licensed under the CDDL, includes more than 200 DTrace scripts and shell scripts that call DTrace. There are scripts for monitoring CPU events, disk I/O events, and network events; as well as scripts for observing function calls in programming languages such as Java, JavaScript, Perl, PHP, Python, Ruby, Tcl, and UNIX shells.

Interestingly, you will find that the output of several traditional monitoring programs such as vmstat and snoop has been duplicated using DTrace, providing more accurate or more detailed information on system activity. For example, the functionality of the vmstat tool has been duplicated as shown in Figure 9-6.

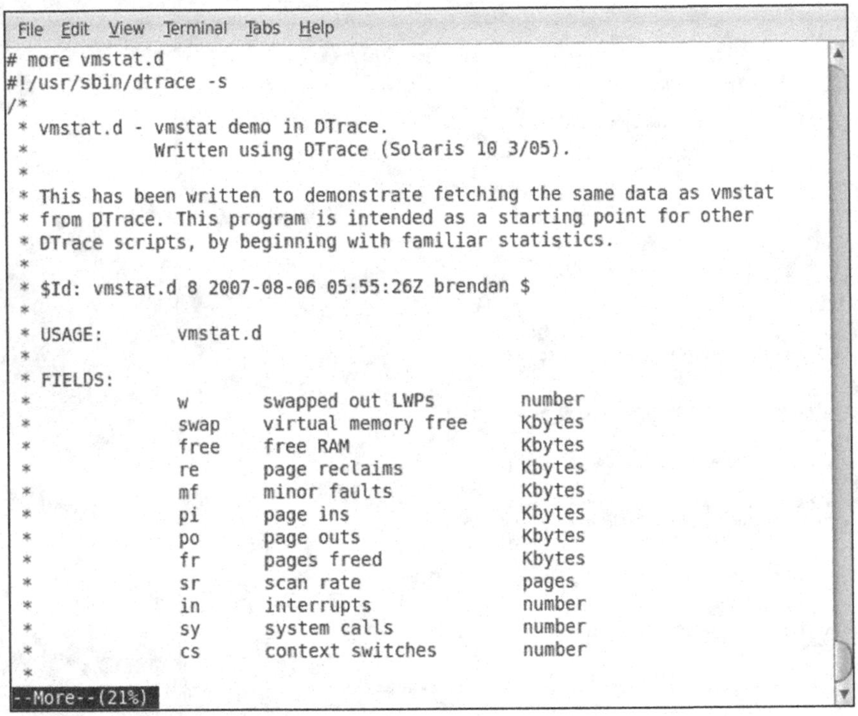

```
File  Edit  View  Terminal  Tabs  Help
# more vmstat.d
#!/usr/sbin/dtrace -s
/*
 * vmstat.d - vmstat demo in DTrace.
 *            Written using DTrace (Solaris 10 3/05).
 *
 * This has been written to demonstrate fetching the same data as vmstat
 * from DTrace. This program is intended as a starting point for other
 * DTrace scripts, by beginning with familiar statistics.
 *
 * $Id: vmstat.d 8 2007-08-06 05:55:26Z brendan $
 *
 * USAGE:        vmstat.d
 *
 * FIELDS:
 *        w       swapped out LWPs         number
 *        swap    virtual memory free      Kbytes
 *        free    free RAM                 Kbytes
 *        re      page reclaims            Kbytes
 *        mf      minor faults             Kbytes
 *        pi      page ins                 Kbytes
 *        po      page outs                Kbytes
 *        fr      pages freed              Kbytes
 *        sr      scan rate                pages
 *        in      interrupts               number
 *        sy      system calls             number
 *        cs      context switches         number
 *
--More--(21%)
```

Figure 9-6. *The DTrace version of* vmstat

To use the script, simply execute it (as root), wait a while, and terminate it using ^C, as shown in Figure 9-7.

Wow. Something on our system is doing a lot of system calls and context switching! We can find that out by running the syscallbyproc.d script, as shown in Figure 9-8.

We can see from this script that Xorg (the X Window System) is churning away at something, and there's an awful lot of find and ls activity, possibly a user searching the entire system. In fact, we've been running the Java 2D demo in another window in addition to searching for files; the DTrace script has identified the program names for us. You can use the syscallbypid.d script to identify these programs' process ID numbers.

DTrace is a scripting language that must be learned, practiced, and used along with other monitoring tools. Once you become familiar with it, you will have a powerful utility for discovering application and OS performance issues.

```
File  Edit  View  Terminal  Tabs  Help
*
* FIELDS:
*           w       swapped out LWPs      number
*           swap    virtual memory free   Kbytes
*           free    free RAM              Kbytes
*           re      page reclaims         Kbytes
*           mf      minor faults          Kbytes
*           pi      page ins              Kbytes
*           po      page outs             Kbytes
*           fr      pages freed           Kbytes
*           sr      scan rate             pages
*           in      interrupts            number
*           sy      system calls          number
*           cs      context switches      number
*
# ./vmstat.d
 w     swap      free    re     mf  pi  po  fr  sr   in     sy   cs
 0   848552   105880    12    156   0   0   0   0   327  62073  1620
 0   848536   105720  8508 115712   0   0   0   0   282  82472  2890
 0   848536   105720     0      8   0   0   0   0   330  55646  1880
 0   848536   105720     0      8   0   0   0   0   396  69205  1729
 0   848076   105212  1496  20948   0   0   0   0   329  72587  1774
 0   848536   105724  6864  94656   0   0   0   0   284  79825  2558
 0   848536   105724     0      0   0   0   0   0   332  57817  1621
 0   848536   105824     0      0   0   0   0   0   327  64049  1586
 0   848152   105396  4480  60548   0   0   0   0   310  76116  2116
^C

#
```

Figure 9-7. *Output of the DTrace* vmstat.d *script*

```
File  Edit  View  Terminal  Tabs  Help
# ./syscallbyproc.d > d.out
dtrace: script './syscallbyproc.d' matched 235 probes
^Ctail -20 d.out
  nautilus                             52
  gnome-panel                          54
  gnome-settings-d                     60
  clock-applet                         65
  xscreensaver                         77
  gnome-terminal                       89
  sleep                               103
  bash                                129
  mixer_applet2                       197
  gnome-netstatus-                    528
  dhcpagent                           834
  Xephyr                             1292
  java                               1963
  dtrace                             2105
  nscd                               2653
  compiz-bin                         4569
  firefox-bin                        8373
  find                               9276
  ls                                22440
  Xorg                             266718
#
```

Figure 9-8. *Output of the* syscallbyproc.d *script*

The Chime GUI for DTrace

One of the graphical DTrace tools, developed to illustrate DTrace's Java providers, is Chime (`http://opensolaris.org/os/project/dtrace-chime/`). This program lets you select and run preconfigured DTrace scripts and has the ability to graph their output as time series; it also includes many of the scripts in the DTrace Toolkit. You must download and install Chime directly from the OpenSolaris web site since it is not yet available in any of the package repositories. Chime installs itself in the `/opt/OSOLOchime` directory; you then run the `/opt/OSOLOchime/bin/chime` shell script to start the program and display its GUI (Figure 9-9).

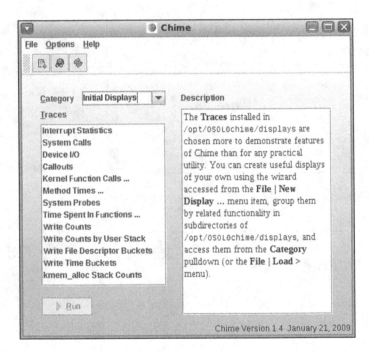

Figure 9-9. *The Chime GUI for DTrace*

Chime's built-in graphical displays let you display real-time plots of system statistics that you can use to identify "hot spots" or imbalances in your configuration. For example, you can monitor interrupts on CPUs, NICs, and USB devices (Figure 9-10). You can also use Chime as a DTrace learning tool since it can categorize and list available probes (Figure 9-11) for the OS and for applications such as *Apache*.

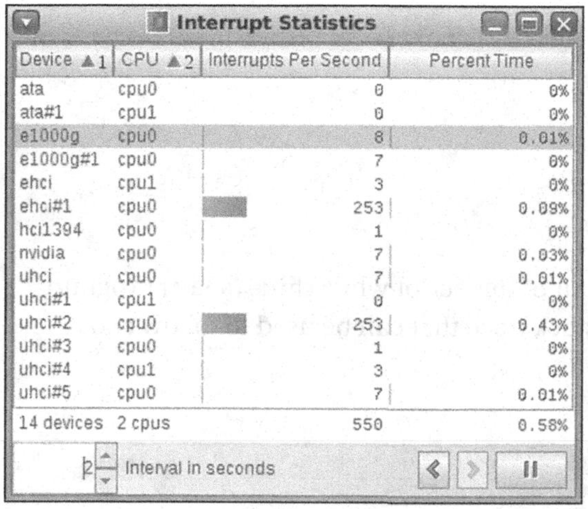

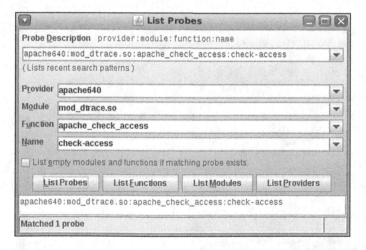

Figure 9-10. *Monitoring device interrupts using Chime*

Figure 9-11. *Using Chime to list available probes*

DTrace and Java

For Java developers, DTrace includes numerous probes for monitoring actions of the Java 6 JVM. This allows you to watch object creation and garbage collection, to display the method call hierarchy, and to observe the time spent within methods. Here's a very simple script that prints a stack trace each time the JVM makes the pollsys system call:

```
#!/usr/sbin/dtrace -s
syscall::pollsys:entry
/ execname == "java" /
{
jstack(16);
}
```

Figure 9-12 shows a portion of the output of this script while chime (a Java program itself) is running; it shows a portion of the stack trace that can be used to follow code paths through your Java programs.

```
dtrace: script './example2.d' matched 1 probe
CPU    ID                    FUNCTION:NAME
  0  63065                    pollsys:entry
            libc.so.1`__pollsys+0x7
            libc.so.1`poll+0x4c
            libmawt.so`performPoll+0xe8
            libmawt.so`waitForEvents+0x24
            libmawt.so`Java_sun_awt_X11_XToolkit_waitForEvents+0x15
            0xfb358fc7
            0xfb3909fc
            0xd9e5bcf0

  0  63065                    pollsys:entry
            libc.so.1`__pollsys+0x7
            libc.so.1`poll+0x4c
            libjvm.so`__1cIos_sleep6Fxb_i_+0x1b7
            libjvm.so`__1cCosFsleep6FpnGThread_xb_i_+0xb2
            libjvm.so`__1cNWatcherThreadRun6M_v_+0xbb
            libjvm.so`java_start+0xf9
            libc.so.1`_thrp_setup+0x7e
            libc.so.1`_lwp_start

  0  63065                    pollsys:entry
            libc.so.1`__pollsys+0x7
            libc.so.1`poll+0x4c
            libjvm.so`__1cIos_sleep6Fxb_i_+0x1b7
            libjvm.so`__1cCosFsleep6FpnGThread_xb_i_+0xb2
--More--
```

Figure 9-12. *Displaying the stack trace of a Java program using DTrace*

The Java directory on OpenSolaris contains more examples of how to use DTrace's JVM probes in `/usr/jdk/instances/jdk1.6.0/sample/dtrace/hotspot`, and of course there are many community-developed examples such as those at `http://www.sun.com/bigadmin/features/articles/java_se6_observability.jsp` and `http://opensolaris.org/os/project/dtrace-chime/java_dtrace_api/`.

The Tracker Utility: Where's That File?

Tracker extracts and stores information (metadata) about the contents of the files on your system so that they can be searched easily and quickly, similar to Apple OS X's Spotlight program.

Using Tracker you locate a file by searching for a word that's in it. Tracker can search many document and media formats such as programs, PDF files, OpenOffice documents, saved emails and web pages, and even music files. For example, in Figure 9-13, we used Tracker to search our system for files containing the word *apache*. Tracker not only found all such files, including OpenOffice, PDF, Java, and even music files, but it listed the *context* of the search term in each file, displayed available information about the file, and lets you click the file to display or run it using the appropriate application.

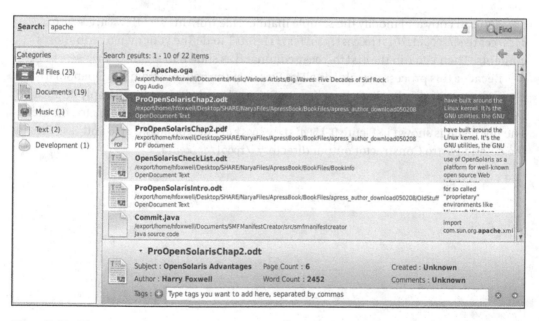

Figure 9-13. *The Tracker search utility*

The OpenSolaris Distro Constructor

You may want to create a collection of OpenSolaris packages including the kernel and use it to provision other systems or even to distribute your own customized version of the OS. The Distribution Constructor (http://dlc.sun.com/osol/docs/content/2008.11/ DistroConst/index.html) is a tool you can use to build redistributable, bootable Open-Solaris images. Using an XML manifest file as input, you specify and build an ISO or USB image much like the Live CD image you used to install OpenSolaris 2008.11. You can define in the manifest file the packages you want to include in the distribution, thereby creating a custom OpenSolaris initial installation environment. The manifest file is an XML document that includes the following information:

- *Distribution name*: A name for your distribution, such as ProOpenSolaris or MyDistro

- *Default package repository*: Where the constructor will obtain its packages, usually http://pkg.opensolaris.org/release

- *Packages*: A list of packages to be included in the distribution

- *Build area*: A temporary directory for copying the distribution files

You can copy and modify the sample manifest file from http://dlc.sun.com/osol/ docs/content/2008.11/DistroConst/manifestfile.html to define your own distribution's contents. Then you run the distro_const command as shown in Figure 9-14.

Because this process downloads all its files over the network from the OpenSolaris package repositories, it takes a long time to finish. This example, which simply duplicated the manifest and files for the OpenSolaris 2008.11 CD, took nearly *two hours* to complete. The net result is shown in Figure 9-15; distro_const created bootable .iso and .usb files in the default Distro Constructor output directory, /rpool/dc/media.

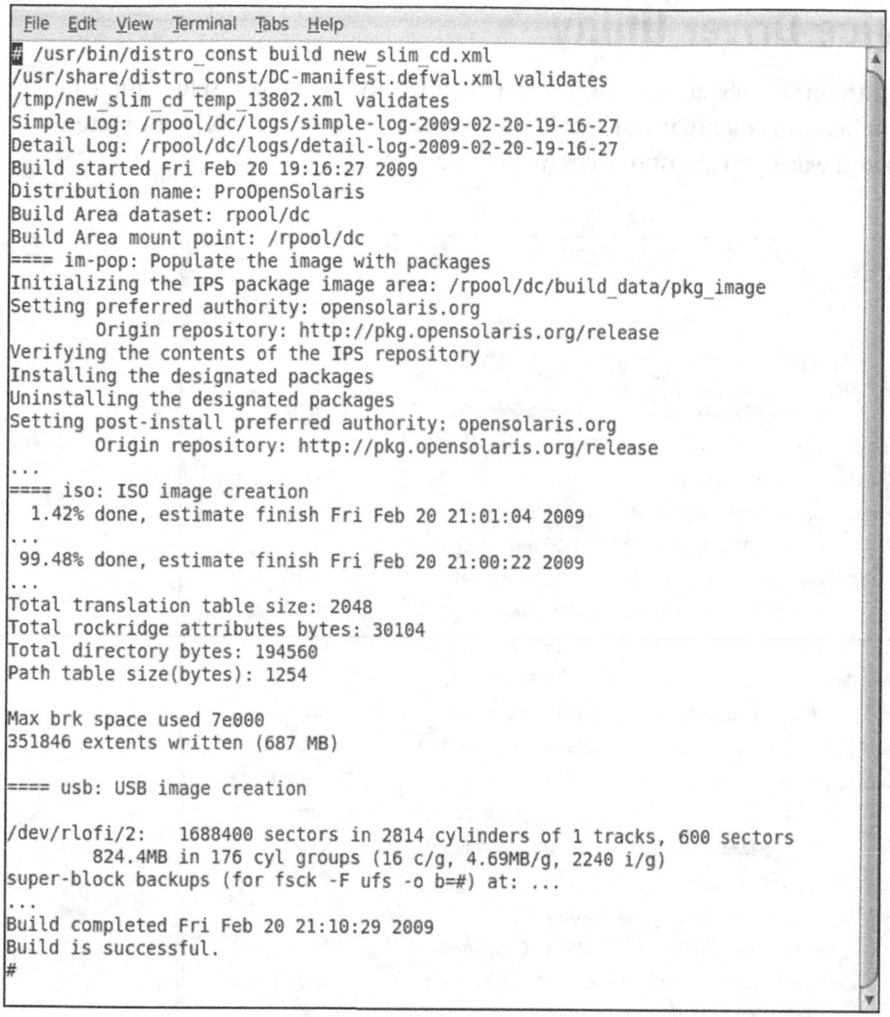

```
File  Edit  View  Terminal  Tabs  Help
# /usr/bin/distro_const build new_slim_cd.xml
/usr/share/distro_const/DC-manifest.defval.xml validates
/tmp/new_slim_cd_temp_13802.xml validates
Simple Log: /rpool/dc/logs/simple-log-2009-02-20-19-16-27
Detail Log: /rpool/dc/logs/detail-log-2009-02-20-19-16-27
Build started Fri Feb 20 19:16:27 2009
Distribution name: ProOpenSolaris
Build Area dataset: rpool/dc
Build Area mount point: /rpool/dc
==== im-pop: Populate the image with packages
Initializing the IPS package image area: /rpool/dc/build_data/pkg_image
Setting preferred authority: opensolaris.org
        Origin repository: http://pkg.opensolaris.org/release
Verifying the contents of the IPS repository
Installing the designated packages
Uninstalling the designated packages
Setting post-install preferred authority: opensolaris.org
        Origin repository: http://pkg.opensolaris.org/release
...
==== iso: ISO image creation
  1.42% done, estimate finish Fri Feb 20 21:01:04 2009
...
 99.48% done, estimate finish Fri Feb 20 21:00:22 2009
...
Total translation table size: 2048
Total rockridge attributes bytes: 30104
Total directory bytes: 194560
Path table size(bytes): 1254

Max brk space used 7e000
351846 extents written (687 MB)


==== usb: USB image creation

/dev/rlofi/2:   1688400 sectors in 2814 cylinders of 1 tracks, 600 sectors
        824.4MB in 176 cyl groups (16 c/g, 4.69MB/g, 2240 i/g)
super-block backups (for fsck -F ufs -o b=#) at: ...
...
Build completed Fri Feb 20 21:10:29 2009
Build is successful.
#
```

Figure 9-14. *Creating your distribution using* distro_const

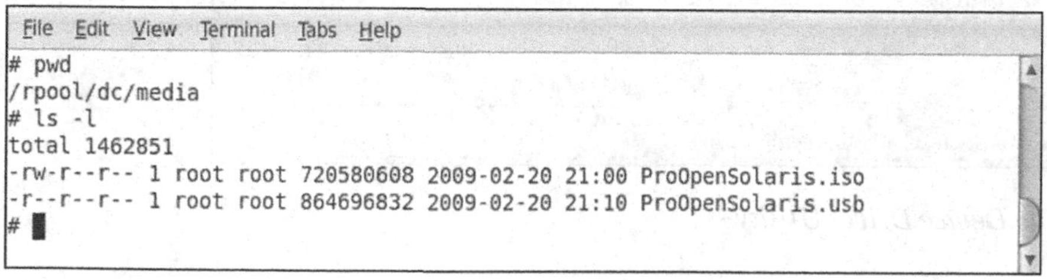

```
File  Edit  View  Terminal  Tabs  Help
# pwd
/rpool/dc/media
# ls -l
total 1462851
-rw-r--r-- 1 root root 720580608 2009-02-20 21:00 ProOpenSolaris.iso
-r--r--r-- 1 root root 864696832 2009-02-20 21:10 ProOpenSolaris.usb
#
```

Figure 9-15. *The output* .iso *and* .usb *files of* distro_const

The Device Driver Utility

A handy program in OpenSolaris is the Device Driver Utility. When you select and run it from the Applications menu, it will list all the installed device drivers on your system (Figure 9-16) and warn you about devices without drivers.

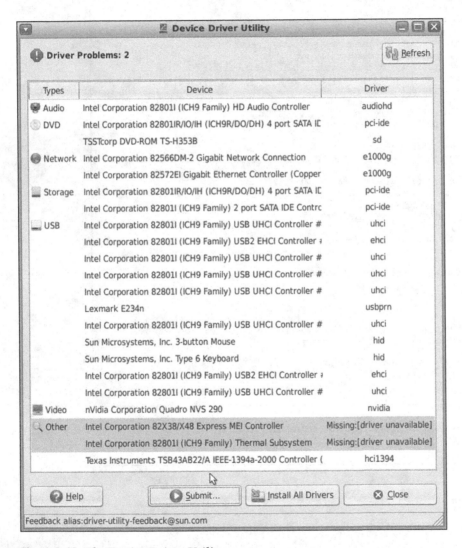

Figure 9-16. *The Device Driver Utility*

The Device Driver Utility not only lets you use the Image Packaging System repositories to search the device drivers on your system to find devices that do not have drivers attached to them, but it also lets you share your working configuration details on the

OpenSolaris OS Hardware Compatibility List (HCL) so that others can see "Reported to Work" information for systems like yours (Figure 9-17).

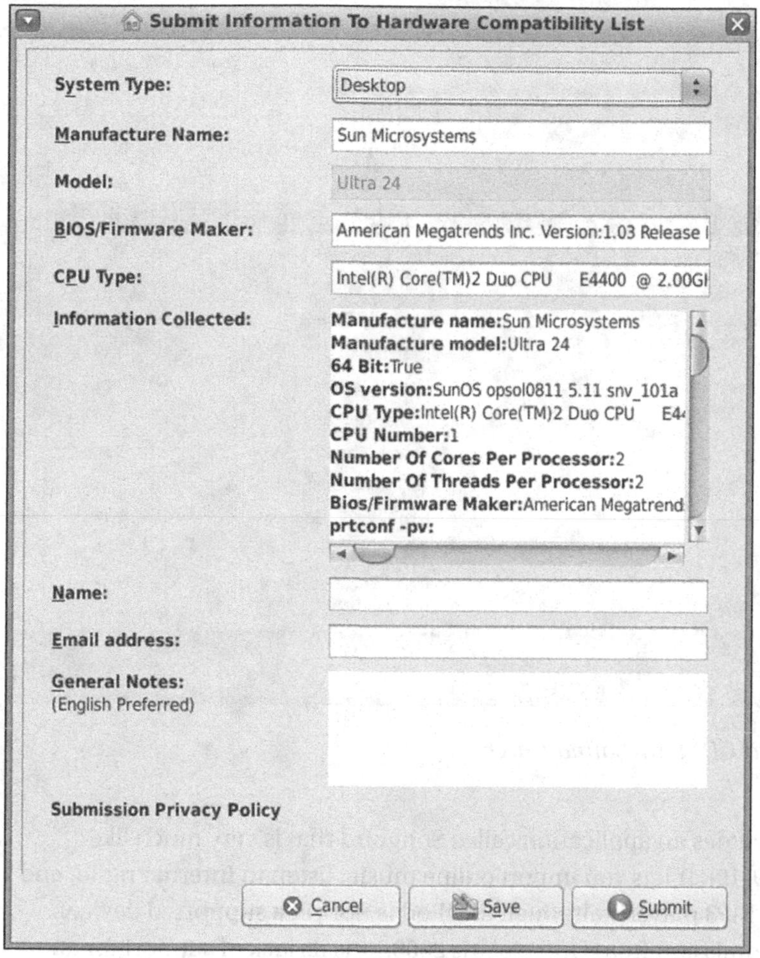

Figure 9-17. *Reporting your configuration to the OpenSolaris HCL*

And Now for a Little Entertainment

Like most Linux distributions, OpenSolaris includes a number of multimedia programs including the popular Sound Juicer, which is a CD ripper; Rhythmbox, a music player; and Totem, a movie player. You can use Sound Juicer to extract tracks from your music CDs (Figure 9-18) into your $HOME/Documents/Music directory and to play them on your laptop or workstation; many audio devices already have drivers included in OpenSolaris to support this.

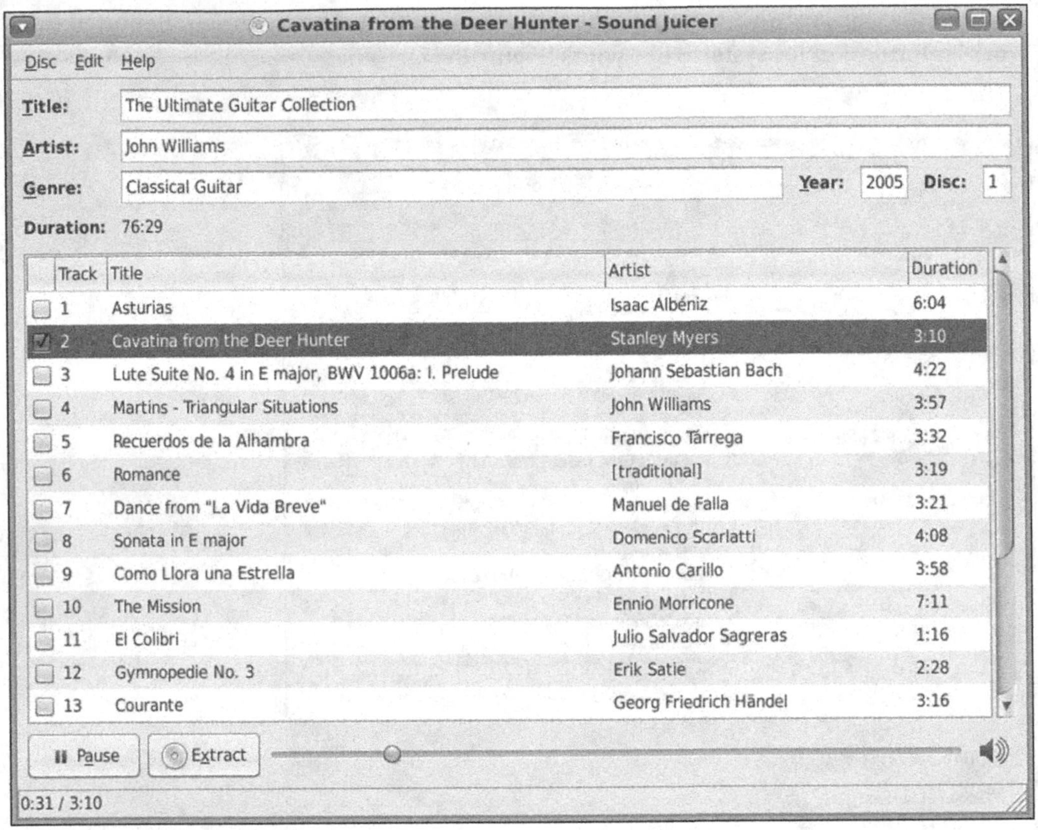

Figure 9-18. *Playing music CDs with Sound Juicer*

But OpenSolaris includes an application called Songbird that is very much like Apple's iTunes (Figure 9-19). It lets you import online music, listen to Internet radio, and create playlists for your MP3 players (although the iPod is not yet a supported device).

One disappointing omission from OpenSolaris 2008.11 is its lack of support for an open source DVD player with required codecs. In part, this is because of Sun's strict adherence to restrictions against providing unlicensed codecs even though some Linux distributions, notably Ubuntu, seem to have no problem allowing you to download and install such "restricted software." The Totem movie player is included with OpenSolaris, but it's not configured by default to play your DVDs and none of the repositories includes the needed codecs. Sun's current solution to this problem is to point you to a distributor of licensed codecs, Fluendo (http://www.fluendo.com/, Figure 9-20). Of course, you have to *buy* this software for 28 euros (about $35 USD as of this writing), which may go against the philosophy of many open source purists. But that's the current solution.

Figure 9-19. *The Songbird music player*

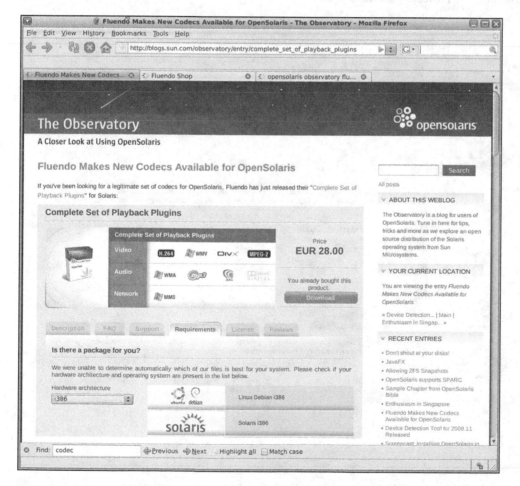

Figure 9-20. *Fluendo makes new codecs available for OpenSolaris.*

OpenSolaris Educational Resources

In this book we have only scratched the surface of all that's available concerning Open-Solaris. Additional resources are available to you if you want to learn more about operating system concepts, and a new online service lets you try OpenSolaris without having to install anything.

The OpenSolaris Curriculum Development Resources

If you're a computer science educator teaching about operating systems, there's an entire curriculum based on OpenSolaris developed by the Academic and Research community at http://opensolaris.org/os/community/edu/. The curriculum includes instructor and student guides (Figure 9-21) and covers general operating system concepts such as process scheduling, memory management, and synchronization; as well as OpenSolaris-specific topics such as zones, ZFS, and DTrace.

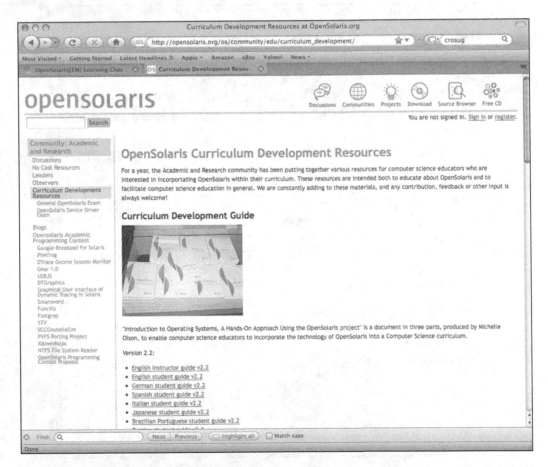

Figure 9-21. *The OpenSolaris curriculum development resources web site*

OpenSolaris Learning Cloud Service

If you want to try OpenSolaris online without installing anything on your own system, there is a Learning Cloud Service that you can register for and then start a Java-based remote display of a complete OpenSolaris session. Figure 9-22 shows the registration and login instruction web site.

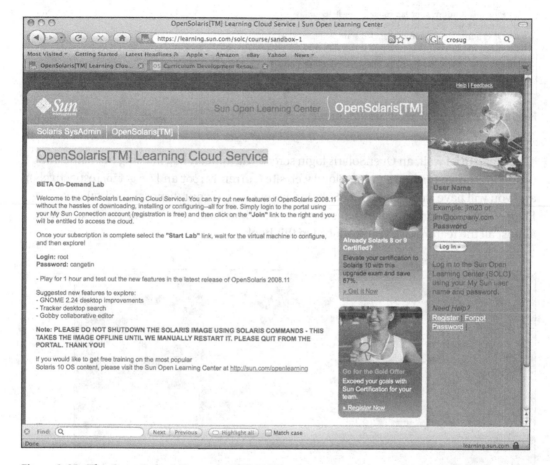

Figure 9-22. *The OpenSolaris Learning Cloud Service web site*

After you log in and click Start Lab, a Java applet will start, as shown in Figure 9-23.

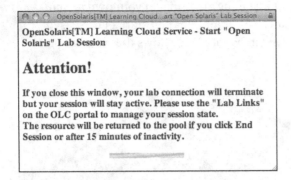

Figure 9-23. *The initial Lab Session applet*

After a brief wait, an OpenSolaris login screen will appear. Log in using the name and password shown on the Learning Cloud web site (currently root and cangetin, respectively), and you will have a complete OpenSolaris environment at your disposal, as shown in Figure 9-24. The performance of this service is less than ideal, but you can use it to explore almost all the features we've introduced in this book.

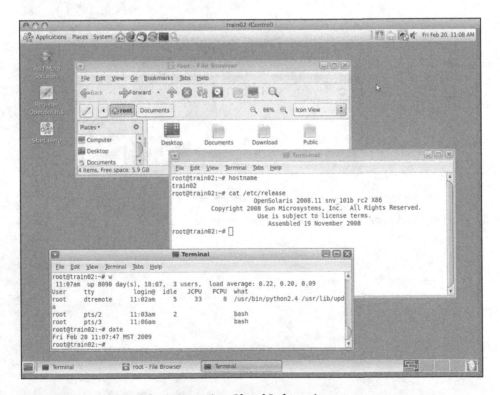

Figure 9-24. *An OpenSolaris Learning Cloud Lab session*

Summary

OpenSolaris contains a rich and growing collection of community-developed programs, information sources, and educational resources for assisting your application development, general productivity, daily Internet activities, and multimedia entertainment. This chapter has mentioned just a few of these; you'll have fun exploring the rest!

PART 4

Appendixes

APPENDIX A

Recommended Reading and Viewing

In this book we have emphasized the key features of OpenSolaris and have organized the chapters in a way that builds up to the practical examples in Chapter 8. But you can use numerous additional resources to enhance and extend what you've learned here. In this appendix we list some valuable documents, videos, and communities that are part of the growing body of OpenSolaris knowledge.

Books

Although there are as yet very few books devoted exclusively to OpenSolaris, there are some that cover both Solaris and OpenSolaris including these by McDougal, Mauro, and Gregg. For readers interested in the internal architecture and source code of OpenSolaris, the *Solaris Internals* book is very instructive. For those interested in performance tools, especially in DTrace, the *Solaris Performance and Tools* book is required reading:

Richard McDougall and Jim Mauro. *Solaris Internals: Solaris 10 and OpenSolaris Kernel Architecture*, 2nd ed., Upper Saddle River, NJ: Prentice Hall, 2007.

Richard McDougall, Jim Mauro, and Brendan Gregg. *Solaris Performance and Tools: DTrace and MDB Techniques for Solaris 10 and OpenSolaris*. Upper Saddle River, NJ: Prentice Hall, 2007.

Software developers will find much value in publications for Solaris, since OpenSolaris has many features identical to or derived from those in Solaris 10. Daryl Gove's book can give readers a head start learning about programming in this new environment, especially for the new multicore, multithread processors:

Gove, Darryl. *Solaris Application Programming*. Upper Saddle River, NJ: Prentice Hall, 2008.

Blogs and Wikis

Sun engineers and OpenSolaris community member regularly blog about new OS features, new tools and techniques, and the future of OpenSolaris. You can participate in their discussions and can often get your technical questions answered by the original designers of the software. Here are a few representative blogs worth reading regularly:

Jeff Bonwick's blog, `http://blogs.sun.com/bonwick/`. ZFS wisdom from one of its designers.

Darryl Gove's blog, `http://blogs.sun.com/d/`. Darryl is a Sun compiler engineer specializing in SPARC programming.

Jim Grisanzio's blog, `http://blogs.sun.com/jimgris/`. Jim is Program Manager for OpenSolaris development. He travels the world promoting OpenSolaris communities.

Brian Leonard's OpenSolaris blog, called the Observatory, `http://blogs.sun.com/observatory/`. Brian is a senior software engineer for Sun Microsystems; he blogs about software and web stack development on OpenSolaris.

OpenSolaris wiki, `http://wikis.sun.com/display/OpenSolaris/OpenSolaris`. A collaborative web site of OpenSolaris news, events, documentation, and ideas.

Developer Resources

Sun has extensive online resources focused primarily on Solaris development, but more OpenSolaris material is being included for new open source developers:

OpenSolaris Subscription Service, `http://www.sun.com/service/opensolaris/`. Paid subscription support for OpenSolaris production users.

Sun Developer Network, `http://developers.sun.com/`. A free community for Sun developers, including an OpenSolaris group.

Learning and Training

The OpenSolaris community encourages academic and commercial educators to teach OpenSolaris and to use it as a platform for learning about open source operating system and application development. Free training and curriculum resources are available:

OpenSolaris Curriculum Development Resources, `http://opensolaris.org/os/community/edu/curriculum_development/`. Resources for computer science educators teaching OS concepts using OpenSolaris.

OpenSolaris Learning Cloud Service, `https://learning.sun.com/solc/course/sandbox-1`. Try out new features of OpenSolaris for free without downloading, installing, or configuring it; just log in and learn.

OpenSolaris Technical Essentials Guide, `http://www.sun.com/training/catalog/courses/WS-1000-OS.xml`. A free web course on installing, using, administering, and distributing OpenSolaris.

Linux to OpenSolaris Translation

One of the most useful online documents for UNIX and Linux administrators is Bruce Hamilton's Rosetta Stone for UNIX, at `http://www.bhami.com/rosetta.html`. It lists dozens of commands and their equivalents for Linux and for all of the major UNIX implementations. It includes a feature that lets you generate a table that lists typical OpenSolaris tasks and programs and their Linux counterparts.

Newsletter

The monthly newsletter OpenSolaris Ignite, `http://www.sun.com/emrkt/opensolaris/ignite/`, is by, for, and about the OpenSolaris community, featuring news, how-to articles, tech tips, and reviews.

User Groups

Participating in user groups is one of the best ways to learn about new technologies, to share ideas, and to grow the community. More than 110 OpenSolaris user groups are currently active; details on how to start a user group are also included here:

Join or start an OpenSolaris user group, http://opensolaris.org/os/usergroups/. You can see a map of user groups in almost every continent on the planet (none *yet* in Antarctica!).

Videos

Educational videos about OpenSolaris features are a good way to learn from community experts. Here are a few such videos, and you can find more on Sun and YouTube:

A 10-minute video about partitioning your hard drive if you have multiple boot partitions, http://frsun.downloads.edgesuite.net/sun/07C00892/media/demos/ OpenSolarisDualBoot-Step2-Partition.html, January 2009. How to install OpenSolaris in a multiboot configuration.

A 10-minute video about using the Package Manager GUI for installing packages, http://webcast-west.sun.com/interactive/09B01790/index.html, January 2009. Learn how to use the OpenSolaris Package Manager.

OpenSolaris & Intel Xeon Processors, http://www.youtube.com/watch?v=VIb8VIgOJMO, April 2008. Intel Open Source Technology Engineer talks about OpenSolaris.

CSI: Munich—How to Save the World with ZFS and 12 USB Sticks, http://video. google.com/videoplay?docid=8100808442979626078, March 2007. An amusing but educational demo of key ZFS features using UFS memory sticks.

Web Sites

Here are some additional web sites for OpenSolaris developers, administrators, and end users:

OpenSolaris Communities, http://opensolaris.org/os/communities/. Developers and users of all the evolving OpenSolaris features.

OpenSolaris Projects, http://opensolaris.org/os/projects/. Collaborative work on new and problem areas of OpenSolaris.

Resource Collection: OpenSolaris, `http://www.sun.com/bigadmin/collections/opensolaris.jsp`. OpenSolaris tips and tools for administrators.

Solaris Information Center—Community: OpenSolaris, `http://www.sun.com/bigadmin/hubs/documentation/community/opensol.jsp`. The OpenSolaris community at Sun's BigAdmin site for system administrators.

Solaris Information Center—How To: OpenSolaris Installation and Image Packaging System, `http://www.sun.com/bigadmin/hubs/documentation/howto/install-nev-current.jsp`, January 2009.

Solaris Internals and Performance FAQ, `http://www.solarisinternals.com/wiki/index.php/Solaris_Internals_and_Performance_FAQ`.

Towards Running Trusted Extensions with OpenSolaris 2008.11, by Christoph Schuba, `http://blogs.sun.com/schuba/entry/running_trusted_extension_with_opensolaris`, September 2008.

White Papers

More detail on the security features of zones; references Solaris 10 but fully applicable to zones on OpenSolaris:

"Security Advantages of the Solaris Zones Software," by Christoph Schuba, `http://wikis.sun.com/display/BluePrints/Security+Advantages+of+the+Solaris+Zones+Software`, December 2008.

"Understanding the Security Capabilities of Solaris Zones Software," by Glenn Brunette and Jeff Victor, `http://wikis.sun.com/display/BluePrints/Understanding+the+Security+Capabilities+of+Solaris+Zones+Software`, December 2008.

APPENDIX B

∎∎∎

OpenSolaris 2009.06

The OpenSolaris update cycle plans for new stable binary releases approximately every six months. At the time of this book's publication, the next such release is expected to be OpenSolaris 2009.06. This appendix covers some of the new features *anticipated* in this release.

SPARC Support

The first two releases of OpenSolaris (2008.05 and the current 2008.11) were for Intel and AMD processors only. Now that the boot process for SPARC processors has been updated to recognize ZFS file systems, OpenSolaris 2009.06 will be installable on these systems, although support for Logical Domains (LDoms on the UltraSPARC Sun4v architecture) is planned for a later release. The http://pkg.opensolaris.org/dev repository has already been updated to include SPARC packages for this build. At this time, however, you need to use the OpenSolaris *Automated Installer* (AI; http://www.opensolaris.org/os/project/caiman/auto_install/) for SPARC systems; detailed instructions for this installation method are at http://www.opensolaris.org/os/project/caiman/auto_install/AI_install_server_setup.html.

We look forward to this release so that the OpenSolaris community will have access to a SPARC development platform and can learn to exploit the parallelism of multicore/multithread SPARC processors.

Project Crossbow

As a complement to virtualization technologies for OS environments, network virtualization techniques are now being developed and will begin to appear in OpenSolaris 2009.06. The OpenSolaris Crossbow Project (`http://opensolaris.org/os/project/crossbow/`) provides tools for virtualizing the entire network software and hardware stack and for managing the resource allocations for specific protocols. The project page says this:

> *Each virtual stack can be assigned its own priority and bandwidth on a shared NIC without causing any performance degradation. The architecture dynamically manages priority and bandwidth resources, and can provide better defense against denial-of-service attacks directed at a particular service or virtual machine by isolating the impact just to that entity. The virtual stacks are separated by means of H/W classification engine such that traffic for one stack does not impact other virtual stacks.*

Crossbow tools will allow you to create and configure multiple virtual NIC devices (VNICs) per hardware NIC, assigning a VNIC to each VM or zone, and to set bandwidth and priority limits for services and protocols assigned to each VNIC. Crossbow will also allow you to model and simulate complex networks within your OpenSolaris system. You can download and try early access builds of the Crossbow software at `http://opensolaris.org/os/project/crossbow/snapshots/`.

Encrypted ZFS File System

This project (`http://opensolaris.org/os/project/zfs-crypto/`) implements on-disk encryption of ZFS file systems in the OpenSolaris kernel, enabling data security on any ZFS file system from laptops through enterprise servers. This feature will provide encryption of the ZFS I/O data stream and will include key management for ZFS file systems. All dataset data, metadata, and properties will be encrypted. File system encryption is becoming a requirement in many government agencies and in organizations that require encryption to guarantee client data privacy. It's also becoming essential for protecting data on laptops in the event of theft. OpenSolaris with encrypted ZFS will provide this level of data security.

CUPS Printing

Although you can manually install the CUPS printing service on OpenSolaris 2008.11, full support for this service is planned for OpenSolaris 2009.06 (`http://opensolaris.org/os/community/printing/Documentation/cupsprint/`). CUPS is an open source, IPP-protocol system for managing local and network printers and print queues. It lets you discover and install new printers through a web browser interface.

Other Anticipated Features

According to the announcements and developer discussions on the OpenSolaris web site, there will be continued improvements in the 2009.06 release for current features such as network automagic, package management, automated install, and a host of new software in the network package repositories. Watch the `http://opensolaris.org/os` web site for news about new OpenSolaris releases and features.

Index

Symbols

.d file extension, 210
/etc/release file, 48
/usr/bin/bash, as default shell, 55
/usr/gnu/bin directory, 55–56

A

access control model, 163
accessing root account, 56–57
acroread PDF reader, 147–148
action flags, service administration
    tasks, 76
Administration menu, 54
administrative tasks
    new users, adding, 62–64
    printing, 64–65
administrator tools with Linux
    distribution equivalents, 56
advantages of OpenSolaris
    DTrace, 24–25
    scalability, 23
    security features, 25–26
    service management, 23–24
    support for virtualization, 25
    ZFS file system, 24
aggregations (DTrace), 210–212
allocating memory to VM, 144
AMP (Apache, Perl, PHP, MySql) stack
    getting, 154
    pkg command and, 156–162
amp-dev package
    amp package compared to, 157
    contents of, 157
    installing, 154
    NetBeans IDE and, 175–178
    Subversion and, 179
amp package, amp-dev package
    compared to, 157
Andreessen, Marc, 17

Apache
    httpd.conf file, 130
    server, starting, 161
Apache 2 web server, installing, 129
application components included with
    desktop environment, 51–54
applications
    OpenSolaris as running high-quality, 22
    qualifying for zones, 164–165
Applications menu, 52, 175
application virtualization, 113
assigning storage space for VM, 142

B

bash shell, choice of, 55
beadm command
    file system snapshots and, 57
    for managing boot environments, 108
binary versions, 47
blogs, recommended, 234
books, recommended, 233
Boot Environment Manager GUI, 59
boot environments, managing with ZFS,
    108–110
booting, 30, 57–59
boot milestones, 74
boot techniques
    Live CD, 30, 34–36
    multiboot installation, 36–37
branded zones, 145
BrandZ, 145–148
browser tool, online source code, 19
bugs, viewing and filing against
    OpenSolaris, 193
build number, 47

C

CAB (Community Advisory Board), 12
CD distribution of OpenSolaris, 28, 53

CDDL (Common Development and
        Distribution License), 11
CDE (Common Desktop Environment), 51
checkout (Subversion), 180
Chime GUI for DTrace, 216–218
Clarke, Dennis, 205
CLI (command line interface), for the
        GUI-averse, 55–56
cloning feature (VirtualBox), 45
cloning zones, 127–128
Cloud Computing products, 112
commands
    beadm, 57, 108
    ctstat, 81
    ctwatch, 81
    format, 96
    isainfo, 134
    pkg, 156–158
    pooladm, 131
    poolcfg, 132
    prstat, 125
    psrinfo, 134
    su, 56–57
    Subversion
        svn add, 181
        svn commit, 182
        svn delete, 181
        svn diff, 182
        svn move, 181
        svn update, 182
    svcadm, 71, 75–76, 139
    svcadm clear, 80
    svccfg
        description of, 71
        SMF repository, interacting with, 200
        verifying file is valid using, 85
    svcprop, 71
    svcs, 71, 139
    svcs -a, 72
    svcs ssh, 78
    svcs -x, 78
    svcs -x ssh, 78
    top, 125
    uname, 47

zfs
    description of, 94
    examples using, 98–100
    snapshot, creating with, 103
zpool
    description of, 94
    examples using, 96–98
    options for, 95
Common Desktop Environment (CDE), 51
Common Development and Distribution
        License (CDDL), 11
communities
    device drivers, 8
    DTrace, 212–214
    laptop Issues, 30
    LDom developer, 149
    printing, 64
    Xen, 115
Community Advisory Board (CAB), 12
community contributions (DTrace),
        212–214
community-developed software
    vendors releasing, 6
configurable zone resources, 132
configuring printer, 64–65
container architecture, 116
container environment
    discrete privileges and, 163–164
    qualifying application for zones,
        164–165
containers
    building application inside, 162–163
    description of, 113, 132
    installing Tomcat in, 165–172
    zones compared to, 118–120
contract ID, viewing, 161
contributing developers FAQ, 8
Copy on Write model, 93
Crossbow Project, 113, 240
C Shell, 55
ctstat command, 81
ctwatch command, 81
CUPS printing service, 241
curriculum development resources, 226

D

.d file extension, 210
data sharding, 163
data storage
  prefixes for decimal multiples of bytes, 90
  techniques for, 89
default shell, changing, 55
delegation, zones and, 162
desktop environment
  application components included with, 51–54
  CLI, for the GUI-averse, 55–56
  GNOME as default, 51
  su command, 56–57
developer resources, 234
developer tools included with OpenSolaris, 22
development environment
  AMP stack
    getting, 154
    pkg command and, 156–162
  containers and, 162–163
  overview of, 154
  production environment compared to, 161
Device Detection Tool (Sun), 21, 32
device drivers, resources on, 8
Device Driver utility, 222–223
device interrupts, monitoring, 217
direct bare-metal installation, 36
disabling ssh service
  for current boot session only, 77
  and not restarting, 77
  using Services GUI, 76
  using svcadm command, 75
discrete privileges, zones and, 163–164
Distribution (Distro) Constructor, 220–222
DomUs, 137
DomU VM, installing, 144
downloading
  OpenSolaris, 27
  programs from software repositories, 48–50

DTrace

  aggregations, 210–212
  architecture of, 206
  Chime GUI, 216–218
  community contributions, 212–214
  description of, 24–25
  Java and, 218–219
  kernel probes, 207–208
  overview of, 205
  privileges and, 164
  production environment and, 206
  providers, 208
  OneLiners, 212
  root privileges, 209
  script example, 209–210
  scripts, 208–209
  syscallbyproc.d script, 214
  Toolkit, 213
  vmstat and, 214

E

editing service manifest file, 86–88
educational resources, 226–228
enabling
  Apache and MySQL servers, 161
  MySQL, 173
  sshd logging, 190
  SSL for Tomcat, 168
  Subversion, 190
  tomcat5.xml, 172
/etc/release file, 48
evince PDF reader, 147
extended ACL, viewing, 158

F

FAQ, for contributing developers, 8
fault isolation, zones and, 162
Fault Managed Resource Identifiers (FMRIs), 70–71, 156
file extensions, .d, 210
files
  See also Time Slider file manager
  Apache httpd.conf, 130
  /etc/release, 48
  my.cnf, 172
  Subversion, managing, 179–180

Filesystem Hierarchy Standard, 168
file systems
    See also ZFS file system
    disk-based, problems with, 90
    goal of, 89
file system snapshots, advantages of, 57
File menu, Boot Environment Manager, 59
flash memory drive, booting from, 30
Fluendo, 224
FMRIs (Fault Managed Resource
        Identifiers), 70–71, 156
format command, 96
freely sharable software, 5
full OS virtualization, 113

■ G

gcc compiler, installing, 48
global zone, 118
global zone environment, 124–127
GNOME user environment
    as default desktop, 51
    typical user session in, 7
GNU General Public License (GPL), 11
Gregg, Brendan, 212, 213
GRUB boot screen, 42
guest operating system, platforms for, 115
guest VM, installing as, 37–47

■ H

Hardware Compatibility List (HCL), 21,
        31, 222
hardware emulation, 113
hardware partitioning techniques, 111
hardware platform, OpenSolaris as
        running on commodity, 20–21
history of OpenSolaris, 9–10
hosted hypervisor, 115
hosting web servers with local zones, 129
hypervisor
    description of, 37, 113
    Type 1 architecture, 115
    Type 2 architecture, 115

xVM
    installing, 138–145
    overview of, 136–137

■ I

IDE. See NetBeans IDE
Image Packaging System (IPS), adding
        software using, 47–50
image-update process, 59–60
initializing web stack, 158–161
installation
    choices for, 29–30, 34
    direct bare-metal, 36
    as guest VM, 37–47
    Live CD booting, 34–36
    multiboot, 36–37
    system requirements, 30–34
Installer Welcome screen, 34, 43
installing
    amp-dev package, 154
    Apache 2 web server, 129
    DomU VM, 144
    gcc compiler, 48
    lx zones, 146
    MySQL, 172–175
    SUNWtcat package, 166
    Tomcat in container, 165–172
    xVM hypervisor, 138–145
intent log, 93
IPS (Package Manager) GUI
    adding software using, 47–50
    description of, 200
    opening, 154
    overview of, 156–162
    packaging web app into, 200–203
isainfo command, 134

■ J

Java, and DTrace, 218–219
Java Community Process (JCP), 12
Joy, Bill, 9

■ K

kernel build, updating, 59–60
Korn Shell, 55

∎ L

LAMP stack, 4
laptop issues, community for, 30
LDoms, 148
Learning Cloud Service, 227–229
licensing of source code, 11
lightweight virtualization, 113
Linux
    history of, 9
    OpenSolaris programs with Linux
        distribution equivalents, 56
    reputation of, 27
    trademark owner, 12
Linux applications, open source
    applications as, 4
Linux developer, 3
Linux Extended File System, 89
Linux to OpenSolaris translation, 235
Live CD booting, 30, 34–36
local zone
    description of, 118
    DTrace and, 209
    using, 129–130
local zone environment, 124–127
locating install media, 142
login screen, 45
lx zones, 145–146

∎ M

maintenance state of service, clearing, 80
manage access control method
        (Subversion)
    public/private key pair, generating,
        187–191
    simple svn remote access, 183–185
    svn + ssh access, 185–186
managing
    boot environments with ZFS, 108–110
    zones, 128–129
manifest files for services, 81
memory, allocating to VM, 144
metadata blocks, 93
metapackages, 157
MilaX distribution, 30

milestones, Service Management Facility,
        74
mirrored pool with spare (ZFS), creating,
        97
monitoring
    device interrupts, 217
    local zone resources from global zone,
        127
multiboot installation, 36–37
multimedia programs, 223–224
Murdock, Ian, 9, 17
my.cnf file, 172
MySQL database, starting, service
        manifest example for, 85–86
MySQL server
    installing, 172–175
    starting, 161

∎ N

naming VM, 141
National Security Agency (NSA), security
        features and, 26
native OS virtualization, 113
NetBeans IDE
    description of, 175–178
    integrating
        with Subversion, 193–200
        with Tomcat, 191–193
Network Auto-Magic Daemon (nwamd),
        51
network device, selecting for VM, 142
network interfaces, manually setting up,
        51
New Java Project screen (NetBeans IDE),
        176
New Project dialog box
    NetBeans IDE, 176
    Subversion, 196
newsletter, monthly, 235
Nexenta storage products, 102
nonglobal zone. See local zone
NSA (National Security Agency), security
        features and, 26
nwamd (Network Auto-Magic Daemon), 51

■O

online source code browser, 19
opening NetBeans IDE, 175–178
Open Software Initiative (OSI), 11
OpenSolaris
  See also advantages of OpenSolaris;
    OpenSolaris.org
  CD distribution of, 28
  Community Advisory Board, 12
  contributing developers FAQ, 8
  goals and future directions for, 10–11
  origin of, 9–10
  qualities of
    free, 18
    open source, 19
    runs high-quality application
      software, 22
    runs on commodity hardware
      platforms, 20–21
  software support subscription, 22
  typical user session, 7
  user and developer tools included with,
    22
OpenSolaris 2009.06, anticipated features,
    239–241
OpenSolaris.org
  bug-tracking and RFE page, 14
  community web page, 12
  device drivers community, 8
  LDom developer community, 149
  Observatory blog, 12
  public road maps, 10
  Source Code, 19
  Zones and Containers FAQ, 129
open source software
  description of, 5–7
  Linux applications as, 4
open source solutions developer, 3
open source user and developer stack,
    typical, 4
operating system (OS), installing as virtual
    machine, 30. See also Linux
OSI (Open Software Initiative), 11
OS virtualization, 113, 116

■P

Package Manager (IPS) GUI
  adding software using, 47–50
  description of, 48, 200
  opening, 154
  overview of, 156–162
  packaging web app into, 200–203
Package menu, Install/Update, 154
packages
  amp, 157
  amp-dev
    amp package compared to, 157
    contents of, 157
    installing, 154
    NetBeans IDE and, 175–178
    Subversion and, 179
  SUNWspnego, 190
  SUNWtcat, 166, 192
  viewing published IPS, 202
paravirtualization, 113
passphrase, empty, 187
password, setting for mysqld, 173
path-based authorization, 184
PDF reader (acroread), 147–148
performance of ZFS, 101–102
permission profile, setting for user, 62
pfexec program, 57
pkg command, 156–158
platforms, OpenSolaris as running on
    commodity hardware, 20–21
pooladm command, 131
poolcfg command, 132
portability, zones and, 163
Preferences menu, 53
Primary Administrator role, 44, 57
printer, configuring, 64–65
Print Manager, 64
PRIV_FILE_DAC_READ privilege, 163
privileges
  processes and, 169
  qualifying application for zones and,
    164–165
  zones and, 163–164
PRIV_NET_RAWACCESS privilege, 164
PRIV_SYS_TIME privilege, 164
probes (DTrace), 207–208

processes, privileges and, 169
process ID, viewing, 161
process rights management, 163
production environment
    development environment compared
       to, 161
    diagnosing application or OS
       performance issues in, 206
    query logging and, 173
projects, starting in NetBeans IDE, 176
providers (DTrace), 208
prstat command, 125
psrinfo command, 134
public/private key generation, 187–191

Q

qualifying application for zones, 164–165
quantize function (DTrace), 212
query logging, 173

R

RAID-Z, ZFS and, 93
RBAC (role-based access control), 57
rc service scripts, 70
rebooting, 57–59
removing devices from storage pool, 98
reporting configuration to OpenSolaris
    HCL, 222
repos (software repositories), down-
    loading programs from, 48–50
resource isolation, zones and, 162
resource management, zones and,
    130–132
resources
    See also web sites
    blogs and wikis, 234
    books, 233
    for developers, 234
    device drivers, 8
    educational, 226–228
    learning and training, 235
    Linux to OpenSolaris translation, 235
    newsletter, 235
    source code, 8
    user groups, 236
    videos, 236
    white papers, 237

resource virtualization, 113
Ritchie, Dennis, 9
role, assigning for user, 62
role-based access control (RBAC), 57
rolling back file system to earlier state, 103
root account/administrator
    accessing, 56–57
    default shell for, 55
    local zones and, 118
    MySQL and, 174
root and user account setup screen, 44
root privileges, DTrace and, 209
run levels, 74

S

scalability
    of OpenSolaris, 23
    zones and, 162
scheduling classes, 130
scripts (DTrace), 208–210
SDN (Solaris Developer Network), 28
security features, 25–26
security isolation, zones and, 162
server, 113
service
    definition of, 70
    states of, 72, 80
Service Management Facility (SMF)
    action flags, 76
    creating services, 81–85
    description of, 23–24
    editing services, 86–88
    Fault Managed Resource Identifiers
      and, 70–71
    milestones, 74
    overview of, 70
    ssh service example, 74–81
    tools, 71
    using, 72–73
service manifest
    components of, 82–84
    creating, 81
    editing, 86–88
    example for starting MySQL database,
      85–86
    online documentation references, 84
    template for, 82
    validating, 85

service programs, challenges of, 69
shares, assigning to local zones, 131
shell, choice of, 55
silos, 163
SMF manifest
    Subversion, 190
    Tomcat, 170–171
SMF Manifest Creator, 86
SMF service for IPS server, 200
SMF (Service Management Facility)
    action flags, 76
    creating services, 81–85
    description of, 23–24
    editing services, 86–88
    Fault Managed Resource Identifiers
        and, 70–71
    milestones, 74
    overview of, 70
    ssh service example, 74–81
    tools, 71
    using, 72–73
snapshots
    file system, advantages of, 57
    taking (ZFS), 103–104
software
    See also hypervisor; tools
    community-developed, 5–6
    freely sharable, 5
    open source, 4, 5–7
    OpenSolaris as running high-quality, 22
software repositories, downloading
        programs from, 48–50
software support subscription, 22
Solaris Developer Network (SDN), 28
Solaris Dynamic Tracing Guide, 209
Solaris for x86 systems, reputation of, 27
Solaris Performance and Tools
        (McDougall, Mauro, and Gregg),
        205
Solaris 10
    DVD distribution of, 28
    goals and future directions for, 10–11
    Linux criticisms of, 55
    Linuxification of, 10
    reputation of, 17
Songbird, 224
Sound Juicer, 223

source code
    licensing of, 11
    resources on, 8
    web site for, 19
SPARC support, 20, 239
srcheck tool, 165
sshd logging, enabling, 190
sshd service daemon, 70–71
SSH key generation, 187
ssh service
    contract_id, 81
    dependencies, 83–84
    disabling, 75–77
    example of, 74
    manifest file for, 81
    missing dependency example, 78
    name tag, 83
    offline or maintenance state of, 80
    state and dependence details for, 77–78
    URL with error details, 80
SSL, enabling for Tomcat, 168
stack trace of Java program, displaying,
        218
Start Here with OpenSolaris page, 46
starting
    MySQL database, service manifest
        example for, 85–86
    Subversion server, 183
    Tomcat manually, 171
start method (Tomcat), 170
states of services
    list of, 72
    maintenance, clearing, 80
stop method (Tomcat), 170
stopping sshd, 75
storage appliances based on OpenSolaris
        and ZFS, 102
storage of data
    prefixes for decimal multiples of bytes,
        90
    techniques for, 89
storage pools
    creating
        zfs command and, 98–100
        zpool command and, 96–98
        zpool command options, 95
    overview of, 91–94

Storage 7000 product (Sun Microsystems), 102
storage space for VM, assigning, 142
subscription support services (Sun Microsystems), 6
Subversion
    files, managing, 179–182
    importing project into, 198
    integrating NetBeans IDE with, 193–200
    manage access control method
        public/private key pair, generating, 187–191
        simple svn remote access, 183–185
        svn + ssh access, 185–186
    new project, creating, 196
    output window, 198
    repository, creating, 179
    selecting directory to check out, 194
    selecting location of files for project, 196
    specifying local directory, and checking out, 194
    specifying location of repository, and logging in, 194
su command, 56–57
sudo program, 57
Sun Microsystems
    Device Detection Tool, 21, 32
    Hardware Compatibility List, 21, 31, 222
    history of, 9
    Linuxification of Solaris by, 10
    Storage 7000 product, 102
    subscription support services, 6
SUNWspnego package, 190
SUNWtcat package
    installing, 166
    NetBeans IDE and, 192
svcadm clear command, 80
svcadm command, 71, 75–76, 139
svccfg command
    description of, 71
    SMF repository, interacting with, 200
    verifying file is valid using, 85
svcprop command, 71
svcs -a command, 72
svcs command, 71, 139
svcs ssh command, 78

svc.startd, automatic restarts by, 75
svcs -x command, 78
svcs -x ssh command, 78
svn add (Subversion), 181
svn commit (Subversion), 182
svn delete (Subversion), 181
svn diff (Subversion), 182
svn move (Subversion), 181
svn update (Subversion), 182
syscallbyproc.d script, 214
system requirements for installation, 30–34
System menu
    Administration submenu, 54
    Applications submenu, 52
    Preferences submenu, 53
    Users and Groups submenu, 62

T

TCP/IP, zones and, 120
terminology overview, 5–6
testing zone configuration, 131
thick hypervisor, 115
thin hypervisor, 115
Thompson, Ken, 9
Time Slider file manager
    description of, 93
    enabling, 104
    icon for, 106
    slider bar, 106
Tomcat
    installing in container, 165–172
    integrating NetBeans IDE with, 191–193
Tomcat manifest (tomcat5.xml), 170–171
tools
    developer, included with OpenSolaris, 22
    Device Detection, 21, 32
    Device Driver utility, 222–223
    Distribution Constructor, 220–222
    for monitoring local zone resources from global zone, 127
    online source code browser, 19
    in Service Management Facility, 71
    srcheck, 165
    Tracker search utility, 219–220
    virt-manager GUI, 140, 145

tools *(continued)*
    Webmin, 86–88, 128
    zonemgr, 128
    zonestat, 127
top command, 125
Torvalds, Linus, 9, 12
total pool of memory or storage, 91
Totem movie player, 224
Tracker search utility, 219–220
training resources, 235
Trusted Extensions, 26
tunnel mode, launching svnserve in, 189
Type 1 and Type 2 hypervisors, 37, 115

■ **U**

Ubuntu 8, running as guest VM, 136
UltraSPARC T2 processor chip, 148
uname command, 47
UNIX
    history of, 9
    service management and, 69
UNIX File System, 89
updating kernel build, 59–60
USB flash memory drive, booting from, 30
user domains, 137
user groups, recommended, 236
user list for MySQL, viewing, 174
users
    adding new, 62–64
    default shell for, 55
    Primary Administrator role, 57
Users and Groups menu, 62
user tools included with OpenSolaris, 22
/usr/bin/bash, as default shell, 55
/usr/gnu/bin directory, 55–56

■ **V**

variables, setting for Tomcat, 167
videos, recommended, 236
viewing
    bugs, 193
    extended ACL, 158
    privileges, 164
    process ID and contract ID of services,
        161

published IPS packages, 202
user list for MySQL, 174
virt-manager GUI tool, 140, 145
VirtualBox
    boot device and network configuration,
        39
    cloning feature, 45
    description of, 38
    installing new guest VM in, 134
    running guest VM on OpenSolaris
        using, 136
    selecting and mounting guest VM CD,
        DVD, or .iso file, 134
    virtual disk type selection, 39
    welcome screen, 39
virtual devices, 94
virtualization
    choosing type of, 115–116
    Cloud Computing products and, 112
    definition of, 5
    installation and, 30
    overview of, 112
    support for, 25
    technologies for
        BrandZ, 145–148
        LDoms, 148
        overview of, 133
        VirtualBox, 134–136
        xVM hypervisor, 136–145
    types of, 113–115
    zones
        cloning, 127–128
        containers compared to, 118
        creating, 120–124
        example configuration of, 120
        global and local environments,
            124–127
        managing, 128–129
        resources, managing, 130–132
        using, 129–130
virtual machine monitor, 113. See also
        hypervisor
virtual machine (VM)
    installing as guest, 37–47
    installing operating system as, 30
vmstat, DTrace version of, 214

W

Webmin tool, 86–88, 128
webservd (user)
    assigning privilege to, 169
    starting Tomcat as, 169
    starting Tomcat manually as, 171
webservd:webservd UID, 167
web servers, hosting with local zones, 129
web sites
    Chime GUI for DTrace, 216
    Crossbow technology, 113
    curriculum development resources, 226
    device drivers, 8
    for downloading OpenSolaris, 27
    essential, 15
    Fluendo, 224
    Gregg, Brendan, 212
    lapto issues, community for, 30
    Learning Cloud Service, 227–229
    manifest files for services, 81
    OpenSolaris .org
        bug-tracking and RFE site, 14
        community web page, 12
        device drivers community, 8
        LDom developer community, 149
        Observatory blog, 12
        public road maps, 10
        Source Code, 19
        Zones and Containers FAQ, 129
    recommended, 236
    service manifest template, 82
    SMF Manifest Creator, 86
    software repositories, 48
    Solaris
        Developer Network, 28
        Dynamic Tracing Guide, 209
        error conditions, 80
        public road maps, 10
    source code, 8
    Subversion information, 191
    Sun Microsystems
        Device Detection Tool, 21
        Hardware Compatibility List, 21
    VirtualBox, 39, 134
    virtualization technologies, 114, 133

Webmin tool, 86–88
Xen community, 115
xVM Server, 137
ZFS file system, 90–91, 102
zonemgr tool, 128
zone or container resource allocation, 132
zonestat tool, 127
web stack
    description of, 154
    initializing, 158–161
white papers, recommended, 237
wikis, recommended, 234
Windows XP, running as guest VM, 136
workload containment, 5, 111

X

Xen community, 115
xVM hypervisor
    installing, 138–145
    overview of, 136–137
xVM Server, 115, 136

Z

zfs command
    description of, 94
    examples using, 98–100
    snapshot, creating with, 103
ZFS file system
    booting and rebooting from, 57–59
    description of, 24
    development and design goals of, 90
    extended ACL and, 158
    features of, 91–93
    managing boot environments, 108–110
    on-disk encryption of, 240
    performance of, 101–102
    snapshots, taking, 103–104
    storage pools
        creating, 95
        overview of, 94
        zfs command and, 98–100
        zpool command and, 96–98
    Time Slider, 104–106
    virtual devices, 94
    web sites related to, 90–91, 102

zlogin program, 120
zoneadm program, 120, 122–124
zonecfg program, 120–122
zonemgr tool, 128
zonename program, 120
zones
    branded, 145
    cloning, 127–128
    containers compared to, 118
    creating
        configuration files directory, 121
        overview of, 120
        zoneadm program, 122–124
        zonecfg command, 121
    discrete privileges and, 163–164
    example configuration of, 120
    global and local environments, 124–127

    local
        description of, 118
        DTrace and, 209
        using, 129–130
    lx, 145–146
    managing, 128–129
    overview of, 163
    qualifying application for, 164–165
    resources, managing, 130– 132
    running application inside, 162–163
    using, 129–130
Zones and Containers FAQ, 129
zonestat tool, 127
zpool command
    description of, 94
    examples using, 96–98
    options for, 95

You Need the Companion eBook

Your purchase of this book entitles you to buy the companion PDF-version eBook for only $10. Take the weightless companion with you anywhere.

We believe this Apress title will prove so indispensable that you'll want to carry it with you everywhere, which is why we are offering the companion eBook (in PDF format) for $10 to customers who purchase this book now. Convenient and fully searchable, the PDF version of any content-rich, page-heavy Apress book makes a valuable addition to your programming library. You can easily find and copy code—or perform examples by quickly toggling between instructions and the application. Even simultaneously tackling a donut, diet soda, and complex code becomes simplified with hands-free eBooks!

Once you purchase your book, getting the $10 companion eBook is simple:

❶ Visit **www.apress.com/promo/tendollars/**.

❷ Complete a basic registration form to receive a randomly generated question about this title.

❸ Answer the question correctly in 60 seconds, and you will receive a promotional code to redeem for the $10.00 eBook.

2855 TELEGRAPH AVENUE | SUITE 600 | BERKELEY, CA 94705

Offer valid through 10/09.